PHILANTHROPY
in an
Age of
Transition

The Essays of
Alan Pifer

The Foundation Center
New York • 1984

These essays were originally published in the annual reports
of the Carnegie Corporation of New York, a philanthropic
foundation established in 1911 by Andrew Carnegie for the
advancement and diffusion of knowledge among the people
of the United States and certain countries which are or were
members of the British overseas Commonwealth.

Contents

Foreword

Newcomers to the world of private giving for public good, and old hands alike, will savor this series of seventeen essays by Alan Pifer marking year by year his thoughtful concerns as an observer and a leader in his field over an unusually eventful span.

When I first came to The Foundation Center after many years in universities, and from a part of the grove remote from foundation grantseeking, Alan Pifer's essays became one of the solid sources of my new education. The Tax Reform Act of 1969 was about to take effect. His commentary on the background and meaning of that unsettling event was especially useful to me. I began to read the earlier essays and to anticipate each new one. Even then, I thought they should be collected in a single volume.

The full collection of essays, first appearing in Carnegie Corporation annual reports and now published by The Foundation Center, represents an important historical record of a period of great change in the philanthropic community and in American society, as well as a thought-provoking agenda of issues that will be of concern for a long time to come. They deserve the broadest audience possible. The introduction by Carnegie Corporation's Board Chairman John C. Taylor, 3rd, tells about the origin of the essays and provides an overview of the work.

The Foundation Center is very pleased to present this valuable addition to the literature on America's voluntary sector.

Thomas R. Buckman
March, 1984

Acknowledgements

The essays in this volume that were published in Carnegie Corporation's annual reports for the years from 1970 to 1982 benefitted enormously from the imaginative assistance and tough-minded editing of Avery Russell. I wish to thank her warmly for her invaluable help.

I would also like to express again my thanks and appreciation to my colleagues on the staff and board of trustees of the Corporation, and especially to John C. Taylor, 3rd, Chairman of the Board, who prepared the excellent introduction to this volume.

Alan Pifer

Introduction

The essays in this book are a record of the evolving ideas and concerns of Alan Pifer, head of Carnegie Corporation from 1965 through 1982 and the ninth president since its founding by Andrew Carnegie in 1911. The essays were first published as introductions to the Corporation's annual reports.

A foundation leader typically uses the annual statement to review the organization's policies and take a backward glance at the year's grant activities. Alan Pifer, following the custom of Corporation presidents before him, elected instead to present his own views about issues of current interest which, although broadly related to the Corporation's policies, only occasionally reflected its specific programs. Alan did address the Corporation's work directly in three of the essays—in 1973, when he presented highlights of the foundation's activities during the 20 years he had been a member of the staff; in 1980, when he discussed the Corporation's long-term support of educational programs in South Africa; and in 1981, when he described the Corporation's 20-year initiatives to advance equality of opportunity and social justice for the nation's minority groups and women and to improve the status and well-being of children.

In the main, however, the essays divide into three subject areas: the role and vitality of the nonprofit sector generally in American life—a concern which preoccupied the early years of his presidency and altogether inspired seven of the seventeen essays; the functions and responsibilities of the field of higher education, to which the Corporation devoted nearly one-half of its grants over the years; and the public and private policy needs arising from profound economic, social, and demographic changes taking place in American society.

Few foundation leaders have devoted such tireless energy as has Alan Pifer toward safeguarding the vitality of nonprofit organizations and creating public understanding of the contribution of nonprofit organizations to the diversity and strength of American life. The very first essay of his presidency, published in

1

1966 as "The Nongovernmental Organization at Bay," discussed the financial uncertainty of these organizations amid their growing responsibilities in the nation and the world. Their social value, Alan pointed out, was increasing in response to the steadily broadening aspirations of the society and to the nation's expanding international commitments, yet sharply increased costs were threatening to limit their future usefulness and undermine private charitable endeavors through which the nation was accomplishing some of its most important objectives. This and succeeding essays explored in depth the nature of the historic partnership of public and private commonweal endeavor and provided a history and typology of nongovernmental organizations that is still applicable today.

In the "Quasi Nongovernmental Organization" (1967),* Alan analyzed the conflict between the requirements of independence and of public accountability besetting the new government-financed, private non-profit enterprises that had emerged in previous decades to deal with complex national problems. Calling such organizations a "half-way house between government and the private sector," he noted that while they had been set up variously to meet the government's need for specialized services and to provide it with unbiased judgment and flexibility of action, their very effectiveness rested on maintaining their freedom from governmental intervention. Reconciling the two requirements, he said, was the central challenge of such organizations and one that he believed had received too little public attention. In the essay, he suggested a set of operating principles by which both the independence and accountability of quasi nongovernmental organizations could be assured.

Three years later, in "The Jeopardy of Private Institutions" (1970), Alan returned to the financial straits of the nonprofit sector, asserting that, "The steady, unrelenting deterioration of their position has now, for the first time, raised doubts about the continued viability of our traditional system of shared responsibility between public and private endeavor." To Alan, the plight of private institutions ultimately derived from lack of clear appreciation by the nation's top political leaders and by the public of what the collective presence and vitality of these institutions mean to the nation. Voluntary associations have been credited with reinforcing our democratic political system in several ways: distributing power widely in the society and permitting the individual to share in it; enabling the ordinary citizen to participate in and understand the processes of democracy; and offering a mechanism for the continued promotion of social change. Fuller understanding of this role, he suggested, might be brought about by a national commission to "arouse public interest in the private service institution and concern over its future," a task that was later undertaken by the Filer Commission on Private Philanthropy and Public Needs.

In 1972, turning to practical measures for overcoming public "antipathy or

---

*A term which in Britain was turned into the acronym "Quango" and became the subject of intense political debate.

just ignorance and indifference" toward charity and for revitalizing the sector, Alan called for changes in the charitable deduction to make it more equitable to all taxpayers and to enable the support of charitable organizations and institutions to become more democratic. One of the specific proposals he put forward was to extend the charitable deduction to those taxpayers who take the standard deduction. This recommendation was later adopted by the Filer Commission and in 1981 was added to the tax code.

In 1968, 1969, and then 1974, Alan elaborated on the nature of foundations and their unique attributes of freedom and flexibility to respond to policy needs engendered by rapid technological and social change—attributes which, ironically, had become so controversial by 1969 as to invite government scrutiny, in part because of some notable abuses of privilege by certain foundations. In "Foundations at the Service of the Public," he traced the history of various legislative committees, from 1915 on, which had investigated foundations and considered the possible need for measures to place them under greater restriction. Each investigation had wrestled with the dilemma of how to hold foundations publicly accountable without at the same time destroying the essential elements that give them their peculiar value, and each had eventually declined to recommend legislation to bring foundations under substantive governmental review. By 1969, however, it appeared likely that foundations would be brought under such control, and in the essay, "Foundations and the Unity of Charitable Organizations," Alan made a vigorous case against proposed legislation that almost certainly would have dealt a life blow to the field. In "Foundations and Public Policy Formation," he went further, upholding the right and need of foundations to support activities directed at public policy formation. In Alan's view, the "greatest justification for foundations continuing to enjoy tax-exempt status lies in their making the maximum contribution they can, within their spheres of interest and competence and within the limits of the law, to the development of enlightened public policy for the nation."

Of great concern to Alan during his presidency of a foundation with a 60-year history of support for American higher education was the health of the field. By 1971, higher education was coming through the most turbulent period in its history, a time in which no social institution was spared the disequilibriums resulting from the baby-boom generation coming of age, our participation in a protracted and unpopular war, and the rising aspirations of the nation's minority groups and women. All of these changes helped foster a mood of skepticism toward large organizations, and higher education was high on the list of those criticized. In 1971, Alan turned analytical attention to "The Responsibility for Reform in Higher Education," in which he elucidated a wide range of functions that higher education institutions had assumed over time and suggested reforms that would lighten their burdens while strengthening their capacity to serve the needs of the nation. In 1975, concerned again about public disenchantment with higher education, Alan, in "Higher Education in the Nation's Consciousness," called for a new consensus regarding the position of higher education, asking academic institutions to take the lead in defining their proper functions, pressing ahead with administrative and educational reforms, cutting costs, and heightening the moral dimension of academic life.

The year 1976 represents a turning point in Alan's concerns. Beginning with "Women Working: Toward a New Society," he explored over a period of four years the public and private policy implications of major social trends of the past two decades. In "Women Working," he noted the powerful forces that were drawing American women into the labor market, giving rise to role conflicts between men and women in the home and workplace and raising serious questions about their combined impact on the health and well-being of children. The problem, he observed, lay not in the fact that these changes in social practice were occurring, but in the lack of adequate policy response to them. Rather than look upon women as the cause of these new stresses, decision makers, he urged, should pay attention to the ways that working women were making a positive contribution to social change and assist their efforts. "If we pass up this opportunity to use accommodation to the new reality of large numbers of women working as a spearhead for much broader change," he said, "we will not only be inflicting needless hardship on numbers of our fellow citizens but also denying to all of us the chance of living in a more humane and equitable society."

This general theme was echoed in the 1978 essay, "Perceptions of Childhood and Youth," in which Alan suggested that the enormous changes in the age composition of the population, specifically the shrinking proportion of the young in relation to older age groups, might be linked to growing negative public attitudes toward children. Once more he made a plea for public and private policies that would assure the well-being of children in light of these trends and adapt as well to the changing nature of the family and the increasing numbers of working mothers. The grounds for such action, he stated bluntly, were not only humanitarian but practical: "Every child alive today or born in the years ahead . . . will be a scarce resource and precious asset as an adult. At that time the nation's standard of living, its capacity to defend itself—perhaps its very viability as a nation—will be almost wholly dependent on the small contingent of men and women who are today's children."

Essays for the years 1977 and 1979 addressed social policy needs regarding the nations's two largest minorities and the special obligations of American society to respond to their claims for just treatment. In "Black Progress: Achievement, Failure, and an Uncertain Future" (1977), Alan weighed the substantial gains that blacks had made in education, jobs, income, and social position since the early 1960s against their failure to attain parity with whites in these areas. Decrying current claims that black advancement had become self-sustaining, he maintained that, on the contrary, active white resistance and lack of the political will to break the barriers to racial equality helped to perpetuate the lag between the promise of equal opportunity and its reality. The increasing class

4

differentiation between blacks and competition for the nation's attention by other groups also served in subtle ways to dilute the commitment to racial justice. For these and other reasons, Alan said, "it may well be fruitless for black leaders to continue to make their appeal to white conscience on racial grounds alone. Rather they should be putting their effort into building a broad coalition of all those who have interest in common—those who suffer from discrimination, poverty, unemployment, poor housing, poor education, and inadequate health care—and seeking gains for blacks within this context."

In 1979, in "Bilingual Education and the Hispanic Challenge," Alan examined the impact of the rapid growth in the Hispanic population in the United States on general education policy and the forces that divided Americans on the issue of whether bilingual education was an effective and appropriate means by which "linguistically different" children could adjust to the English-language curriculum. Coming out in favor of bilingual education, Alan nonetheless cautioned that "advocates of bilingual education should be wary of advancing rationales for it that go beyond its strictly educational purpose of helping children to acquire the intellectual skills they will need to compete successfully in the American mainstream."

In "Final Thoughts," Alan took the occasion of his last essay to discuss forthrightly the values and beliefs informing his leadership over 18 years and to hearken once again to the practical need for heavy national investment in human resource development and equal opportunity for all. In his view, the rapidly rising numbers of elderly people, combined with the precipitous drop in the numbers of children born since 1970, pose two principal challenges in the coming years: How to make the most of the limited number of productive workers there will be relative to the number of retired Americans, and how, in a period when resources will inevitably be limited, to reconcile the insatiable demand for expenditure of public and private funds on the elderly with the competing needs and claims of younger age groups. Deploring current efforts to dismantle many of the social programs established over preceding decades, many of which benefit children, Alan emphasized that these programs "were not confined simply to helping those members of the society who are least able to help themselves but were aimed broadly at developing the nation's human potential." He went on to urge Americans to understand the longer-term negative consequences for the nation's economy and for its security of a prolonged failure to invest adequately in human resources.

These "final thoughts" are most fitting for a president who has devoted his entire foundation career to the pursuit of equal justice and opportunity and to the special needs of the young. Alan Pifer's leadership in these important and controversial areas has been a source of pride to Carnegie Corporation's trustees and to all who have had the good fortune to be his colleagues. The board and staff are grateful that Alan will be continuing to exert the fullest efforts to help build the kind of society in which he believes so strongly—one, as he expresses it, "that is humane, caring, and provident in developing the talents of all its people." In these endeavors we wish him Godspeed.

John C. Taylor, 3rd
Chairman of the Board
Carnegie Corporation of New York

The Nongovernmental Organization at Bay

An occupational hazard of philanthropy is repeated exposure to the financial plight of others. While the reaction may at times be a kind of relieved "there but for the grace of God . . . ," more often it is one of deep concern, even anxiety. Why do so many of our private nonprofit organizations seem to have perpetually engrossing financial problems? Why should the men who run them have to spend so much time and effort making the rounds of potential donors, hat in hand, often with disappointing results and always at the expense of their primary administrative and program function? Has the system for maintaining these organizations become basically unsound?

These are questions that each year become more insistent as the social value of nongovernmental organizations continues to mount in response to the steadily broadening aspirations of our society and to the nation's expanding international commitments. Indeed, the financial uncertainty of these organizations in the face of growing responsibilities and sharply increased costs threatens to limit their future usefulness and undermine the private side of a public-private partnership through which the nation is now accomplishing some of its most important public business.

Definition

The term "nongovernmental organization" is used in several ways and is often ambiguous. As used here, it is arbitrarily limited to those organizations that have a private and nonprofit status but are *not* universities, colleges or schools, hospitals, fully endowed foundations, or religious missions. It includes scholarly, professional, educational, scientific, literary, and cultural associations; health, welfare, and community action agencies; nonuniversity research institutes; agen-

7

cies providing overseas technical assistance; defense advisory organizations; and agencies that have educational purposes but are not part of the formal educational system. Thus, the term takes in only part of that heterogeneous list of approximately 100,000 organizations that are tax exempt and to which contributions are deductible under federal income tax law.

A few hundred of these organizations have national or international purposes and are individually important to the nation at large. The remaining thousands operate only at the local level but have national significance collectively as a vital part of our system of democratic pluralism. In both groups, but especially in the former, are to be found an ever growing number that derive part of their income, and in certain cases a goodly portion of it, from federal grants and contracts. Some of these organizations have moved into the federal orbit by choice, seeing there new sources of financial support. Others have entered it in response to a call for help from Washington. Still others were created by, or as the result of an initiative from, a federal agency.

The kinds of services offered to government by these private nonprofit organizations are too varied and numerous to catalogue here. Indeed, it is a striking fact that nowhere in the Federal Government does there exist a central record of these services, the organizations providing them, and the volume of expenditure involved, and even at the department or agency level this information is not readily available. "We just don't look at it that way," is the explanation offered, and so separate statistics are hard to come by.

Nevertheless, the use of nongovernmental organizations to carry out public functions, a rare occurrence before World War II, is now accepted policy in most parts of government. Gone are the days when most people in Washington would agree with the once widely held view that public money should be spent only by public agencies. A more flexible approach to the art of government, which also includes an expanded use of universities and private business firms, is growing steadily.

In the Government's Service

Examples drawn at random from current government operations illustrate the variety and ingenuity to be found in the ways private nonprofit organizations are serving government.

The United States Employment Service of the Department of Labor has recently contracted with the National Travelers Aid Association to provide supportive social services in the relocation of families from areas of labor surplus to areas with a labor shortage. The Office of Regional Economic Development of the Department of Commerce, to assist local industrial growth, purchases research services having to do with new products and new markets from such nonprofit organizations as the Midwest Research Institute, the RAND Corporation, and the New England Economic Research Foundation.

The Bureau of Educational and Cultural Affairs of the Department of State uses the services of the National Social Welfare Assembly for planning and administering travel programs of some foreign visitors to this country. The same bureau has for a number of years relied on the Conference Board of Associated Research Councils and the Institute of International Education to assist in the selection of American scholars and students for research, teaching, and study abroad under the Fulbright Program.

The Agency for International Development employs International Voluntary Services for rural development work in Laos, and the American Institute for Free Labor Development to train labor leaders from Latin America. It contracts with the African-American Institute for a variety of educational services in many parts of Africa, and with the Near East Foundation for agricultural education and extension services in Dahomey. It finances a program under which CARE is assisting Algerian doctors to develop their capability to run an ophthalmological clinic. Peace Corps volunteers are being trained by the Tucson, Arizona, branch of the YMCA for service in Venezuela.

The National Science Foundation under its course content improvement program has given substantial contract support to Educational Services Incorporated for curriculum work in science, mathematics, and social studies. The U.S. Office of Education, under its ERIC (Educational Research Information Center) program, an enterprise that also involves ten universities and two private business concerns, has recently contracted with the Modern Language Association and the Center for Applied Linguistics to set up clearinghouses for information on, respectively, the common and the less taught foreign languages. The Office of Education has also provided contract support to CONPASS, a newly formed consortium of professional associations, including the Association of American Geographers, the American Historical Association, and others, to make possible a continuing appraisal of the $33 million annual National Defense Education Act program of teachers institutes in such fields as foreign languages, geography, English, history, reading, and the arts.

In the poverty field well over half of the 900-odd newly created community action agencies supported by the Office of Economic Opportunity are private nonprofit organizations. The OEO also finances demonstration programs carried out by long-established private agencies. An example in the community action area is the Office's support of Project ENABLE, jointly sponsored by the National Urban League, the Family Service Association, and the Child Study Association. A second example is OEO's support of programs of the National Legal Aid and Defender Association. A third is the contract with the YMCA to help meet the costs of a job-training program for young people in the Bedford-Stuyvesant area of New York City. The Department of Labor and Office of Education also contribute to this program.

The Food and Drug Administration has recently engaged the National Academy of Sciences to carry out a reassessment of the efficacy of all new drugs marketed in the years between 1938 and 1962. Previously, at the request of the same federal agency and with funds provided by it, the Public Administration Service, a private organization in Chicago, had made a study of state and local food and drug control procedures to help the Federal Government determine its area of responsibility.

Government by Contract

These are but a few instances of one aspect of the rapidly growing phenomenon of government by grant and contract. The phenomenon will almost certainly continue to grow despite the opposition of some members of Congress, who believe it would be preferable for federal agencies to develop their own internal capacity to take on all the new tasks society is assigning to Washington rather than hire others for this purpose. These critics contend that contracting is no more than a subterfuge by which government gets around its own regulations and salary scales. More importantly, some have real doubts as to how far federal agencies should go in delegating their public responsibilities to private contractors. Can the elected officials of a democratic government, they ask, be held fully accountable to the public for tasks that appointed officials have contracted with others to perform?

This is a fair question. At the same time the greatly increased use of nongovernmental organizations to serve government ends is the product of a powerful and pervasive new force that is not to be denied. This force is the growing complexity of the domestic and international problems with which government must cope—complexity that is rooted in scientific and technological advance, in population growth, in urbanization, in international tensions, and in still other factors. Solution of these complex new problems requires ever greater specialization, both of facilities and professional and technical manpower. Government cannot hope to build up and maintain such a capacity within its own bureaucracy. It has no alternative but to buy the specialized help it needs from the universities, from private enterprise, and from the nongovernmental organizations.

Beyond this reason, however, are other sound justifications for the government's use of nongovernmental agencies to carry out the nation's public purposes. These agencies by their very nature should have the kinds of attributes that an alert federal administration needs today, if it is to have an adequate sense of responsibility for the nation's well-being. Not all private organizations have these qualities, but many do. They include the capacity to move swiftly, flexibly, and imaginatively into a new area of critical need; the power to arrive at a disinterested, objective appraisal of a situation free of political influence; the freedom to engage in controversial activities; the ability to experiment in an unfettered manner—and if need be fail; and finally the capacity for sympathetic personal attention to the variety of human problems that beset our increasingly dehumanized world.

10

A New Partnership

Realizing the need for access to such qualities, Washington officialdom has in recent years authorized an ever greater use of nongovernmental organizations, and Congress has provided the necessary funds to buy their services and support their projects. A partnership has been sealed, as it was between government and the universities in scientific research and development. The result is that just as we now have the "federal grant university," so also we have the "federal grant nongovernmental organization." And just as we have learned to worry about the impact on the universities of large-scale, mission-oriented federal support, we must also develop a concern about the impact of this kind of money on the weaker partner in the new alliance between government and the nongovernmental organizations.

At the moment such a concern both within and outside government has not arisen, as it did in regard to the universities. Why? One explanation is simply that the volume of governmental contracting with the private organizations is smaller than it is with the universities. This in turn is explained by the predominant part research and development have played in government's need for outside assistance and the universities' special—though not exclusive—capability in this area. Federal contract and grant support, much of it for research, now represents a substantial part of the annual income of many of our leading universities. No sensible person in government or the universities can ignore the implications of this development. But among nongovernmental organizations research is a much more limited activity, and no other single area of government dependence on these organizations has yet been great enough to arouse concern.

Nevertheless, important as research and development requirements remain, other types of government needs have been growing rapidly, especially for the kinds of operational and management services that nongovernmental organizations of the types we are considering here may provide more appropriately than universities. As the nation increasingly grapples with its domestic problems of educational expansion, urban blight, poverty, housing, race relations, health, and environmental pollution, as well as with its international responsibilities, the use of the nongovernmental organization must inevitably continue to mount.

Concern developed slowly over the implications of government dependence on the universities for research. Originally federal agencies believed they could simply buy research from the universities as a kind of commodity, much as the army once bought mules. This simple notion was later replaced by a more sophisticated realization that to get the research it needed government would also have to support the research universities wanted to do. There developed, therefore, a dual system of relationships, one based on contracts, the other on grants. Gradually, however, the distinction between the two has faded as the result of changing procedures, until the grant and the contract are now virtually indistinguishable.

More recently the government has recognized that it not only must administer its university research support flexibly but also must help build up the basic long-term strength of the universities. It is doing this through the new institutional grant programs of the National Science Foundation, through general research support and grants for facilities to the medical schools by the National Institutes of Health, through the "sustaining university" grants of the National Aeronautics and Space Administration, and through Office of Education grants to the universities for buildings and equipment.

Finally, in the new international education legislation Congress and the Administration are contemplating yet another step. They are now proposing to give general support to universities to enable them to develop the capability with which to provide international technical assistance, not only in research but for training and operational services as well.

Let the Seller Beware

Clearly the university case has been well made. But the same case has never been made for using public money to develop the general capacity of nongovernmental organizations to do their jobs more effectively. The standard government position here is that it is simply buying services as a commodity and has no responsibility for the basic health of the suppliers. Therefore it must pay for a whit more (and often less) than the tangible products it receives, whether research or services; it must buy at the lowest possible price; and it must limit its support to the program and administrative costs of a carefully defined project with a specified terminal date.

This kind of support is in the long run harmful to the nongovernmental organizations. It tends to produce mushroom growth and to place them in a position where they must continually seek further project support of the same nature to prevent the laying-off of staff and closing-down of programs. Thus, the paths of these organizations become characterized by frequent changes of direction induced by Washington's concerns of the day, rather than deliberate courses set by the organizations' own board of trustees. This process in turn can diminish the interest of the trustees, and hence their sense of responsibility—which is the very heart of effective voluntary private service in the public interest.

The probability is that project support alone will in time make these organizations little more than appendages of government. What may also develop, since government officials cannot in the very nature of their jobs take consistent responsibility for the affairs of private organizations, are situations in which responsibility falls somewhere between government and trustees, with no effective check on the activities of staff. The dangers here are obvious.

The management of a nongovernmental organization, guided by its own sense of what is best for the organization, does, of course, have a free choice of whether to accept or reject government contracts. This can be said to be a basic part of management's responsibility. One can say, therefore, that if the organization begins to exhibit hyperthyroid or schizoid tendencies as the result of an overdose of government contracts, it has no one to blame but itself. In practice, however, many organizations have found the rejection of government business extremely difficult because of their unwillingness to appear—and be— unresponsive to the national need. In some instances also it is their own iden- tification of a pressing problem that leads them to take the initiative in seeking government support. Finally, they know that organizations that consistently give a higher priority to their own stability than to venturesome growth run the danger of removing themselves from the battle altogether.

Why have the private nonprofit organizations not come together and made their case to government as the universities did? Perhaps it is merely a matter of not yet having had time. A more likely explanation, however, is that they have no ready means of cooperation, so great is their diversity and so amorphous the field of which they are members. Each of these organizations has a con- stituency of its own and inhabits a world that rarely intersects or overlaps that of another organization. The men responsible for their affairs often do not even know each other. There has, therefore, never been a concerted initiative for the creation in Washington of a single voice to speak for the interests of the nongovernmental organizations field, a voice such as that provided for higher education by the American Council on Education. Perhaps, given the diversity of the field and its lack of integration, this is the way it has to be, but the result is a babel which amounts to no voice at all.

A New Approach

Were government now to recognize the need for building a long-term service capability in organizations with unique or special talents, it would seem an easy matter for federal agencies to begin to apply to the private agencies on whose services they depend the same principles now applied to the universities. For example, "sustaining grants" to such organizations could provide funds for ad- ministrative costs not allocable to contracts. Such grants could also provide "venture capital" for programs which, though not of current interest to the government, would develop the general competence of these organizations, and hence their longer-range usefulness to government.

From government's point of view several problems stand in the way of a new approach of this kind. Many Washington officials and members of Congress who believe in the public-private partnership would still hesitate to see gov- ernment provide general support to private organizations, because they believe this would turn them into veritable arms of government, thereby destroying the very qualities that make them indispensable. General support, they point out, would oblige government to audit the full accounts and monitor the entire program of an organization being helped, whereas with contract or grant support the auditing and monitoring need apply only to a specific project. Others in Washington disagree with this conclusion, saying that if the will existed, there could be as much latitude in government's approach to the nongovernmental organizations as there is in its flexible and generous new attitude toward the universities.

A more serious difficulty from Washington's point of view is that some private organizations seem to be badly run and others are apparently still addressing themselves to yesterday's problems, while still others give the impression of being nothing but lobbying groups promoting the selfish interests of particular professions or occupations. Liberalized financial policies that included such organizations might, it is suggested, simply reward inefficiency, obsolescence, and venality. While the point can be made that government has no business using the services of such organizations anyway, the argument is, nonetheless, generally persuasive, and it indicates that any change of policy must be applied selectively and with discriminating care.

This argument also points up a fundamental difference between universities and nongovernmental organizations. The very nature of the academic enterprise provides a kind of built-in system of responsibility upon which government can rely. Each scholar is accountable not only to colleagues at his university, including boards of trustees or regents, but also to a wider circle of scholars in his discipline at other universities. And at the institutional level, individual universities are accountable to a national—even international—community. This system of self-audit within the academic enterprise has its moments of failure. But on the whole it is remarkably reliable, and it provides a substantial assurance that the money will not be misspent when government gives public funds to the universities.

Nongovernmental organizations, on the other hand, being more disparate, lacking intercommunication, and possessing no sense of community and tradition do not have such a built-in system of discipline. In their case, responsibility is a more localized matter and lies primarily with their boards of trustees. Government's protection in its grants to these organizations is to make sure that the trustees recognize their responsibility and discharge it. Where the trustees are strong and active, the protection afforded government can, in fact, be even greater than that provided in grants to universities.

Responsibility for Support

Most people in Washington believe responsibility for the basic financial health of nongovernmental organizations lies in the private sector. The rightness of this view cannot be disputed when we think of philanthropy as a broad, undifferentiated activity in which the individual is free to give his dollar, or million dollars, for any purpose he chooses. Along with hospitals and educational institutions some nongovernmental organizations benefit from this kind of giving. This point of view provides one framework for thinking about these organizations, appropriate for those with purposes that tug at the heart strings—the "sailors, dogs, and children" group, as the British say—but wholly unrealistic in regard to those with less emotional pull.

Another framework is provided by the notion that at least certain nongovernmental organizations are national resources of such importance to the public welfare that their financial health cannot be entrusted to the vagaries of individual philanthropy. Here people in government tend to take the view that financial responsibility lies essentially with the foundations and business, an assumption that neither accepts.

With the exception of a number of quite small, local trusts most foundations take the position that only in exceptional circumstances is the provision of long-term, general support to an organization justified. They tend to be especially wary if the purpose for which a general support grant is requested is simply to put an organization into a position to accept government project grants or contracts. Indeed, the foundations regard project support as *their* particular province and are not ready to have responsibility for some other role thrust on them. Their funds, they argue, are severely limited in size and must be used for the kinds of experimental purposes for which no other funds are available. While this antipathy to general support may be as disappointing to the nongovernmental organizations as is the restricted policy of government, any other attitude would soon tie up foundations' funds and destroy the very flexibility that gives them their unique value.

Within the business community the general rule seems to be that corporate giving, beyond donations to educational institutions, hospitals, and the usual private charities, should be restricted to purposes at least indirectly related to a company's interests. Thus, a firm with markets in Latin America is more likely to support a private organization providing technical assistance there than one with the same purposes in Southeast Asia. Or a company manufacturing agricultural machinery may support an organization concerned with farm life but probably not one involved in, say, the arts. This is understandable. But the net effect is that a number of nongovernmental organizations qualify for little or no support from business at all.

Beyond this is the fact that some companies either cannot or do not choose to give. And for all of them there remains the basic consideration that they are by nature profit making, not philanthropic, enterprises. So while it may be argued cogently that business firms should support nongovernmental organizations more heavily, there are some good reasons why, for the present anyway, passing the hat among them is a frustrating exercise.

Finally, those in Washington who regard the private sector as having full financial responsibility for the nongovernmental organizations, even organizations essentially serving important public purposes, seem to be less than fully aware of the enormously increased costs today of operating these agencies. Both administrative and program costs have risen drastically, because salaries have had to be raised to meet the competition offered by rising government and academic salaries.

A more fundamental explanation, however, of why the resources of the private sector are no longer adequate lies in the dramatic rise of our national aspirations. Under Great Society legislation we have launched a frontal assault on many of the nation's most grievous social, economic, and environmental problems—in poverty, civil rights, health, education, welfare, urban renewal, and air and water pollution. The nation has taken on enormous new tasks costing hitherto undreamed of sums. The impact on government has been traumatic. And no less forceful has been the impact on private organizations. They, however, lack within the private sector a new source of funds comparable to the new kinds of Congressional appropriations available to federal agencies.

While comparisons between nations are always hazardous it would appear that the same type of conscious reexamination of the role of the nongovernmental organization, and reassessment of its relationship with government, which have taken place in Britain since the appearance there of the Welfare State twenty years ago must now take place in the United States. Influential in the British reexamination have been Lord Beveridge's book *Voluntary Action*, published in 1948, the report of the Nathan Committee in 1952, and the subsequent Charities Act of 1960. From these and other contributions to the debate there have emerged both a reaffirmation of the value of voluntary effort in a democratic society and a new recognition of the interdependence of voluntary and statutory effort in an era of greatly expanded governmental responsibility for social welfare. The reexamination in this country must, however, be extended beyond simply the social welfare field to other areas, such as international education and technical assistance, where nongovernmental organizations are now in partnership with government. Furthermore, the process here will be more complex because, among other reasons, our three-tier system of government provides a greater variety of relationships with the nongovernmental organizations.

The Central Issue

Nonetheless, the real issue is beginning to emerge clearly. Is the nongovernmental organization of the future to be simply an auxiliary to the state, a kind of willing but not very resourceful handmaiden? Or is it to be a strong, independent adjunct that provides government with a type of capability it cannot provide for itself?

If it is to be the latter, and for most Americans the question is one that is likely to admit of no other answer, then we must face up to the difficult problem of how we are to finance these organizations. More can be done on the private side, as private responsibility will—and should—continue. For example, there might perhaps be some advantages to be found in experimenting more widely with the notion of cooperative fund raising which has worked so well for some community chest organizations. But the question must also be raised as to whether responsibility for the general financial health of at least the most important of the nongovernmental organizations should not now be shared by the Federal Government. Certainly the time has come for a comprehensive and careful study of the problem from both the governmental and nongovernmental sides.

If such a study should confirm the findings suggested by informal evidence and indicate the need for a new approach by government, three problems will then have to be considered: the mechanism for distribution of general support, how such support can be given without compromising the independence of the organizations aided, and how quality can be maintained. Would a new central mechanism in Washington, created with a broad charter, to act as a sort of analogue to the National Science Foundation, prove feasible as a device for channeling general support grants to the nongovernmental organizations? It would seem so in theory, but there would be many problems that might make the idea unworkable. A more practical approach, but one that also contains potential dangers for the organization seeking funds, would be to have each federal agency decide for itself which organizations it considered essential for its purposes and then determine the amount of general support each should receive. As noted above, such a process would have to be rigorously selective, with a wary eye open for possible incompetents and self-servers. The process would also have to be based on criteria politically defensible to Congress and the public.

Preserving the independence of the organizations aided would not appear to be an insoluble problem, although it may be a more difficult one than guaranteeing the independence of the universities has proven to be. It would require on the part of many people in the administration and in Congress a new attitude of greater trust in the nongovernmental organizations. It would entail new administrative practices, based in some cases on new regulations or even on new legislation but in other cases simply on a more liberal interpretation of existing regulations. Lastly, it would demand of the nongovernmental organizations that they continue to seek a wide diversification in the sources of their income, and linkages to as many constituencies as possible.

Government acceptance of a shared responsibility for the financial health of those nongovernmental organizations on whose services it most depends would not solve the problem of how other organizations, not linked to government, are to be adequately financed in the world of tomorrow. But it would be a specific response to the pressing difficulties of at least some of our most valuable private agencies. If we want to avoid an ever more extensive and powerful Federal Government, it would seem that we must now, paradoxically, use federal money to ensure that we have a viable alternative—a network of vigorous, well-financed nongovernmental organizations ready to serve government but able, in the public interest, to maintain their independence of it. This further financial burden on government may be unpalatable to many. But the logic of it is hard to escape.

The Quasi Nongovernmental Organization

In recent years there has appeared on the American scene a new genus of organization which represents a noteworthy experiment in the art of government. Lodged, through the normal process of legal incorporation, in the private sector of society, this new entity has in many respects the countenance of the private, nonprofit enterprise and even some of the characteristics of the true voluntary association. Yet it is financed entirely, or in large part, by the federal government, it was created as the result of federal legislation or other governmental initiative, and it serves important public purposes as an instrument of "government by contract." We may call it the *quasi nongovernmental organization*.

What precisely is this new creature? Why has it come into being? What unique purposes does it serve? Why is it quasi nongovernmental? What is its probable future?

These are questions that have on the whole been little considered. They should interest anyone who is concerned about the future of private institutions in our society. They should also intrigue anyone who is concerned about how— indeed whether—our national government can remain an effective force in the face of the mounting complexity and increasing extent of the problems with which it must grapple. For this new social form has, like previous inventions such as the government corporation and the government foundation, come into being not for capricious reasons but because it is an indispensable response to new conditions. Our society needs it and accords it an honored, if indeterminate, place among our panoply of national institutions. What is different about this new development, however, is that although it stems from government, it is not, like its predecessors, located within government. And, therefore, it raises some novel questions.

Quasi nongovernmental organizations seem to be principally a phenomenon of the past two decades. How many of them there are now or how much money government spends through them annually, no one knows for sure because of the difficulty of defining the genus precisely and because of the lack of any centralized information about it. The genus would, however, seem to include the following distinct and quite different species: several dozen so-called "not-for-profit corporations" providing advisory and other services to the Air Force, Navy, Army, Department of Defense, Atomic Energy Commission, and National Aeronautics and Space Administration; a small number of agencies related to the Department of State or the Agency for International Development providing educational, informational, cultural, and technical assistance services overseas; a score of regional educational laboratories sustained by the United States Office of Education; and about three-quarters of the more than 1,100 community action agencies, which receive most of their support from the Office of Economic Opportunity. The list would also include the limited group of organizations which have until recently been wholly supported by the Central Intelligence Agency.

Probably not yet to be classified as quasi nongovernmental organizations are many additional agencies which, unlike the ones just described, have genuine origins in the private sector but which in recent years, with large-scale government financial support, have increasingly become instrumentalities for carrying out public purposes. These agencies are found in the fields of health, welfare, and education, in the international area and in other domains. If the special relationships which they are developing with government become appreciably closer, they too will be denizens of the halfway house between government and the private sector already occupied by the quasi nongovernmental organization. One must, therefore, keep these additional organizations in mind as potential recruits to the new genus.

Characteristics

The quasi nongovernmental organization has many of the attributes of the true private organization. Typically, it has a board of trustees or directors that is supposed to govern it and that, in theory, is ultimately responsible for its affairs. The members of its staff are private employees, not civil servants. It is not housed in a government building or located on federal property. Its employees are in most instances free from security clearance except when working on classified government business. In theory, it determines its own program and carries this out as it sees fit. Frequently, it receives some, though usually limited, financial support from sources other than the federal government. It may, occasionally, even extend the privilege of membership in itself to individuals meeting certain qualifications, thus giving it the appearance of the voluntary association. Lastly, as we have seen, it is legally incorporated as a private institution, and it enjoys tax-exempt status.

But the quasi nongovernmental organization has other characteristics which seem to deny it a place in the tradition of voluntary associations in American life or, indeed, fully in the private sector at all. Most importantly it was created as the result of federal legislation or administrative action in Washington, rather than on the initiative of private citizens. It is dependent financially for its very existence on Congress and the particular federal department, agency, or service to which it is related. The accounts it keeps on its federal funds are examined not only by private but also by government auditors. It may, indeed, even be subjected to a searching investigation of its books by the General Accounting Office on the order of a member of Congress. Its most active channel of authority, therefore, tends to run between its paid staff and a Washington bureaucracy, and its program is likely to be heavily influenced by Washington's needs, regulations, and whims of the hour. At bottom, its freedom of action, compared with that of a truly private organization, is considerably restricted because the necessity for public accountability is built into its very nature.

In the circumstances, the quasi nongovernmental organization is unlikely to be able to put down a deep and vigorous root system in private soil. However fine an organization it is and however useful, it remains an exogenous growth, never entirely accepted as either truly voluntary or fully private.

Reasons for Existence

The existence of each type of quasi nongovernmental organization has at one time or another being seriously called into question. And yet in each instance there was a convincing basic reason for its establishment. An urgent national need had been identified that no other institution in the society was meeting, or, seemingly, could meet.

In the case of the "not-for-profits," the defense establishment, responding to new scientific and technological challenges, needed two products which it could neither develop in house nor buy from private industrial firms. These were, first, certain specialized technical skills derived from a scientific, scientific-engineering, or social science knowledge base and, second, highly specialized advice given with absolute objectivity. The capacity of the "not-for-profits" to pay salaries higher than those which government could offer of course enhanced their ability to attract particularly well-qualified personnel.

The regional educational laboratories were a governmental response to growing public awareness of failure in the nation's educational system. In theory, it would have been possible simply to give the funds to university schools of education for additional research of the type they were already doing. Their research record, however, was considered sufficiently questionable to make this an unpromising alternative. While it was clear that university scholars from many disciplines would have to participate in a new national research effort in education, it was also clear that some new mechanism was needed as a base for the effort, a mechanism in which a number of resources not previously directed towards the problems of our educational system could be brought together. The independent nonprofit corporation was considered to be the best device for the purpose.

In the case of the CIA-sponsored organizations, a national need had appeared in the early fifties for some means through which American intellectuals could make their presence felt, and have their arguments for a free society heard, in the confrontation that had developed with the Communist camp. It was obvious that the Communists were organizing a variety of intellectual activities around the world aimed at winning uncommitted people to their side. We had to do the same, and yet we had no effective means at hand for the job.

One possibility would have been to use government funds openly to expand existing government educational and cultural exchange programs, but there were members of Congress and others in government who doubted the wisdom of such a course. Equally important, however, was the view held then within government that the United States, having private institutions, should use them in the struggle against totalitarianism because their very involvement would be an advertisement for a free society such as ours. The problem, however, was that in a number of instances we lacked private agencies with the appropriate mission and competence.

So the expedient of using CIA funds to create new private organizations specially for the purpose (and in some cases to subsidize existing agencies) was adopted. It was in the circumstances a quick, imaginative, and effective solution to a serious problem. But it was a solution that was bound in time to become embarrassing because of the incongruity of covert financing with the nature of free intellectual institutions. The need, however, for communication with intellectual and artistic leadership throughout the world remains, and, as before, it will have to be met very largely by government funds—but this time given on an open basis and by a more appropriate agency of government.

Sponsorship by the Agency for International Development and its predecessor agencies of new private organizations to provide technical assistance to developing countries came about for the straightforward reason that, in the administration of the aid program, there proved to be a distinct need for certain specialized kinds of services that no existing private agency or university was able to provide and that could not be developed as economically or efficiently within the governmental bureaucracy itself.

In the case of the community action agencies sponsored by the Office of Economic Opportunity, there was, again, a pressing national need not being met. This need was to develop an understanding of the causes of poverty, the will to attack it, and the capacity to do this on the basis of a broad participation of all elements in the community, including the poor themselves. The job was simply not being done by existing public and private agencies, nor was it thought, could it be; they were considered too fragmented in their approach and too set in their ways, and they were also seen as being too middle-class, too white, too paternalistic, and too alien to be acceptable to those who were most deeply mired in the "culture of poverty." Clearly, the solution was to create a wholly new kind of mechanism to deal with the problem, the community action agency, and in most instances the most workable form for this to take proved to be that of a private, nonprofit agency heavily supported by federal funds.

The quasi nongovernmental organization has, therefore, been established to fulfill a number of specific purposes. These may be summarized under three general headings: to meet government's need for specialized services not else-where available, to provide it with independent judgment, and to offer it the kind of flexibility required for fresh solutions to complex and novel problems. Each of the quasi nongovernmental organizations has had, in varying degree, these basic purposes. And in every case it has been deemed essential to achievement of the purposes, not only that a new organization be created, but that it be located in the private, nonprofit realm of American life.

The Voluntary Association

To understand why the quasi nongovernmental organization can never be fully integrated into the voluntary tradition in American life, we need to reflect for a moment on the characteristics of the true voluntary association. The term itself is elusive. Theoretically, it includes not only all kinds of private enterprise, both nonprofit and for profit, but even the institutions of a democratic form of government as well—in short any activity by private citizens undertaken in concert and on their own volition. A more usual definition, however, and the one we are concerned with here, restricts the term to *private, nonprofit* activities, that is, action outside the initiative and authority of the state but not in the profit-making sector. This definition can include such diverse enterprises as religious organizations, political parties, trade unions, private educational institutions, voluntary hospitals, private museums and libraries, professional associations, mutual insurance companies, cooperative savings and loan associations, foundations, research organizations, fraternal societies, social clubs, and so forth. (Sometimes use of the term is restricted even further to apply only to nongovernmental service organizations in such fields as health, welfare, and recreation. These organizations, however, are then usually referred to as "voluntary agencies.")

Those who have studied voluntary association in American life have maintained that they seem to satisfy two basic social needs. They offer the individual an opportunity for self-expression, and they provide a means through which he can promote his interests or beliefs, or satisfy his altruistic impulses, by way of collective action. Thus, most voluntary associations fall into one of two types, the expressive and the instrumental, or in some cases represent a combination of the two. An example of the former might be an amateur choral group; of the latter, a national health agency; and of a mixture of the two, a national sports society.

Voluntary associations have been credited with reinforcing our democratic political system in three ways. They distribute power widely in the society and permit the individual a share in it. They enable the ordinary citizen to understand better the processes of democracy by providing him a means to participate in it in ways directly meaningful to himself. They provide a mechanism for the continual promotion of social change.

It is fundamental, therefore, to the true voluntary association, that it exists primarily to serve the *individual citizen,* providing him with a means for self-expression and collective action outside the aegis of the state. Voluntarism is, furthermore, based on the assumption that the maintenance of a democratic society depends not alone on the preservation of democratic governmental institutions, but also on the existence of nongovernmental institutions which serve a variety of democratic purposes outside the area of state action and responsibility.

On close inspection the quasi nongovernmental organization, although in some cases having volunteer workers associated with it, proves not to be a true part of the voluntary tradition. In carrying out its mission it may quite possibly serve the needs of the individual citizen. Certainly, in the case of the community action agencies, it often does. But in the final test it must serve public purposes, and if these do not coincide with the individual's purposes, government's interest must prevail. Moreover, the quasi nongovernmental organization does not have as a primary concern the safeguarding of the essential nongovernmental aspects of a democratic society. Its concerns are, rather, with the collective interests of the polity and with the discharge of government's responsibilities.

Thus, the quasi nongovernmental organization is at bottom as foreign to the tradition of voluntary association as is the formal structure of government itself. It has been created by forced draft and has not sunk its roots into the social structure as has the true voluntary association. No matter how much it is made to resemble the voluntary association, it can never be quite the same thing. It will always have a kind of "as if" or "as it were" quality to it, which leads us to attach to it the qualifying (but by no means disparaging) term *quasi.*

The Nonvoluntary Voluntary Association

In actual fact many voluntary associations today no longer meet the criteria for being truly voluntary, to such a degree have they become professionalized and bureaucratized, or so much has their *raison d'etre* become one of responding to governmental needs. Such voluntary organizations no longer exist primarily to serve the individual, and he has little or no say in their management. Nor do they serve particularly to strengthen the voluntary aspects of democracy. "Voluntary" organizations such as these are, in a sense, severed heads no longer related to a body. They are answerable not to a membership, but to themselves—that is, to paid professional staffs—and self-perpetuating boards of trustees. These organizations are legitimized in society by the social utility of their programs rather than by their status as the representative organs of defined bodies of the citizenry.

This type of "voluntary" organization can perhaps best be called simply a private service agency. It is in most instances a highly valuable instrumentality performing essential services for society. Nothing that has been said about it, therefore, should be regarded as deprecatory. It exists as simply a distinct type of private, nonprofit organization clearly distinguishable from the true voluntary association.

There would, on the face of it, seem to be considerable resemblance between the quasi nongovernmental organization and the private service agency in that neither truly belongs within the great tradition of voluntarism in American life. But the likeness is, in fact, more apparent than real. The basic difference between them is revealed if we ask where the ultimate power and the ultimate responsibility lie for each type of organization. For the private service agency they lie solely with its board of trustees. It is this body alone which has to see to it that the organization is adequately financed and well managed and that its programs are relevant to society's needs.

In the case of the quasi nongovernmental organization, however, power and responsibility are shared uneasily between a board of trustees and government. While in a showdown the trustees, it is true, could threaten to dissolve the corporation, government on its side has the power at any time to starve it to death financially, or use its financial power to shape the organization's program. And since financial power of this kind implies the acceptance of responsibility, a measure of the final responsibility for these organizations must inevitably remain in Washington, in a federal agency in the first instance, but ultimately with the Congress.

This is why all the organizations which make up this new genus, the defense advisory "not-for-profits," the agencies created by AID and the CIA, the regional educational laboratories, the majority of the OEO-supported community action agencies, and others are unlikely ever to become fully integrated into the private side of American life. However much they have the appearance of the typical private service organization, they will remain at bottom something essentially different. They are founded on the notion of "maximum feasible participation" of the private citizen in their governance, but, when the test comes, "maximum" must, of course, fall somewhere short of the absolute power possessed by the trustees of the fully private agency.

Independence and Accountability

The most difficult problem which has arisen in connection with the quasi nongovernmental organization is how to reconcile its dual needs for independence and accountability to government. It was placed outside government by its originators for good reasons—among them that this would help ensure its freedom. Freedom was considered to be an essential requisite to the functioning of this new type of organization.

On the other hand, the quasi nongovernmental organization, as we have seen, serves public purposes and remains almost totally dependent on the federal tax dollar for its existence. This makes necessary a close accountability by it to government. It was, therefore, in a sense, born in a dilemma, and it has never escaped from the constant inner tension this has produced as it has been buffeted by the conflicting claims of independence and governmental accountability.

The case for independence rests on the simple proposition that for government to reap the real benefits that these organizations offer, they must be *genuinely* independent. If they are anything less than this, their effectiveness will be compromised. Among the benefits, as we have seen, can be a special capacity for experimentation, objectivity, the ability to recruit specially trained or talented personnel, flexibility, economy, and efficiency. Each of these benefits is a direct function of the quality of the management of these organizations, and this in turn is a function of the degree of independence which management is accorded. In short, able men know that freedom of action is essential to their own highest performance, and they will demand it. Having won it, they will resist all attempts by government to erode it.

There would appear to be three minimum freedoms which the quasi nongovernmental organization must enjoy if it is to have real independence: freedom of program, freedom of administration, and freedom of communication. It must be able to decide for itself (within the limitations set by the legislative authority under which its governmental sponsor must operate) what programs to pursue and what to abandon, and relative priorities among the former. And certainly it must have absolute freedom to determine the nature of any part of its total program supported by private funds. It must have the right to hire and fire employees and determine their duties, compensation and prequisites, and where and how they shall be quartered. Lastly, it must be free to reach its own conclusions on both technical and policy questions and, within the minimum limitations of security requirements, communicate these without restraint publicly or privately to anyone interested.

The case for governmental accountability derives ultimately from the representative character of our democratic political system. In such a system those who govern do so on the sufferance of the people and in turn are accountable to the people. The citizen, therefore, has an inalienable right to know what his government's policies and programs are and how his tax dollar is being used.

In the American system of a separation of powers, both the President and Congress are accountable to the people and both, through appropriate methods, must satisfy themselves that when government funds are given to a private organization under grant or contract they are used for the purposes specified and in ways that do not result in personal gain to any individual above fair compensation for his services.

Thus, on the face of it, both the executive and legislative branches of government would seem to have a positive duty to exercise direct supervision over the affairs of the quasi nongovernmental organization, for how else can they discharge their responsibility to the people? This is also to some degree the case whenever government grants public funds to a private organization or individual, no matter how small the amount. But in practical terms does not government's responsibility for supervision rise in relation to the proportion which government funds represent in an organization's total budget, reaching a maximum degree in the case of the quasi nongovernmental organization? It has seemed so.

Also relevant is the degree of complexity of the activity being supported by government funds. The more abstruse and technical this is, and the further it is removed from the personal experience of the responsible civil servant or interested member of Congress, the greater is likely to be the freedom from supervision accorded it. Finally, there is some evidence to suggest that an organization's degree of independence is related to its general prestige and standing. If these are high, government is likely to treat it with greater respect.

If, in meeting its responsibility for supervision, government is not satisfied with the performance of a quasi nongovernmental organization, it must either withdraw its support or persuade the organization to mend its ways. Government then faces a dilemma. It cannot very well do the former, because it has a moral responsibility for the organization's very existence. To put it out of business would in some cases simply be to deny government services which it needs, and in other cases would be a politically embarrassing admission of the failure of a costly program. To intervene directly in the organization's administration is, however, equally distasteful, because this can very quickly succeed in killing off the organization's independence—the very thing which government most needs it to have.

Thus, independence and accountability to government seem to be irreconcilable when the theoretical implications of each are made explicit. And yet, paradoxically, the concept of a quasi private agency created as the result of government initiative and financed by public funds seems to work and in many instances work well. It works because there are constraints operating on both the governmental patron and its organizational protégé which most of the time enable them to avoid head-on confrontations. Most importantly, there is a job to be done in the national interest with no readily apparent alternative way of getting it done. This makes for a willingness to compromise on both sides, so that the requirements of neither independence nor accountability are ever fully met.

The quasi nongovernmental organization exists, therefore, in a state of constant uneasiness. To keep it functioning, there has to be on the part both of Congress and the particular executive department to which the organization is related a constant appreciation of the high value which its independence has to the nation and the greatest restraint in encroaching on this. And in the quasi private organization there must be irreproachable standards of conduct and common sense in regard to such matters as salaries and perquisites. There must, furthermore, simply be a constant awareness of the need for accountability to the people whenever public money is involved, however complex or professional the business at hand or however burdensome the process.

Essential also to the continued viability of the quasi nongovernmental organization is a clear definition of its responsibilities in relation to those exercised by government. While the former should have some role in government policy formation, this is essentially the responsibility of the latter. It is all too easy for government to abdicate this responsibility when an issue is extremely complex or highly technical. The danger here is that the nongovernmental partner will become so deeply implicated in government policy through having in effect been the creator of it that it will sacrifice its position of detachment and objectivity, and hence its ultimate independence.

Finally, nothing can reduce a quasi nongovernmental organization to ineffectuality more quickly than to have government exercise its responsibility for supervision at too detailed a level. The necessity to clear petty and routine decisions with Washington not only causes inefficiency, delay, and wasteful duplication of effort but also makes it almost impossible for the private organization to hold good staff. At bottom, this sort of practice corrodes the basis of trust which is essential if the relationship between sponsor and protégé is to prosper.

The Future

One can only speculate about the future of the quasi nongovernmental organization. It is at present a highly useful, perhaps even indispensable, adjunct to government and, all things considered, has been a success. And one must remember that it was established as a response to new social needs that were not being met in any other way. Yet the very ambiguity of its status is bound to be cause for disquiet.

Throughout our history we have had two ways of getting things done in this society, by voluntary action (either profit-making or nonprofit) or by direct government action. The dividing line between these two spheres has always been indistinct. But gradually, in response to powerful new forces, especially population growth, urbanization, the thrust of new technologies, and the changing nature of the economy, the area of governmental responsibility has, perforce, greatly expanded. Many Americans have regretted this, because of a deep-seated belief in the value of voluntary action and accompanying distrust of government. This belief is part of our history and of our mores. A natural reaction, therefore, has been to strengthen the failing voluntary sector with public funds as a way of redressing the public-private balance. We have been doing this in the past few decades on an ever increasing scale with federal grant and contract funds.

The quasi nongovernmental organization does not, however, represent simply an intensification of this trend. It is, as we have seen, something new because it emanates not from the private sector but from government. Nevertheless, the questions that it raises in an acute form are the same questions which must ultimately be faced by every private organization receiving an increasing share of its income from public funds: Is it possible in these circumstances to keep one's independence? Is independence important?

The latter question can be answered only with a resounding affirmative. It *is* important to the nation's future—vitally so—that we maintain strong, independent, nongovernmental institutions.

But how to do this in the face of increasing dependence of these institutions on public funds is a question that has received too little attention. There is, therefore, an urgent need to turn all of our powers of political and social inventiveness to this task. As we do so, a good place to start will be with the quasi nongovernmental organization, for if we can find ways to protect its independence, then surely we can solve the problem of guaranteeing the freedom of the truly private organization.

High on the priority list will be to find ways to give financial security to the quasi nongovernmental organization, because financial stability is an essential ingredient of independence. Here, fortunately, there is a device that is already working successfully for the defense-related organizations: the fee paid to them by their governmental sponsors over and above contract costs and overhead. This fee, which averages around 5 per cent of contract value, is unrestricted money, to be used as the organization sees fit. The fee arrangement seems to be the best device presently available for bringing to a nongovernmental organization the general support, free of project obligations, which it so desperately needs. The device could, and should, be extended to all organizations of the quasi nongovernmental variety and possibly to private organizations generally which receive substantial government funds.*

Also to be examined will be all aspects of the issue of accountability, for the present uneasy arrangement could fall apart at any moment. It seems probable that in the interests of meeting new public needs of the nation through the device of the government-established, quasi private organization there is going to have to be considerable "give" on the side of traditional modes of account-

---

*The financial plight of nongovernmental organizations at large and their need for general, unrestricted funds in addition to project funds was discussed in an introductory essay entitled "The Nongovernmental Organization at Bay" that appeared in Carnegie Corporation's annual report for 1966.

ability to government. In short, independence will have a higher value than this kind of accountability because of the direct relationship that independence bears to quality of performance. And it is the latter that will matter most to the society.

To compensate for this "give," however, there will have to be an intensification in these agencies of the type of broad accountability to the public exercised by the staff and trustees of fully private, tax-exempt organizations generally. If this kind of accountability, which must include periodic public reporting, can be regarded as acceptable by government and the public, there is no reason why it cannot be fully as effective as accountability *through* government.

It is possible that because of the Vietnam war only a limited number of additional quasi nongovernmental organizations will be created in the months immediately ahead. A look into the farther range future, however, suggests the likelihood of a considerable growth of this type of institution, because the basic forces which have produced the present crop are more likely to become intensified than to diminish.

Also, it is none too early to consider what the mood of the country may be after the war ends. The American people may be eager then to turn to new and more satisfying endeavors and may show themselves ready to support major new governmental programs for the advancement of social welfare at home and economic and social development in Asia, Africa, and Latin America.

If this is so, there will be fresh pressure to create new quasi nongovernmental organizations to help do the job. Now is the time, therefore, before that pressure comes, for both government and the private sector to think this new organizational form through, in order to clarify its status, to strengthen it, and to find for it a more secure place in our society.

Foundations at the
Service of the Public

If there is an evident lesson to be learned from the turbulence of the times in which we live, it is that the nation has no higher requirement today than a flexible capacity for rapid change in its social institutions. So forceful is the impact of pervasive new technologies and of new, energetically-pressed expectations of the American people, especially segments of it formerly voiceless and powerless, that intransigence to change can nowadays turn revered, influential, and proud institutions into noisy battlegrounds, or leave them as decaying edifices where the main road used to run.

The kind of conservatism which regards organizational forms and procedures as ends in themselves rather than as no more than present means for accomplishment of the ever changing purposes of society is increasingly doomed. The dodo (*didus ineptus*), a bird with a large, heavy body and tiny wings, could not adapt to the coming of predatory man to its habitat in Mauritius and perished. Our institutions today need slim bodies and well-developed wings!

In the light of this national imperative, every agency which can serve the common good by facilitating the processes of institutional change toward a more just, healthier, better educated, and more universally prosperous national and world society has a very special value, and perhaps none more so than foundations. Indeed, many observers, while denying the foundation a role as *active leader* of the more militant movements of social change, would say that its chief value to society today lies in its capacity to anticipate the need for institutional transformations and help bring these about by speedy deployment of its funds to critical points of leverage and potential breakthrough. In this view, foundations have a restricted ability to lead change but an unusual capacity to help it along. The two are not the same. The former may be more romantic, but the latter, perhaps, more realistic and productive!

The means available to foundations for facilitating change are varied. They include traditional activities such as the support of research and dissemination of its findings, the financing of experimental projects by established institutions, and the organization and financing of special studies and national commissions of enquiry. But they may also include the encouragement and support of aggressive new community organizations which have sprung up as the result of social dissatisfaction and which the comfortable stratum of American life would consider disturbing and perhaps even dangerous.

The types of social institutions affected may be as specific as a university, a nonprofit organization, or a government bureaucracy, or as broad as an entire profession or a great national program. While in some cases a foundation may find it necessary to take the initiative in establishing a wholly new enterprise, in most cases its effectiveness will depend on the availability within an existing institution of a nucleus of able individuals ready to bring about internal reforms. It is the foundation's role to seek out these men and women and give them the support they need.

The willingness to accept a continuous responsibility for the discernment and furthering of required social change provides an exceedingly tough standard against which foundations may be measured. No foundation, obviously, has the prescience or courage to meet this responsibility all of the time. A few try and do reasonably well at it, but most foundations make the effort seldom or not at all. Should they?

The Obligations of Freedom

Among the vast array of institutions, public and private, profit-making and non-profit, which comprise the fabric of contemporary American society there is none which possesses greater freedom than the foundation. Unlike a business enterprise, it is not subject to the discipline of the market place nor, like public agencies, of the ballot box. It is not dependent on others for funds. It does not have to be responsive to the claims of a membership or of alumni, students, or faculty. It is not subject to periodic accreditation or licensing or obligatory compliance with a set of traditional professional standards. In short, it enjoys less constraint by the usual forms of accountability to society than does, perhaps, any other type of institution.

As a corollary to this freedom the grant-making foundation possesses uncommitted funds which can, within the limits specified in its charter, be directed by its trustees to whatever philanthropic purposes they think best. These funds are in most cases remarkably free both of stated or implied obligations for their use. No particular cause, group, or institution has a "right" to them. No individual has a special claim on them.

It is these two associated characteristics of the foundation, its freedom and the generally uncommitted nature of its funds—not its size, not its prestige, and not its past reputation—which make it a unique agency in our national life and potentially one of such enormous value. No other has as great liberty, and consequently such an awesome responsibility, to diagnose the need for institutional reforms, however controversial these may be, and to help bring them about. The foundation can put itself above the special interests which restrict the vision of most organizations and the parochial concerns of the professions and consider only what is for the common good—tomorrow and on into the more distant future.

This is a noble vision which, if accepted, leads to the conclusion that a foundation does have a special obligation to try to use its particular strengths to help along those types of social change that will make for a better world. Conversely, a foundation would seem to have a special responsibility not to dispense its funds in such a way that they simply perpetuate sterile institutional forms and procedures left over from the past—comfortable and familiar though many of these are likely to be.

These objectives are, perhaps, obvious, but they are more difficult to achieve than they may seem to be. In some cases, foundations are fettered by overly restrictive charters. In others, the close control exercised by individual donors or corporations prevents them from taking full advantage of the unusual freedom given them by society. The capacity of these foundations to support social innovation is often severely circumscribed by the special interests of their sponsors. Foundations with these limitations serve many useful purposes. But the touchstone of the true foundation, some would say, in the form in which it can have its highest value to society, is absolute unfettered independence protected by trustees and staff whose sole loyalty is toward the long-run public good.

The Public Stake in Foundations

The foundation is, paradoxically, both private and public in its nature. It is private because it is incorporated as a private, nongovernmental institution, derives its assets from private donors, and is privately controlled by a donor-appointed or self-perpetuating board of trustees.

There is a common misunderstanding that the public character of the foundation, and hence the public stake in it, derives from its tax-exempt status. How frequently has one heard it said that foundations are really spending public money, and therefore should be subject to greater governmental control. Such a view, however, is based on fallacious reasoning and reveals either surprising ignorance or a dangerous disavowal of one of the basic tenets of the American system.

Throughout our history we have believed in pluralism and have practiced it. We have recognized that the nation's public purposes are considerably more extensive in scope than its governmental purposes, and, through the aegis of the state, we have enabled a wide variety of private institutions, including foundations, to be chartered to accomplish certain *public,* though *nongovernmental,* purposes. We have also, through the aegis of the state, given tax exemption to these institutions to facilitate their work and have regarded this as being eminently in the public interest. Therefore, to attribute the public stake in the foundation to its tax-exempt status or to regard this status as a "privilege" is wholly erroneous. It is, in Professor Milton Katz's pithy phrase "to mistake an effect for a cause."

The true origin of the public aspect of the foundation lies in the nature of its activity. It is public because it devotes its funds to purposes in which the total society has a vital interest, such as education, health, and welfare. Grants in these fields do without question affect the public, and hence the public has a legitimate stake in the foundations which make them.

But there is an even more important sense in which the foundation is public in character. It is public because the public cannot afford to regard with indifference how foundation funds are spent, so precious are they, as we have seen, in the vital process of social change, and so limited are they in amount. The $1.3 billion spent by foundations in 1967 was, for example, less than 0.2 per cent of the Gross National Product, less than 9 per cent of total voluntary giving, and only 3 per cent of the federal government's expenditure for health, education, and welfare.

Foundation funds, in short, offer a case where a technically private asset is of such potential value to the nation that it must, perforce, be regarded as a public asset. The implications of this proposition are far reaching.

The Dilemma Posed by Foundations

If, then, the larger society's stake in foundations rests, in its highest form, on the preciousness of their funds for the anticipation and easing of social change, one may well ask how society can be sure these funds are being used as effectively as they might be to that end.

This question probes to the heart of the special dilemma which foundations have always posed to the nation. On the one hand, their principal value derives directly from their unusual freedom. It is to be found in their ability to support controversial causes, to help establish tomorrow's orthodoxy by backing today's heresy, to be bold and of independent mind, even seemingly whimsical or arbitrary. The foundation, as we have seen, cannot in the best sense really be a foundation without freedom.

On the other hand, it is under the generous mantle of freedom with which society has clothed foundations that there can also lurk such anti-social characteristics as mismanagement, short-sighted judgment, complacence, and downright rascality. With regard to the last of these faults, investigations by the Internal Revenue Service have indicated that the foundation device is unquestionably in a few cases being misused for personal gain. The present rate of establishment of new foundations, nearly 2,000 a year, is in itself enough to make even the casual observer wonder whether foundations are in all instances serving genuinely philanthropic purposes.

It is also apparent that some foundations are ineptly managed. Their funds are not invested in such a way as to provide an adequate balance between annual income and growth of the corpus, their administration is slipshod, or they are unnecessarily secretive in their operations. These are faults which should be put right by their trustees, but sometimes are not. The newly instituted registration of foundations in the State of New York is turning up some uncomfortable evidence along these lines.

Lastly, there is complacence and short-sightedness to be found in some foundations, probably some in all of them. This is not surprising, as these natural human failings are present to some degree in all social institutions.

The dilemma faced by society has, then, always been how to hold foundations accountable without at the same time killing off the very thing that gives them their peculiar value—their freedom. How is their need for independence to be reconciled with society's need that they serve the public interest?

The Limitations of Governmental Regulation

Committees of Congress have on several occasions, most notably in 1915, 1952, 1954, and currently, investigated foundations and considered the possible need for legislative measures to place them under greater restriction. The Treasury Department, following an intensive study of foundations in 1964, made a number of suggestions for possible legislative measures. From time to time there have been limited modifications of federal tax laws affecting foundations. But, fortunately, Congress has never yet been persuaded that it should pass legislation to bring foundations under substantive federal regulation.

At the state level there has in recent years been a gradual movement to register foundations, and 12 states now require this, including, as we have seen, New York, where about 25 per cent of all foundations are located. This appears on the whole to have been a constructive development, although registration can and does, mean different things in different states and can only be effective if the attorney general or other appropriate state official is provided with adequate authority and sufficient well-trained staff for the job.

What the future may bring in the way of regulation no one can say, but thus far it has seemed to most concerned individuals, inside as well as outside government, that the functions which public authorities, both at the federal and state levels, should perform in the regulation of foundations must be specific and limited. The accepted objectives of regulation include preventing use of the foundation device for personal gain or for control of a profit-making business, ensuring conformity to charters and deeds of trust, and enforcing regularity in the handling of funds.

If regulation were to extend much beyond these types of controls into the realm of attempting to ensure that all foundations are *effective* in their operations, a number of serious problems would quickly become apparent. In the first place, such regulation would presume that a legislative body had been able to agree on a clear definition of what constitutes foundation effectiveness—obviously a dubious possibility, as each legislator would have a different notion of this based on a particular cause or institution in which he happened to be interested.

Secondly, it would represent a dangerous attack on the basic American belief in pluralism, of trusting private institutions to carry out public purposes with a minimum of interference. True, this attack would, on the face of it, be directed at only one part of the private sector. But, philosophically, on what grounds could regulation of the effectiveness of foundations be justified if other types of private, nonprofit institutions were not similarly subjected to regulation? Furthermore, would not regulation of foundations in effect also constitute a form of regulation of the potential recipients of foundation funds?

Thirdly, it might cause a drying up of private donations to foundations for unrestricted, general purposes, thereby not only throwing a greater burden on government agencies and the public purse but also inhibiting the establishment of new foundations of a type with the greatest potential usefulness.

Lastly, and most importantly, it would destroy the independent character and spirit of foundations, wherein, as we have seen, lies their highest value to society.

And so it would seem that of the four anti-social characteristics exhibited here and there in the foundation field, government has a legitimate role to play only in controlling out-and-out rascality and some aspects of mismanagement. It cannot legislate against myopia and sloth in foundations any more than it can root these shortcomings out of government itself! And even less can government regulate foundations in such a way that the highest test of their effectiveness—their ability to facilitate social change—will be more fully met. This is a responsibility which foundations themselves alone can assume.

Difficulties in Self-regulation

The danger which foundations have faced in recent years, and perhaps never more so than today, is that public loss of confidence in them, occasioned by limited, but continuing and well-publicized disclosures of abuses, will become great enough to precipitate Congress into a hasty and clumsy piece of legislation. The suggestion has, for example, been made by Congressman Patman of restricting the life of *all* foundations to 25 years—a remedy tantamount to using a jack hammer to crack a walnut.

It is evident, therefore, that the foundations which are carrying out genuine philanthropic purposes, which are well managed, and are making a strong effort to serve the public interest, must take energetic steps themselves to put the foundation house in better order. They have no grounds for thinking that because they have escaped restriction in the past they will necessarily continue to do so in the future. A field which has grown from less than 200 members 40 years ago to 20,000 today and has an *annual increment* of 2,000 will, of course, come under ever closer scrutiny by public authorities. And the concern of these officials, once aroused, may not stop at regulation which simply prevents wrongdoing or the grosser forms of mismanagement, however inappropriate more extensive government regulation may be.

But for the "good" foundations to take publicly convincing measures to put the foundation house in order is no easy matter and has always proved baffling to those who have contemplated it. The reasons for this are not at all difficult to find.

First, there is the enormous variety of size, purpose, governance, and style of operation among the large and growing number of foundations. No two are exactly alike and most are widely different from each other. Nearly all foundations, some rather strongly, still reflect the strengths, interests—and idiosyncrasies—of their founders and in many cases have an attachment to the founder's domain which makes for a kind of aloofness not only to the public but even to other foundations. The task of building a sense of common identity or community—of common participation in a select activity—which might serve as the basis for collective responsibility and self-imposed standards of conduct, is well nigh impossible among such a large and heterogeneous group.

The second reason is somewhat akin to the first. Because of their origins, many foundations have a strong orientation toward the realm of personal or corporate private charity. They are essentially simply a useful institutionalization of the giving which a wealthy man or a corporation might otherwise do directly, without the benefit of an intermediary mechanism. Other foundations, however, especially those in being for some length of time, are oriented entirely toward the public and consider themselves to be semi-public institutions, or in transition toward that status. There is, therefore, a basic dichotomy in the field which tends to work against the development of the kind of unifying élan that might provide a basis for the acceptance of a common set of standards. The gulf between these differing orientations is broad and deep.

Lastly, there is a long tradition, not unlike that found in some other fields, which makes it a breach of good manners for one foundation to criticize another. It is a little like telling a member of your club that he could use a good bath and clean shirt. It just isn't done! An unwritten code such as this can be a powerful deterrent.

External Forms of Foundation Accountability

In the popular mind, the term accountability usually has the restricted meaning of answerability for fiscal regularity in the handling of funds over which one has stewardship. In government it has come to have a wider meaning which includes fiscal regularity but also connotes answerability for adherence to budgetary prescriptions and for efficiency in administration. In the professions, for example medicine or law, accountability implies conformity to certain customary and statutory standards, basically of an ethical nature. Accountability can be of a well-defined, direct, or immediate sort, as to a superior within an administrative hierachy, or it can be indirect, undefined, or even quite vague—something one simply feels as a consequence of his own professional, moral, or ethical standards. Finally, it can apply either to individuals or collectively to organizations. In all cases it implies the obligation to be prepared to give reasons for and explanations of one's conduct to the public.

There are already in existence several forms of public accountability by foundations, some of which are outside foundation control and some of which are within their control. Among the former the most important is the federal requirement that foundations, in consideration of their tax exemption, file a report annually with the Internal Revenue Service. This report, known as Form 990-A, includes information on income disbursements, administrative expenses, assets and liabilities, as well as other pertinent matters such as whether any funds have been used to influence legislation or participate in a political campaign. Information in this form, with one exception, is made available to the public. The annual submission of Form 990-A to the federal government is important but is, of course, restricted in the purpose it can serve to the relevant provisions of the Internal Revenue Code. With state regulation, which has been discussed above, it constitutes the only form of governmentally imposed public accountability by foundations and is strictly limited in nature.

A second external form of public accountability by foundations is press comment. Theoretically, this could be a powerful instrument for calling foundations to the bar of an informed public opinion. In fact, the press has generally not shown itself to be well informed or sophisticated in its treatment of foundations. Major exceptions can, of course, be found here and there among writers for certain newspapers, news magazines, and journals of opinion. Blame must also be placed on the foundations themselves. Some have actively, even brusquely, discouraged press interest and others have refrained from trying to interest the press in their activities because of an old-fashioned and virtuous, but perhaps optimistic, belief that good works should be done in secret and will in time provide their own advertisement.

Internal Forms of Accountability

Among internal forms of accountability, there is the type provided by organizations which the foundation field has itself created, chiefly the Foundation Library Center and the Council on Foundations. The former, though having other functions, is essentially what its name implies, a library. The latter is a membership organization open to any grant making foundation. Both are supported by foundation contributions. Through their meetings, counseling services, research, and publications, these two organizations help to raise standards in the field.

The Council, which has a broad membership of all types of foundations—general purpose, community, family and corporate, both American and Canadian—serves as a general forum for the exchange of views among foundation officers and trustees. The Library Center, by means of the current *Foundation Directory* which it prepares, its collection of annual reports and other reference materials, and its willingness to answer enquiries, provides the public with a readily available source of information about foundations. With headquarters in New York City and a branch in Washington, D.C., it maintains depositories in seven locations in other parts of the country.

But neither of these organizations, valuable as they are, is in a position to criticize foundations directly and specifically by name. Their suggestions and exhortations have to be broad and general in nature, and experience shows that the foundations which could profit most from such criticism are least likely to listen to it.

A second internal form of accountability, tenuous and subtle in nature but nonetheless real, is that imposed on foundations by the concern which their staffs are likely to have for their own professional reputations. These concerns are of two quite different kinds: a desire for distinction as a foundation practitioner, wise, skilled and fair-minded in discerning the public interest, and for professional recognition within a discipline. Of the two the former is probably the more important to the public. The latter, if it assumes too great importance to a foundation officer, can even be antithetical to the public interest because it may diminish the officer's capacity to recognize the general good and to give this precedence over the special, and sometimes selfish, interests of a particular discipline or profession. This form of accountability is, of course, limited by the failure of many foundations to employ any professional staff at all, a shortcoming which many informed people regard as one of the principal liabilities of the foundation field.

A third and extremely important internal medium for public accountability is provided by foundation boards of trustees, whose principal duty as directors of a philanthropic agency is to serve the public interest and have a sense of obligation for accountability to the public. But, paradoxically, the trustees are also there to carry on the donor's interests, and, as time goes by and conditions change, these may well begin to fall a good deal short of what independent observers would then consider to be of greatest benefit to the public. Nonetheless, the trustees, out of loyalty to the donor, or a sense of obligation to him or his family, may be reluctant to change with the times.

Andrew Carnegie foresaw this difficulty when in his letter of gift establishing Carnegie Corporation he said:

> Conditions upon the earth inevitably change; hence, no wise man will bind trustees forever to certain paths, causes or institutions. I disclaim any intention of doing so. On the contrary, I give my trustees full authority to change policy or causes hitherto aided, from time to time, when this, in

their opinion, has become necessary or desirable. They shall best conform
to my wishes by using their own judgment.

There is also the problem of board composition. If trustees have a responsibility to serve the public interest, should they then be so selected as to be
representative of the public? Foundations have been equivocal on this question.
Some have denied the need for representativeness and have taken the view
that trustees can best serve the general interest precisely by not being representative of special interests. Other have taken tentative steps to provide
broader representation in their boards but have not admitted the principle in
full. It remains an area of confusion and is one that will probably become
increasingly troublesome.

Taking the field at large, one would have to question whether there is to be
found today in most foundation boards an adequate variety of trustee experience
with current problems of the society. A study of board membership would
probably reveal that trustees are largely drawn from the same social class, the
same age group, the same professions, the same educational background, the
same sex, and the same race.

A final internal form of public accountability is provided by the annual reports
which some foundations publish voluntarily. These reports usually include a
list of trustees and senior staff, a description of the foundation's program interests, a list of its donations for the past year including the purpose, recipient,
and amount of each grant, and a complete financial statement including a
breakdown of administrative expenses. Unfortunately, although the issuing of
such a report is a basic canon of good foundation practice, most foundations
still fail to comply with it. Of the 249 foundations with assets of over $10 million,
less than a third have ever issued a report and fewer than a quarter do so
regularly each year. Various excuses for not publishing reports have been
advanced by foundations over the years, none of them convincing. The record
has improved slightly with time but is still reprehensible.

Potentially, there is no more important form of accountability than these
published reports, especially were they to include some explanation of how the
foundation sees its particular program of grants serving the public interest and
specifically the public interest as it relates to social change. This, of course,
amounts to asking foundations to expose themselves to the full glare of public
scrutiny and possibly of public censure or ridicule as well as approbation. But
it is not too much for society to expect, and perhaps even require, in return
for the unusual freedom which it gives to foundations.

An Independent Appraisal

Various suggestions have been made in recent months as to how the foundation
field could provide itself with a continuing means of independent, nongovernmental appraisal. These proposals clearly reflect a growing feeling that present

forms of public accountability are inadequate to the times and a fear of increased governmental regulation. None of the designs for an appraisal mechanism has been able to answer two hard questions: How can it be adequately financed and yet be—and be seen to be—sufficiently independent of the foundations to win public confidence? And how can sharp enough teeth be put into its work to bring about real reforms in the field?

The need for public accountability by foundations presents a complex set of problems to which there is probably no single solution and certainly no easy one. More likely the answer will lie in a variety of steps.

Perhaps, for example, the foundations, large and small, which see themselves as semi-public institutions oriented principally toward the public, should find new ways of coming into closer association with one another to further their common belief in the necessity for public accountability. In so doing they might begin to refer to themselves as the "independent foundations," signifying their difference from other types of foundations and giving themselves a separate identity in the eyes of the public.

Perhaps the functions of the Council on Foundations and Foundation Library Center should be considerably expanded and in the process each organization provided with a set of sharp incisors. For example, the Council might develop a code of good foundation practice as a basis for membership in it and the Library Center might make its studies and publications more pointedly critical of certain foundation practices.

Perhaps all foundations over a certain minimal size should be required by law to publish a comprehensive annual report for distribution to the public.

Perhaps the foundation field itself should set up an independent commission to review the present state of the field and make recommendations as to how foundations might more effectively serve the public interest. The purpose of such an enquiry would not be inquisitorial, although the commission should not shrink from calling attention to wrongdoing where found, but a constructive effort to help foundations attain the highest degree of social value of which they are capable.

These and other ideas should be given serious consideration by all who value foundations. For otherwise that great social invention which has done so much for American life and, indeed, for mankind over the past half century may find itself first fettered and then destroyed by a society which has lost faith in it. It has happened to social institutions before.

Foundations and the Unity of Charitable Organizations

The following address was given by the Corporation's president in November 1969 before action was completed on the tax reform bill. Although the final version of the bill deleted some restrictions discussed here, we believe the views expressed in the speech on the basic relationship between foundations and the charitable organization field at large have continuing relevance to the future of American society.

The assault this year on foundations, if it reveals anything, tells us that the safety of all types of private charitable organizations—religious, educational, medical, and philanthropic—may now be in serious doubt. The advocacy of pluralism may still make for good political rhetoric, but there seem to be fewer and fewer people at the nation's center of power who really believe in it and are prepared to act on that belief.

From what I have witnessed in Washington in recent months, it is my sad conclusion that the role played by free, private institutions as a bulwark of the American democratic system may be in jeopardy. I say this because I have seen alarming evidence both in the Congress and the Executive Branch of an astonishing lack of knowledge, and hence lack of concern, not just about foundations but about private organizations generally. Beyond that, there is a pervasive atmosphere of suspicion, even hostility, to the very idea of the independence of foundations, and this seems to extend in some measure to other private, tax-exempt institutions as well.

Particularly distressing is the seeming ignorance among high officials of the nature and meaning of certain broad, fundamental concepts which give unity to the entire charitable organization field and which make the welfare of foundations and other types of charitable organizations an indivisible matter.

Many people have been slow to recognize in the current attack on foundations the broader danger to private charitable organizations generally. This is because the foundation field has gradually slipped into a position of extreme vulnerability as the result of a growing loss of public confidence in it occasioned by real and fancied foundation misdeeds.

Lumping the charges against foundations—right or wrong—indiscriminately together, foundations have come to be thought of as tax dodges for the wealthy;

as involved in improper political activity; as the backers and promoters of extremism, Left or Right; as the corrupters of public officials; as representing dangerous concentrations of economic power; as favoring black people, the intellectual elite, and the citizens of other countries at the expense of the "common American"; and so on. The list of fears and phobias has lengthened over the years with each Congressional investigation and has been assiduously kept alive, whether based on truth or falsehood, by relentless and sometimes unscrupulous critics.

What we have seen in the past year is a recrudescence of all the long-smoldering antipathies toward foundations suddenly fanned into a roaring flame by the wind of a taxpayers' revolt—a revolt not just against high tax rates but also against inequities in the system of taxation. And the heat has been felt in Washington. Unfortunately, many observers in other kinds of private institutions have felt that this was not their fight and that the foundation field perhaps deserved at least a good scare. They have, therefore, overlooked the wider dangers inherent in the excessive aspects of the Congressional response to the public heat. They have failed to see that in these excesses could lie the seeds of the destruction not just of foundations but of other private institutions as well.

Granting, of course, that there have been real financial abuses in some foundations, and conceding that specifically tailored measures to prevent these abuses are highly desirable, there are five themes that have appeared in the legislative debate on foundations which are cause for real alarm. Whether the full force of each of these themes will be evident in the law Congress finally passes is still in doubt, but that is not the point here. It is the fact that these ideas have even been seriously considered at one stage or another that is disturbing.

A Tax on Foundations

The first of these themes has had the most public discussion and has aroused opposition from other classes of charitable organizations as well as from foundations. This is the notion that foundations should pay a federal tax on their investment income from endowment, on the theory that all who share in the benefits of government and are thought to be able to pay should contribute to its cost. The opposition to such a tax has centered on the loss of income it would entail to other private organizations, as it would, in effect, be a tax not on foundations but on the charities they support. Thus, foundations are able to help pay the cost of government only at the expense of their beneficiaries.

Important as this consideration is, it is not by any means the chief harm the tax would do. Its worst feature would be that it would for the first time breach the principle of total exemption from income tax of charitable organizations, a principle which has been basic to our social system and served the nation well since a constitutionally based income tax was first introduced in 1913.

A tax on foundations would set a precedent that could in time lead to a similar loss of full exemption by other classes of endowed charitable institutions—private universities, colleges, and schools, voluntary hospitals and welfare organizations, and religious institutions. If it were considered proper by this Congress that foundations contribute to the cost of government, then it could seem logical to some future Congress that these other institutions, which also share in the benefits of government, pay their fair share. A tax would, furthermore, serve as a precedent to encourage other levels of government to levy an income tax on foundations and in time on other charitable organizations.

It might, therefore, be only a matter of a few years before income tax exemption, which is basic to the financial viability of private, charitable organizations, disappeared from our national life altogether. The ensuing enfeeblement and demise of many of these private organizations would in itself spell the end of much of the nongovernmental, pluralistic activity that is essential to the American form of democracy.

An income tax on foundations, because of what it could set in motion, can be viewed as being inimical to the very nature of our kind of society, not, of course, deliberately so but nonetheless potentially as dangerous to it as the threat of foreign ideologies. And that should be cause for the most sober reflection.

The Nature of Foundation Funds

A second disturbing theme of the legislative proceedings in Washington has been the assertion that foundation income is really public money, because it is itself tax exempt and because it derives from endowment funds created by gifts which offered a donor tax advantages; and yet decisions on the use of this income are not subject to the normal forms of government decision-making and public accountability. This frequently repeated statement is usually made in a kind of accusatory manner, with heavy emphasis on the *privilege* of tax deductibility and tax exemption, as if there were something inherently wrong, or contrary to the public interest, about these tax benefits and about private, self-perpetuating boards of trustees having the power to give away foundation funds.

What this kind of statement overlooks, of course, is that if there is validity to it, it must also apply logically to *any* funds derived from a gift that brought tax benefits to a donor and to the investment income of *all* private, tax-exempt organizations, be they educational, medical, religious, or any other. And it must be remembered that these other types of charitable organizations are as much governed by private, self-perpetuating boards of trustees as are foundations.

Those who glibly say that foundation funds are really public funds are in fact raising a fundamental, general question of whether there can be any such thing as really private endowment funds in our society any longer and are thereby, in fact, challenging the very right to existence of tax-exempt, private organizations.

While granting that foundations, and hence foundation funds, do have their

45

public aspects and their funds quite properly should be regarded as being impressed with a public trust, it must always be remembered that, since foundations are formed as private corporations by private individuals, they are *private* institutions, and the funds they possess and spend are *private* funds. In this respect, the tax benefits foundations enjoy should be seen as society's *quid pro quo* for the charitable functions they perform that would otherwise either be a burden on public, tax-derived funds or not be performed at all. They are simply one part, and a vital part, of a group of incentives which the state offers to private citizens to encourage them to perform charitable acts.

Protecting Government from Foundations

A third theme in the legislation, sometimes explicitly stated and always implied, has been that foundations represent a potentially evil influence on government and government must, therefore, be protected from contact with them. The Ways and Means Committee initially proposed restrictions on the influencing of legislation by foundations so stringent as virtually to bar them altogether from participation in public policy formation, and its final proposals were nearly as restrictive.

Aside from being profoundly insulting to many fine public officials, both elected and appointed, by implying that they lack the intelligence, integrity, and courage to make independent decisions in the public interest, such a concept, if given effect in the final legislation, will erect a barrier not only between government and foundations but between government and many valuable experimental projects financed by foundations but carried out by other tax-exempt organizations and institutions. Government—and hence the public—thereby will be denied, in an important respect, the benefits of private sector experience, ideas, and initiative. The public loss will be particularly great in fields such as education, health care, scientific policy, welfare, conservation, and the control of environmental pollution, where substantial general improvements cannot be made with private funds alone but must inevitably entail massive governmental participation.

It is distressing that this notion of insulating the processes of government from the private, nonprofit sector should have come to the fore just at a time when the public interest would most be served by a maximum amount of public/private cooperation. And it is ironic that this should have happened when foundations generally had at last outgrown the deep antipathy that many of them traditionally felt toward cooperation with government.

Control through Taxation

A fourth troublesome aspect of the legislation is the way the power of Congress to tax and to grant tax exemption has been used to institute new program controls over foundations. Under present law, foundations are not permitted to influence the outcome of elections or to influence legislation directly except as an insubstantial part of their activities. But the proposed legislation introduces new controls and outright bans on certain specific activities. For example, a foundation would now be barred from making a direct grant to an individual except pursuant to procedures previously approved by the Internal Revenue Service and would be barred altogether from supporting voter education programs designed to encourage citizens to exercise their democratic right to vote, such as those of the Southern Regional Council and League of Women Voters. This means, simply, that, in areas hitherto reserved for decision by private boards of trustees, government authority would now prevail.

The dangers of such an extension of government authority are manifest. What a simple matter it would be for some future Congress, guided by this precedent, to use its taxing power over private university endowment funds as a convenient weapon to limit the autonomy of these institutions. What a convenient device this could be to stifle dissent—on the campus, in the pulpit, or anywhere else in the nongovernmental sector.

The freedom of private institutions is their most precious asset, and it must be jealously guarded. Erosion of the freedom of one institution normally leads to the erosion of freedom in others. History is replete with examples of societies where liberty has given way to tyranny because their peoples failed to realize that freedom is indivisible. All who value liberty should think hard about the question of how far government should be allowed to go in extending its authority over private institutions through the taxing power, for down this road can lie enormous dangers.

The Forty-year Death Sentence

A fifth theme, which has been evident here and there in the legislation, is a kind of doctrinaire populist opposition to foundations as a matter of democratic principle. Because foundations derive from great wealth, they *ipso facto* must be suspect. This, of course, was a prevalent attitude toward foundations in their early days just prior to the First World War, but one would have supposed the nation had outgrown it years ago simply on the evidence that the vast majority of foundations do in fact serve the public interest. Nevertheless, the attitude persists in some quarters and has manifested itself this year in an extraordinarily harmful decision by the Senate Finance Committee that the life of all foundations should be limited to forty years.

Strictly speaking, of course, Congress cannot terminate the existence of a charitable corporation or trust created under state law, as this would be unconstitutional. All Congress actually has the power to do is to remove the tax exemption of foundations after forty years and require them to pay income taxes. Whether foundations would then choose to dissolve or to pay taxes and stay in business would depend on the level of the tax imposed.

The basic argument used to support the notion of a limited life for foundations is that through this device a wealthy man may bind future generations forever to use charitable funds for the purposes he chooses. And since these purposes may become irrelevant to the later needs of society, the argument continues, it is contrary to the public interest that the donor be allowed to control the nature of the use of the funds for more than a limited period of years. However, it is implied, this death sentence should apply only to foundations, because other types of charitable organizations founded or assisted by charitable bequests, such as churches, colleges, or hospitals, are somehow different, somehow more responsive to the forces of change.

The basic flaw in this argument is revealed by consideration of the history and nature of the traditional concept of private charity. This concept goes back at least to the Roman era and probably earlier, was well understood in medieval times, was given legal definition in England in 1601 in the Statute of Charitable Uses, and has been a feature of the common law of Britain and the United States ever since. The concept involved the granting of certain privileges by the state to private citizens, or groups of citizens, in exchange for their willingness to serve the public good by performing or supporting acts of charity. These recognized acts of charity were first legally defined in the preamble to the Statute of Charitable Uses and since then have undergone varying restatements. The most recent in this country is contained in Treasury Department regulations of June 22, 1959, which define charity as:

> . . . relief of the poor and distressed or of the underprivileged; advancement of religion; advancement of education or service; erection or maintenance of public buildings, monuments or works; lessening of the burdens of government, and promotion of social welfare by organizations designed to accomplish any of the above purposes, or (i) to lessen neighborhood tensions; (ii) to eliminate prejudice and discrimination; (iii) to defend human and civil rights secured by law; or (iv) to combat community deterioration and juvenile delinquency.

The definition is clearly an attempt to restate the meaning of the term charity to conform to the current needs of society.

The important point, however, is that there has been throughout history an evolving definition of charity that encompasses a set of activities *all* of which were considered to be in the public interest and in the interests of the state. And therefore the state has never found it necessary to discriminate between charitable purposes by granting greater privileges for one form of charitable activity than for another. The concept has always been considered to be indivisible.

A second important point is that throughout the entire history of private charity, with minor deviations in some states in this country in the last century, the legal doctrines that shaped and defined the nature of charitable trusts and corporations have remained constant. Two of the most important of these doctrines have always been the right to existence in perpetuity and the possibility of the terms of a charitable bequest being altered at a later date through *cy pres* legal proceedings to adjust the intent of the donor to changed conditions.

In summary, given the assumption of public good inherent equally in all charitable purposes and the power which future generations always have of modernizing any overly restrictive provisions of a charitable bequest through legal proceedings, it has never been considered in the public interest to place an arbitrary limit on the life of any charitable trust or corporation. If they met the test of being charitable, all were considered equally worthy and equally entitled to perpetuity.

What the Senate Finance Committee has now attempted—through the back door of removing income tax exemption—is no less than the abrogation of one of the most ancient, basic, and well-proven principles of the common law tradition: the principle of the indivisibility of the right to perpetuity of all charitable trusts and corporations. I do not have to tell you that this principle has been fundamental to the development of a vigorous voluntary sector in the common law countries and that it has been especially successful in this country in encouraging the kinds of philanthropically supported private endeavors that are an essential feature of our democratic system.

Nor, I am sure, do I have to point out to you the enormous dangers inherent in the destruction of this principle through discriminatory action taken against one form of charitable organization. It is the indivisibility—the unity—of the principle that has given it its great strength. It is the realization that the state would refrain from interposing its judgment that has encouraged private citizens to devote their efforts and their money as *they* best saw fit to charitable ends. Once this principle has been breached, it is dead. Let us be clear that if this effort to use the tax laws to place a limit on the life of foundations is successful, opportunistic moves to do the same to other classes of charitable organizations will come in its wake.

Another argument employed by those who favor limiting the life of foundations is to pose the question of why a donor should be allowed to create an instrumentality that ensures benefits for his descendants in perpetuity. But this argument is really a red herring. The fact is that if a charitable trust or corporation is not serving the broad interests of the public, it is not charitable and its tax exemption can and should be quickly removed. There are trusts intended to benefit only the descendants of the founder, but these are private trusts and the length of their life is already limited by law.

Yet another argument against the perpetuity of foundations is that they must be prevented from developing into vast concentrations of economic power. But a recent study shows that their aggregate assets are actually declining as a proportion of the total wealth of the country and indeed have never been larger than .7 percent. The nation's true concern, therefore, should not be that the assets of this vital sector of philanthropy are too large but that they are too small. And any legislation should be designed to encourage rather than discourage the establishment of new foundations.

In addition to the basic philosophical and legal arguments against setting a limit on the life of foundations, there are, of course, some sound practical reasons for not doing so. In most foundations, and especially the larger ones, the charitable purposes outlined in the charter or deed of gift are so broad as to give the trustees in succeeding years almost complete discretion over how the funds shall be employed. Thus, to suggest that the right to perpetuity allows a foundation donor to prescribe forever the ways its funds will be used regardless of how these conform to society's needs is simply untrue for the vast bulk of these funds.

In fact, in 1967, of the 6,800 foundations which controlled 98.5 percent of total foundation assets, 5,300, with 91 percent of the assets, were operating under broad general charters. And virtually all foundation charters are nowadays drawn up to conform word for word with the broad charitable purposes outlined in the Internal Revenue Code as qualifying a charitable corporation for tax exemption. Where, then, is the evidence on which the Senate Finance Committee was acting? Or was it acting simply on a doctrinaire theory unrelated to fact?

Most donors have been governed by the philosophy that they should leave maximum discretion to future trustees, but it was Andrew Carnegie who perhaps best put the idea into words. He wrote:

> No man of vision will seek to tie the endowment which he gives to a fixed cause. He will leave to the judgment of his trustees, as time goes on, the question of modifying or altogether changing the nature of the trust, so as to meet the requirements of the time. Any board of trustees is likely to become indifferent or careless or to make wrong decisions. In the perpetual trust, as in all human institutions, there will be fruitful seasons and slack seasons. But as long as it exists there will come, from time to time, men into its control and management who will have vision and energy and wisdom, and the perpetual foundation will have a new birth of usefulness and service.

A second practical reason why it is not in the public interest to limit the life of foundations is that the considerable knowledge and experience they accumulate in the course of their work is thereby needlessly sacrificed—squandered—to satisfy a purely theoretical good. If, for example, the Rockefeller Foundation had been forced out of business in 1952 after forty years of life, it would never have carried out the great work, which developed out of its pre-1952 experience, in the dramatic improvement of wheat and rice yields. Without this "green revolution," as it has been called, many millions of people would now be suffering from malnutrition or dying of starvation.

If Carnegie Corporation had shut its doors in 1951 on turning forty, its accumulated experience and expertise in the field of education would not have been brought to bear on the pressing problems of the past two decades. If the Commonwealth Fund had ceased activity in 1958, its notable endeavors of the past decade in the strengthening of medical education, which grew out of its pre-1958 experience, would never have taken place.

These are but a few examples of the price that would have been paid by the nation and by mankind in return for someone having had the theoretical satisfaction of denying perpetuity to charitable bequests. I believe most Americans, if the issue of denying perpetuity to foundations were presented to them in this kind of pragmatic manner, would consider the bargain a poor one. They would quickly see the illogicality of killing off foundations just when they were most able to serve the public interest and when they had had the time to mature into institutions imbued with a strong sense of public trust.

Finally, while it is easy to laugh off the forty-year life issue with the quip that "foundations have thirty-nine years to get this changed," the harm of such a measure would start immediately, first in the inhibiting effect it would have on the establishment of new foundations; and second, in the general negative impact it would have on the morale of existing foundations.

In the final decade of their operations, it would be virtually impossible for foundations to recruit and hold able young staff members, and in the scramble at the end to dispose of their assets many unwise decisions might be made.

This extreme provision came as a shocking surprise to foundations, since it was based on no study of the total foundation record and no consideration of the harmful consequences involved. It seems only common sense for Congress to eliminate it entirely until the effect of other provisions of the legislation is tested.

Legislating in the Dark

No doubt troubled by the implications for other types of charitable organizations inherent in the several kinds of discriminatory restrictions proposed for foundations, the framers of this legislation have sought to establish in it a distinction between what they call private foundations and publicly supported charities—educational institutions, churches, hospitals, and organizations receiving more than one-third of their financial support from governmental funds or from the public.

The legislation is shot through with an assumption, which has been current in certain places in government for some years, that private foundations do not serve the public interest as much as do public charities. For example, a health agency governed by its own self-perpetuating board of trustees, but collecting its income in small donations from the public, would be considered to be more responsive to what the public conceived to be good than would a private medical foundation also governed by a self-perpetuating board, but getting its income from an endowment fund.

This is an assumption which fits the purpose of discriminatory legislation against foundations but is absolutely unsupported by factual evidence. No study has ever been made either outside or within the government that would justify such a conclusion. Indeed, despite the abuses in some foundations, a strong case could be made that they have, on the whole, been managed every bit as much in the public interest as have the so-called public charities. But no facts are available to prove that case either. So the truth of the matter is that this legislation, with all its tremendous consequences to the nation, rests in large part on no more than an untested hypothesis.

Indeed, the bill at large, granting that it does include some well-drawn provisions to deal with specific problems, is an almost classic example of legislating in the dark as an emotional response to the public disclosure of a limited number of abuses. That some of these abuses were particularly egregious does not alter the fact that very little specific, reliable knowledge about foundations exists in Congress, in the Treasury, or in any other arm of government on which farsighted legislation that would really serve the public good could be based.

This in itself is a disturbing matter. But given the import of the legislation to the entire charitable organization field, to the future of private institutions in our society, and to the very nature of the American system of democracy, its broad, sweeping provisions, the fallacious concepts which inform it, and the ignorance and myth on which it is based add up to nothing less than a vast disservice to the nation.

And should this legislation be passed, its disservice will be nowhere greater than to the cause of conservatism in American life. I mean by this, conservatism in the true sense of the word and of the type the great majority of Americans espouse—the conservation of a social and political order in which voluntary, citizen effort, carried out through private organizations and supported by private philanthropy, has an honored and protected place as a partner and as a counterbalance to an otherwise all-encompassing government.

The Fragile Private Sector

I believe that all of us should be deeply troubled about the broader consequences of what has so heedlessly been set in motion in the foundation part of the tax reform bill. The private, non-profit sector of our national life, with all its great importance, is only just keeping afloat. This legislation, if passed, will only make its condition worse. What we desperately need today is not further discouragement to this sector but measures designed to sustain and strengthen it. In no respect has the new Administration, which put itself firmly on record during the campaign as favoring maximum governmental encouragement to the voluntary sector, had a more clear-cut opportunity to give effect to its philosophy than in supporting foundations. Now is our moment of greatest need for that help as the legislative debate moves to its conclusion.

I would like to urge that a broad, national effort be made by private, charitable organizations generally, acting in concert, to reassert their basic unity and to reaffirm to the American people, to the Congress and the Executive Branch, their essential role in our national life. We have too long taken for granted that we were understood and appreciated. But we know now that there is widespread ignorance about us and a growing indifference to our welfare. That trend must be sharply reversed.

Reestablishment of public confidence in foundations is, I realize, obligatory if they are to assume their rightful place in such a united effort. We in the foundations are making this the first item on our agenda, and we have already set about it. We fully expect to be capable of being strong allies of other private institutions in what may be the last great opportunity we have to retain our common position of independence in the nation's life.

While I am by no means certain that the legislation I have been discussing as finally enacted will not have serious faults and dangers in it, the long debate in Washington has, nevertheless, demonstrated that there are many members of both houses of Congress who do understand the seriousness of the issues involved, and for the longer run that is a hopeful portent. With the help of such men and with a maximum effort from private organizations and institutions, I remain confident that the traditional American commitment to the private, nonprofit sector can once again be made as strong as it has been in the past. But there is no guaranty that this will happen. We must work hard and work together to see that it does.

The Jeopardy of
Private Institutions

Private nonprofit institutions serving the public good are one of those special features of American life so much taken for granted they have long since become obscured in a haze of familiarity. And yet, if one has occasion to observe life in a nation where all activities are functions either of the state or of a single, authorized political party, the value of independent private institutions, to our perception of a good society, becomes freshly and arrestingly apparent.

Nevertheless a high proportion of our private educational, cultural, health, and welfare institutions are heading into deep trouble, increasingly affected by social and economic forces they are powerless to withstand. The steady, unrelenting deterioration of their position has now, for the first time, raised doubts about the continued viability of our traditional system of shared responsibility between public and private endeavor. For varying reasons, the American people at large and most of their political leaders seem either unaware of the situation, or unconcerned. In any age notable for the gravity and complexity of its problems, this problem, as important as many others with which we are currently obsessed, has simply failed to make its mark on the national consciousness.

Why do private service institutions matter to our society, and why is their continued existence in jeopardy?

The Private Commonweal Enterprise

The private nonprofit sector of our national life can be thought of as having three parts. The first of these is the spontaneous coming together of citizens in support of causes which enlist their interest or excite their passions. These groups are often transitory, usually operate on limited funds, and seldom have professional staff. Evidence of the vitality of this part of the nonprofit sector was provided in the celebration of Earth Day last April. In the New York area alone, more than 200 voluntary organizations—ranging alphabetically from "Action for the Preservation and Conservation of the North Shore of Long Island" to "Westchester Students for Cleaner Environment"—joined in dramatizing the ecological crisis.

A second part of the nonprofit sector consists of that vast array of private local and national associations, nearly all enjoying tax exemption, that are devoted to the economic or social interests of *particular* groups of the population. Here we find labor unions, trade associations, agricultural organizations, chambers of commerce, real estate boards, country clubs, fraternal and employee beneficial societies, teachers' retirement fund associations, mutual credit unions, mutual insurance companies, and many others. This portion of the nonprofit sector is also thriving.

It is the third part of this sector, the part which is composed of established service institutions and organizations devoted to the common or *general* good, that is in ill health. These institutions are, roughly speaking, of five kinds: Those offering formal education, for example, private schools, colleges and universities, and special professional and vocational institutions; those providing informal education or cultural activities, such as museums, private libraries, zoological and botanical gardens, art galleries, symphony orchestras, and civic theaters; those giving health care, principally voluntary hospitals; those devoted to research; and those providing welfare services to disadvantaged or disabled members of the population.

Although there are great differences among them, private service institutions do possess a set of common characteristics. Originating generally as the fruit of some impulse of personal or religious philanthropy, they have developed into professionally administered enterprises impressed with a broad public trust. Incorporated as nonprofit institutions, they enjoy federal and state income tax exemption and, in most cases, exemption from local property taxes. They are governed, almost always, by self-perpetuating boards of trustees in whom, corporately, their assets are vested. Most importantly, they exist *solely* to provide needed services to the public or some designated part thereof—services which might otherwise have to be provided by government out of tax revenues.

Traditionally, these institutions were supported almost exclusively by the income from endowments, annual gifts by individuals, corporations and foundations, and user fees; but as costs have risen and the demand for services has mounted, these sources of revenue have become increasingly inadequate. In recent years, therefore, many private institutions have begun to seek and receive a measure of governmental support, in the form of grants or contracts for specific purposes, or, indirectly, through subsidization of the purchaser of services, or, occasionally, at the local or state levels, as annual subventions.

Nonetheless, they remain *private* institutions for whose continued state of health no one is legally responsible except their boards of trustees and the administrative staffs employed by these boards. To distinguish them from private associations serving the special interests of self-selected groups, we can call them privately controlled public enterprises, or, perhaps, private commonweal enterprises.

How many of these private institutions there are today no one is certain, although we do know that there are approximately 1,450 colleges and universities, 4,600 secondary schools, 3,650 voluntary hospitals, 6,000 museums, 1,100 symphony orchestras, 5,500 libraries, and 29,000 welfare agencies supported by United Funds. There can be no question that these institutions form a highly important piece of the fabric of American society, important enough to justify—indeed necessitate—our looking at their situations *collectively*. Together they give expression to the concept of private effort for the public good, and it is belief in the efficacy of this concept that has released untold energies and talent to the development of this nation.

Private versus Public

Almost every category of private commonweal enterprise has its tax-supported, publicly controlled counterpart: public schools, colleges and universities, public museums and libraries, public hospitals, public research institutes, and public welfare agencies (albeit virtually no public symphony orchestras or public opera, ballet, and theater companies).

From time to time efforts have been made to demonstrate that the private institution is superior—or inferior—to its public analogue. Extravagant claims have been voiced on each side of the argument, and a good deal of blood, figuratively speaking, has been spilt in the sport. Common sense has always shown, however, that the question of private *versus* public, when posed as exclusive alternatives, lacks even a semblance of validity within this nation's experience. The issue is a handy one for populist or élitist polemics, but that is all. Each set of institutions has its particular strengths and weaknesses, and together they share many characteristics and goals. The case for private institutions, therefore, cannot, and should not, be made in terms of any inherent superiority they may be thought to have to public institutions.

A question that is more to the point is whether, in the aggregate, private institutions provide an essential element to the character of our national life. Would our society be as rich, as varied, as free, as lively, as it is, if these enterprises disappeared entirely from the scene—if all education took place in public institutions, if opera, ballet, drama, and music were performed only by official state companies, if medical care were provided only in public hospitals, if research were done only in governmental institutes, if welfare services were a monopoly of governmental agencies?

Put this way, the question is rhetorical and the answer, to many of us, obvious. Of course we believe in private institutions, and of course their place in the society must be preserved. But rhetoric and sentiment are not enough. A substantial new effort will be required to safeguard the future of these institutions, based on an understanding and appreciation of the unique role they play in our society. The case for a combined public/private system can no longer be assumed to rest on some sort of divine law. It must be explicitly examined and stated.

The Case for the Private Nonprofit Service Institution

Granting that many of the special virtues claimed on behalf of private institutions turn out not to be unique to them, and granting that some of them have in the past been less democratic and less open to change than they should have been, there are, nonetheless, at least four distinctive reasons why it is a matter of compelling importance to retain in our society service institutions that are not under public control.

The first reason is the special opportunity they offer for concerned citizens, through membership on boards of trustees and participation in a wide range of voluntary activities, to accept a significant measure of personal responsibility for the provision to the public of many kinds of essential services. Acceptance of this kind of responsibility enables lay men and women to become informed about pressing national problems. It gives them a basis for judging the performance of public officials and institutions in attacking these problems. It serves as an antidote to the all-too-frequently encountered attitude that as long as one pays one's taxes, the failures, the evils, the pathologies of the world, are someone else's responsibility.

Additionally, voluntary service by trustees and other supporters brings to these institutions special talents and experience they could not possibly command otherwise, in fields such as fund raising, legal affairs, investing, property management, and community relations. Growing recognition of the paramount importance of the last of these fields has stimulated many institutions to broaden membership in their governing boards to include more young people, more women, and more representatives of minority groups.

In this day, when it is increasingly evident that public authority, important as this is, cannot alone solve the nation's growing problems, the need is great for private individuals to accept a real measure of responsibility for these problems themselves. One of their best opportunities to do this—and an opportunity which should be extended ever more widely to all kinds of citizens—is through participation in the work of private service institutions devoted to the common good. In this respect these institutions perform an essential function in our national life.

The second notable reason private service institutions and organizations must not be allowed to disappear is the important role they play in the safeguarding of academic, professional, and artistic freedom. In periods of sharp controversy, when legislative or executive pressure on public institutions become intolerable, private institutions can provide essential reserve protection for these freedoms.

As one looks ahead, it is hard to imagine that the tensions of our deeply divided society will not produce many new storms, each with its own particular threats to liberty of mind and conscience.

This is not to suggest that all private institutions are necessarily impervious themselves to external pressure, or that public institutions have a record of supineness in their defense of freedom. Far from it. It is simply to say that private institutions, because they are not directly dependent on public appropriations, are less immediately vulnerable to restrictions on their capacity to function effectively in the public interest.

It has therefore seemed wise to many Americans to distribute the safekeeping of their nation's most precious asset, its intellectual freedom, among a variety of institutions under the control of private citizens as well as of public authorities. In a totalitarian state, where intellectual orthodoxy is of the highest imperative, this kind of arrangement would be unthinkable because it is one designed to produce a babel of intellectual and artistic claims in the name of truth, perpetual challenges to authority, and a seeming lack of a disciplined sense of national purpose. Despite the attacks on it today by young radicals, and despite the clearly evident imperfections of our present society, our system of shared responsibility is one that has served the American people well, and we would be foolish to abandon it by allowing our private institutions to fail.

A third, purely pragmatic reason for securing the future well-being of these institutions is simply the fact that they do exist and that if they ceased to function as a private responsibility there is no guarantee that the same kinds and quality of service they now provide could or would be provided at public expense. This is particularly true in regard to some types of services provided by religious institutions, where the doctrine of separation of church and state bars public support; but it also applies to situations in which private institutions supply services of such a controversial nature that public agencies would not dare to enter the field. There are other kinds of services, such as those offered by cultural institutions and by some kinds of research institutes, specialized educational institutions, and welfare and public affairs organizations, which many Americans would think ought not, within this nation's traditions, to be totally financed by government.

If commonweal enterprises could no longer be kept afloat through private funding and were to become entirely dependent on tax funds to continue operating, it is a fair assumption that many would have to close down or drastically reduce their services. In many cases, they would not qualify for public support, and where they did, hard-pressed public authorities would be reluctant to give them the necessary priority in the face of already established budgetary claims. It is also probable that if they were to qualify, their services would be made to conform to those offered by comparable public institutions, thereby standardizing them and very possibly destroying some of their special ésprit and quality.

The building of great institutions, be they universities, museums, symphony orchestras, or independent research facilities, is a painstaking process, almost invariably requiring many decades. Each successive generation of trustees, staff, and volunteers adds its increment to the facilities, the range of services provided, the professional standards, the ésprit and the reputation of these institutions, until eventually they stand as mature resources to the society of a value incalculably greater than simply the worth of the "assets" which are listed in their annual balance sheets.

Such institutions are essential to an enlightened, humane, and stable society. They bring to it the perspectives of the past and of world culture. They serve as springboards from which advances are made in basic knowledge or in standards of individual and organizational performance. In an age of relentless change they provide a steadying hand of continuity. And, lastly, they serve to keep alive on a year-in year-out basis important fields of activity during the lean periods when these are out of fashion for public support.

A fourth, and perhaps most important, reason private institutions must not be allowed to decline is that they bring to our national life vital elements of diversity, free choice, and heterodoxy. These qualities are often lumped together and their identity obscured in celebration of the vague and rather overworked concept of "pluralism." But each, in fact, has a quite different connotation, and each has its own special importance.

Diversity suggests the existence of a variety of institutions within a given field, all rather different from one another in the way they are managed, in their perceptions of priorities, and in the kinds of service they offer. The term is value-free in that it contains no suggestion of superiority or inferiority. It says only that there are likely to be a number of ways to accomplish something and that in the long run the competition between several possible approaches is good for everybody. This prevents new ideas from being suppressed, it provides challenge to fat and complacent bureaucracies, it assures experimentation and flexibility, and it lends color to what might otherwise be a monochromatic scene.

Free choice applies to the consumer rather than to the purveyor of services. It implies the existence of a market, wherein those seeking services can shop around and take their trade where they choose. The market is, of course, not an entirely free one because the costs of private services are likely to be higher than those provided by public institutions. But the existence of the market is, all the same, important to the way the consumer feels about his life, for he knows that if a massive public agency whose services he was using were to become rigid, or inhumane, he would at least have the possibility of an alternative.

Heterodoxy describes the permitted presence in a society of unconventional ideas and philosophies and of institutions and organizations which nourish them. Tolerance of this kind is a sign of national maturity and self-confidence and indicates faith in the good sense of the average citizen to sort out what is genuine and what specious. It also recognizes that today's iconoclasm may, as the result of changing conditions, be tomorrow's orthodoxy and that any attempt forceably to stifle the free play of ideas, however seemingly eccentric, may produce stagnation or cause the buildup of powerful social forces that will eventually result in violent upheaval. Thus, the capacity to tolerate nonconformism, trying as this sometimes becomes, is the *sine qua non* of a free society. Without it the imposition of a totalitarian state ultimately becomes inevitable.

Private institutions are not the only contributors to pluralism. Public institutions can and do play a part in it; but their vulnerability in times of crisis places a special burden on private institutions for the preservation of diversity, of free choice, and of the capacity to tolerate heterodoxy—in short, for the preservation of an open society.

Character of the Threat

The developing threat to private institutions is certainly grave, but in pointing it out one risks the accusation of crying "wolf." Any adequate description implies some sort of dramatic, instant fulfillment, whereas the demise of an institution is more likely to be a protracted and inconspicuous process lasting many years and encompassing several stages of progressive debility.

There may be a first stage in which the institution, for financial reasons, becomes unable to manage the growth necessary to meet new challenges. This loss of a cutting edge may bring on a second stage in which the institution's own self-confidence and the public's confidence in it begin to slip, a third in which the recruitment of capable staff becomes progressively more difficult, a fourth in which declining income begins to necessitate the curtailment of important activities and reduction of staff, and so on. Even when the institution is moribund, it may drag on for sometime before it is finally forced to close down. It is at the very first stage, however, when an institution shows itself to be incapable of vigorous response to changed times, that it should be seen to be seriously ill, and it is then that remedial steps should be taken.

Many of our greatest private service institutions are now showing all the symptoms of being in this initial stage of sickness; and in seeking to understand the cause of their illness, they tend to diagnose it as essentially financial. They regard themselves as simply the victims of an inflationary spiral in which for some years now their costs of doing business have mounted more rapidly than their income. Over the past decade, expenses have at least trebled to provide the same amount of service. As service institutions, they have not been able to offset steadily rising labor costs through automation or other increases in productivity, or, alternatively, just to drop unprofitable services, as could a business enterprise. Either course would have constituted abandonment of their very *raison d'être*—to provide services they deem to be good or essential for all or many citizens, and as much as possible on terms which the less fortunate can meet.

During the past year an already serious situation for the private commonweal institution has been further aggravated by cutbacks in federal spending and by the decline in the stock market, with its consequent reduction in charitable giving. The annual operating deficit has now become an all too-common phenomenon among these institutions. Financial exigency has, in many cases, caused positive steps to be taken, such as improvements in efficiency, new efforts at private fund raising, and efforts to reach out to meet new needs for which funding is available. It has also caused some unfortunate compromises, for example, reductions in the quality of services offered, increased charges for these services, encroachments on unrestricted endowment funds for use as annual income, and even short-term borrowing to meet payrolls. But these moves, whether sound or unsound, have provided only temporary relief, not a real solution. They have simply served to stave off the ultimate day of reckoning when many private institutions will either have to become publicly controlled and supported or go out of business.

At bottom, the problem faced by private institutions is very much the same as that faced by public institutions, except for the vital consideration that the latter's support is hitched to the tax dollar. Both have been hard hit by rising personnel costs. Both have found it impossible to offset these costs through increased productivity. More importantly, both have been seriously affected by an enormously heightened public demand, caused by affluence, population growth, changing attitudes, and related factors, for the kinds of educational, cultural, health, and welfare services which traditionally have been, and should be, supplied on a nonprofit basis.

Government, quite properly, has concentrated on the staggering problem of meeting this demand and in so doing has put the major part of its effort into the development of public institutions. This approach, understandable as it is, has been built on assumptions about the continued viability of private institutions as a national resource that have become less and less justified and consequently has precluded the kind of *special* attention they urgently required.

During this period, many Americans have enjoyed an illusory confidence that private giving by individuals, foundations, and corporations, reinforced perhaps by better investment policies, by some increases in user fees, and by some limited access to funds provided through government programs, would be sufficient to maintain the strength of private institutions. They have simply failed to understand that income from private giving, essential as it is because of its unrestricted nature, represents only a small part of the annual budgets of these institutions. They have also failed to appreciate that many private institutions, because they are located in cities, have lost their traditional supporting constituencies through the migration of more well-to-do families to the suburbs. This problem particularly afflicts cultural institutions, so that just when the need for them to reach out further to serve larger numbers of urban residents is being widely recognized, their financial capacity to do so has become woefully inadequate.

If financial debility were the only problem faced by private institutions, there might be grounds for at least some degree of optimism. One might suppose that resolute action and more favorable times would, in due course, begin to restore them to a state of financial health, thus assuring the continued viability of our combined public/private system. But this future appears increasingly to be subject to more fundamental doubts having to do with the basic attitudes and beliefs of the American people. The issue now is whether a majority of our citizens still sees special merit in the retention of a combined public/private system or, conversely, whether substantial numbers would now, for varying reasons, be quite content to see private institutions generally handed over to public control.

The answers to these questions are by no means clear, however distressing this may be to those of us whose faith in our traditional system runs deep. We must recognize, for example, that millions of Americans, because of poverty, discrimination, or disillusion with the society's values, feel alienated from it. To them, private institutions, like government itself, are simply part of what they consider a rotten system and of a *status quo* which they are convinced is entrenched against the kinds of social change they advocate. We cannot expect these Americans to be the defenders of the private commonweal enterprise unless ways are found to relate it far more effectively to their needs and aspirations; but how far it can go in this direction without at the same time alienating other constituencies and jeopardizing its financial support is an even more difficult question.

Another very substantial group of citizens—fearful, insecure, disturbed by the changes that have taken place in American life and inclined to a conservative outlook—may also be disenchanted with private institutions, ironically, for almost diametrically opposite reasons. This group tends to feel that private institutions, especially colleges and universities, have gone much too far to the side of "liberalism,"—that amorphous and enigmatic force in our national life which has, in their eyes, pandered to blacks and other minorities, capitulated to student irresponsibility, undermined law and order, ignored the legitimate needs of people like themselves who are "willing to work their way," and generally raised everyone's taxes in the process. There certainly can be no guarantee that this large group will be passionate defenders of the independent position of private institutions in the society. On the contrary, we can expect such Americans, by and large, to favor measures which bring these institutions under ever greater public control.

Thirdly, there remain in the nation many people, especially in the nation's "heartland," who continue to have a kind of populist distrust of private institutions, associating them with great wealth, privilege, and a social caste system.

They feel more comfortable about institutions which are the immediate responsibility of elected, publicly accountable officials. While it would be an overstatement to say that people of this outlook are downright hostile to private institutions, it would certainly be fair to suggest that one would not find among them the kind of spontaneous, fervent support these institutions now so desperately need.

Finally, there are many people who are simply indifferent to the issue, to the degree that they are even aware of it. They know little of the role of private institutions in our national life, and they care less. From time to time they benefit from what they take to be public services without realizing that these are, in fact, provided by private institutions. Unfortunately, this group probably constitutes a large part of the population.

Lack of a philosophical commitment to the idea of a combined public/private system, ignorance of private institutions and what is at stake in their preservation, and even disaffection toward them as such, among certain parts of the public at large is, not surprisingly, reflected by many public officials. Here and there one finds active and courageous supporters of the cause of private institutions, and their efforts have been helpful and appreciated. The predominant attitude of officialdom, however, is at best one of indifference to the entire issue and at worst one of skepticism bordering on hostility.

Dramatic evidence of the prevalence of these attitudes was offered in the Tax Reform Act of 1969 when Congress placed a 4 percent excise tax on the income of foundations. Foundations opposed this strenuously, pointing out that the tax would simply deny some 50 million dollars of much needed income to the organizations and institutions, *most of them private*, which they customarily support. The argument, though understood, was disregarded. A desire to "chastise" foundations, however illogical the form of punishment, out-weighed the concern that should have been felt about those on whom the real burden of the tax would fall. Most disquieting of all was the fact that an action as damaging as this to private institutions could have been taken with so little protest from the public. That surely was indicative of a state of public apathy toward these institutions that bodes ill for their future.

The Future

In view of the state of public opinion on the question, the general lack of official concern, and the nation's preoccupation with other issues, it seems unlikely that any systematic, coherent effort will develop in the immediate future to alleviate the financial situation of private service institutions. Their relative position in our national life seems destined to decline and with it the special values they bring to our society.

Some types of private service institutions will be less vulnerable than others, particularly those which can go on raising their prices because the consumers of their services are subsidized by public funds or protected by insurance plans; but for other types of institutions, especially those providing informal education and cultural activities in which the demand for service inevitably begins to fall off when charges are raised too high, the day of final reckoning will come much sooner.

Private schools, colleges, and universities, while retaining a leavening of low-income scholarship students, will do best financially by turning their backs on the hard-pressed middle class and concentrating their admissions on the children of affluent families which can best afford ever-rising tuition charges. In so doing, they will pay the price of becoming estranged from the mainstream of the populace, which will only serve to increase their growing insecurity. As for the major private research universities, even substantial tuition increases will help only marginally, so small a part does tuition play in their overall financing.

Any real solution to the plight of private institutions must begin with a clear appreciation by the nation's top political leaders of what the *collective* presence and vitality of these institutions mean to the nation. These leaders, rather than simply mirroring public ignorance and apathy, must educate the public and, where necessary, convert it, to a sense of active concern over the future of our traditional system of shared public and private effort and responsibility; and, in this task, our political leaders must be supported and reinforced by other leadership elements in the nation. Nothing less than this kind of impetus from the top will provide the basis for the great variety of measures which will be needed to preserve and revitalize the position of our private institutions.

Much of the remedial action will, of course, have to be tailored to the special situations of specific types of institutions and will have to be taken by state and local governments as well as in Washington. But other approaches can be broad enough to affect all classes of institutions simultaneously. An example of the latter would be a totally new look at the tax laws which would approach charitable giving not simply negatively as an area for taxpayer abuse, as did the tax reform legislation of 1969, but with the positive attitude that philanthropy is a national virtue that should be given maximum encouragement. Such a reexamination has been recommended by the "Peterson" Commission on Foundations and Private Philanthropy.

Another possibility might be a comprehensive study of the variety of ways in which private institutions could be aided as the result of public subsidization of the consumers of their services, with a view toward extending and broadening this approach. Public funds are already used extensively to provide scholarships tenable at private colleges and universities. Voluntary hospitals are assisted through medicare and medicaid to elderly and less advantaged individuals. Perhaps other kinds of private institutions, such as museums and symphony orchestras, could be assisted indirectly through public subsidy of the users of their services. This form of public support has an advantage in that it reduces the likelihood of government control of the operations of private institutions and preserves the free market.

A third possibility might be a national commission which would think through and articulate the requirements for a massive campaign to arouse public interest in the private service institution and concern over its future. Such a commission would have to determine who should be responsible for launching the campaign, how it should be organized, and how financed. And it would have to ensure that something would really happen as a result of its work.

The time for action, whether of a broad or specific nature, is extremely late. Our historic partnership of public and private commonweal endeavor is in grave danger because of the state of apathy that is permitting the decline of private institutions. Unless this decline is arrested and reversed, we, and our children after us, will almost certainly be living in a society where the idea of *private* initiative for the *common* good has become little but a quaint anachronism largely associated with the mores of an earlier age. Perhaps at that time there will be Americans who are reasonably satisfied with the kinds of lives offered them by a society which functions solely through public institutions. But there may well be others with a great yearning for more variety, more choice, more animation, and more freedom in their lives than such a system would be likely to provide. If so, they will certainly wonder at the heedlessness—the sheer negligence—of the generation before them that could have allowed a system which has these attributes to atrophy.

The Responsibility for
Reform in Higher Education

It will be many years before we begin to understand fully the turbulence of our times. Whether this turbulence, and our uncertainty about its meaning, reflect primarily the trauma of withdrawal from an unpopular and mistaken war coinciding with the strains of a national effort to right three centuries of wrong against American minorities, or whether it signifies the onset perhaps of a fundamental cultural and social transformation, we simply cannot now know. And whether this great change, if it is to come, will ultimately prove beneficial or harmful to the nation, we also have little way of predicting.

Whatever the turbulence may indicate, the disequilibrium it is causing in our national life has brought on a healthy mood of skepticism about the operation of some of our major governmental, social, and economic institutions—institutions as varied as the federal regulatory agencies, the health system, and giant industrial corporations. Searching questions are being raised: Are these institutions serving the best interests of the people? Are they adequately accountable? Have they kept in step with the needs of the times?

Many people would agree that, among the major institutions of the society, none is riper for objective reappraisal than higher education. Indeed, it is now the subject of intensive study and debate—on individual campuses, in legislative and executive bodies, and by national commissions, including the Carnegie Commission on Higher Education. At no time in its 335-year history has American higher education come under such critical scrutiny.

Ironically, the new skepticism about higher education comes close on the heels of two decades of astonishing development which had brought it to a point where it was enrolling eight and a half million students while serving the needs of the nation in a wide variety of other ways. Only a short time ago this extraordinary enterprise seemed to many to be rapidly approaching an apogee of success unparalleled in this or any other country.

Certain simplistic charges against higher education have become familiar to the point of staleness. It is accused by radicals of complicity with the political, military, and industrial forces that have "conspired" to create an "oppressive society" and to involve the nation in an "unjust and immoral war." These critics also believe higher education serves primarily to further entrench the dominant classes in American life and to frustrate the kinds of revolutionary social change they regard as desirable.

Conservatives, on the other hand, argue that higher education, through an abdication of responsibility, has played a major part in helping to subvert the very values on which this country was built. It has, they believe, provided a home for the growth of a new youth culture founded on the use of drugs, permissive sexual relationships, and radical political notions and has turned out a product largely unfitted to contribute constructively to our national life.

Finally, there are large numbers of people, of all political persuasions, who believe that higher education has seriously neglected its teaching mission, the very purpose for which it principally exists.

These and other charges, leveled sometimes at something referred to loosely as "the system" or "the university," sometimes at the faculty, and usually at harassed administrators, have filled the air. Much of this criticism is superficial and based on limited evidence. The prescriptions for reform it generates are usually naive or simply punitive and generally have little practical value.

The desire for reform today, however, is by no means a monopoly of extremists, know-nothings, and political opportunists. There is a growing body of responsible, well-informed people, both on and off the campus, who believe the time has come for substantial changes in higher education. Among these people there is now a questioning of once sacrosanct practices, a new willingness to experiment, a new interest in the needs of students, and a new concern for those who have been denied access to higher education or have not been reached by the conventional system. Whether this new mood has been brought on solely by the successive shocks caused by student unrest, declining public confidence, and financial crisis, or whether it reflects some deeper dissatisfaction with what we have wrought in American higher education is not altogether clear. But whatever the cause, it is apparent that the disposition for reform is quite powerful.

People of this outlook are deeply troubled by the breakdown of the traditional consensus which for so long made the campus a readily manageable community. They are disturbed by such developments as the growing unionization of faculty and the tendency for the concept of "rights" to take precedence over other considerations in governance. They are concerned that the explosive growth of higher education in recent years and the proliferation of functions it performs seem to have destroyed any common sense of purpose within the enterprise.

Finally, they are increasingly uneasy about the curriculum, wondering whether either the liberal arts as taught or the vocational training given is appropriate to the needs of today's students.

As those responsible for the destinies of particular institutions or groups of institutions face the question of reform, they quite naturally look first to what can be done on their own campuses. They take steps to enlarge student participation in decision making, to increase student contact with faculty through smaller instructional units, to allow periods of off-campus work and study, to improve management practices, to eliminate less important activities, and so on. In short, they do the kinds of things that lie within the power of governing boards, administrators, faculty, and students, working cooperatively, to do.

To call this kind of reform simply tinkering or minor repair work would be unfair, for it can affect an institution in quite fundamental ways. Nevertheless, it falls far short of what is required, because the root of the malaise presently afflicting higher education is to be found not so much in the practices and programs of individual institutions, important as it is that these be improved, as in the nature of the relationship which has developed between higher education and society. As this relationship has deepened and broadened over recent decades in response to vast changes in American life, the pressures on higher education have been raised to an intolerable level, and expectations of it have been created that cannot possibly be fully satisfied. It is, therefore, to the basic nature of the relationship between higher education and society that reform of a fundamental character must be directed. Such reform will require the participation not only of these groups or "estates" which make up the campus community, but of external agencies as well—government, industry, parents, and, indeed, the public at large.

The Functions of Higher Education

The most illuminating approach to an understanding of the present nexus between higher education and American life is simply a description of the functions which our universities, four-year colleges, and community colleges, taken together, actually perform. Generally, these are expressed as "teaching, research, and service," but this traditional triad seems to obscure more than it reveals. A listing of the true range of functions yields a startling picture of an enterprise with a very broad range of purposes, all of which are somehow interrelated and yet many of which also seem to be mutually contradictory. Some of these purposes are well known to the public; others are only vaguely comprehended.

The many functions performed by higher education collectively are, of course, found in individual institutions in widely varying degree. No one would claim that the University of Minnesota, the Massachusetts Institute of Technology, Fresno State College, Amherst College, Tuskegee Institute, and Miami Dade Junior College are alike. Differentiation of function among institutions is an important aspect of our higher educational system. Nevertheless, a categorization of functions—of which it is possible to name at least thirteen—yields a composite picture of the total role of higher education in our society that cannot be grasped through analysis of the purposes served by any single institution.

Virtually every American college or junior college devotes some portion of its energy and resources to the *liberal education* of its students. There has always been argument about the precise definition of this concept. Most people would agree, however, that it involves gaining a basic knowledge of man and his societies and the physical world, mastering the language and mathematical skills to reason and express thoughts clearly and logically, and acquiring such habits of mind as intellectual curiosity, the capacity to think critically, and the ability to weigh evidence objectively. There would be less agreement today that the inculcation of any particular set of values constitutes an integral part of liberal education. Few, however, would dispute that the concept does at least include some acquaintance with the principal value systems by which man throughout the ages has attempted to steer his path to some higher destiny.

Collectively, American universities, colleges, and two-year institutions prepare young people for an extraordinary range of professions, subprofessions, and occupations. Some of this training takes place in graduate professional schools, but much of it is at the undergraduate level or in two-year institutions. Although in most instances the credential awarded does not actually constitute a license to practice, the granting of such a license is dependent upon completion of the appropriate training. *De facto*, therefore, higher education not only conducts a vast system of *professional and occupational training* but also serves as a *sorting and selecting mechanism* to route the nation's youth into employment.

Although there are many inefficiencies in the way these two functions are carried out, the contribution higher education makes to our national life in performing them is indisputable. So varied and extensive are these training and sorting activities, the public tends to take them for granted and hence does not fully appreciate their enormous value.

In the United States we place primary reliance on higher educational institutions for the *discovery of new knowledge*. Research is also performed in industry, in independent institutes, and in government installations. Much, however, of the research that ultimately proves to be of greatest value, being unrelated at the time it is done to a recognizably useful product, would never be undertaken except in an academic environment. The significance of university-based research to the nation's economy, to its security, and to the quality of life of its people is incalculable. Not always appreciated, it is one of the great bargains Americans get when their tax dollars are used for the support of higher education.

Beyond the functions they perform in imparting the principal elements of liberal and vocational and professional education to large numbers of young people entering adulthood, and in the discovery of new knowledge, our colleges and universities have a special responsibility for the conservation, and transmission from generation to generation, of existing knowledge in its more complex or abstruse forms. In meeting this responsibility, they serve an indispensable purpose as *custodians of our cultural heritage*. It is to maintain the enormous accumulated store of humanistic and scientific knowledge which mankind now possesses that large sums of money are spent on faculty with highly specialized training and on great libraries, laboratories, and teaching museums. Without this investment we would constantly be engaged in a fruitless rediscovery of old knowledge. Cut off from our history, we would lack that sense of perspective about ourselves and our current social institutions so fundamental to enlightened judgment.

Many colleges and universities also sponsor a variety of cultural events which are available to the public as well as the campus community. This activity is a logical extension of their role as custodians of our cultural heritage.

One of the less understood and appreciated but more important functions of higher education is its responsibility to provide a protected environment for detached, impartial *criticism of the larger society* based on knowledge derived from disinterested study and research. This is a role which other institutions, such as the press, also play, but the resources possessed by higher education to seek truth and express it extend far beyond the capabilities of other institutions. The need to safeguard this function is the basic reason why higher educational institutions, as institutions, must not take partisan positions or engage in partisan activities. So complex are the pressures on urban-centered universities today and so intensely felt the great moral issues of our times, it would be naive to suppose that this proscription can be absolute. But if institutions systematically or aggressively violate the position of neutrality that society accords them, they will not only forfeit one of their principal claims to support but will also jeopardize one of their chief values to society.

A peculiarly American function of our system of higher education is the role it plays in providing the *administrative base for public service programs* of an operational or research nature. These programs are found in fields such as health care, defense, foreign assistance, agriculture, and community service and are generally externally financed. Although they frequently make some contribution to the educational program on campus, their existence is also defended in many instances on the grounds that higher educational institutions have a responsibility for public service irrespective of any direct educational benefits involved. Despite the intrinsic value of many of these programs to external communities and to relationships with those communities, many institutions are coming to see that public service activities of this kind may be in partial conflict with the central functions of teaching and research.

Closely associated with the previous function is the service higher education performs in providing the logistical base for a *pool of specialized talent* which it makes quite freely available to external agencies such as government and industry. Outside consulting by faculty members, especially those serving in graduate professional schools, is an activity that has grown substantially and for some individuals provides a significant part of their income. From the point of view of the user agencies, having such a talent pool available is a distinct bargain, because the consulting fee paid to a faculty member is insignificant compared with the cost to his institution of maintaining his logistical base. It is certainly one of the hidden benefits to the nation for its support of higher education.

Nevertheless, faculty consulting has its severe critics. A great many students and some administrators feel that it causes a high rate of absenteeism among leading faculty members and conflicts with their primary responsibility for teaching and research.

Traditionally, higher education in the United States, as in many other countries, provided a means for the particularly ambitious and able person of middle or working class background to gain entry into a small elite at the top of the society, an elite which enjoyed considerable social prestige. As the proportion, however, of the eighteen to twenty-one year old age group enrolled in higher education steadily expanded—from 5 percent in 1910 to nearly 50 percent today—"going to college" gradually began to serve a different purpose. Today, for most Americans, it is virtually a prerequisite for entry into the middle class, or for remaining in it, if one is already there. Unquestionably this *class certification* function benefits minorities, the poor, and the lowly born in aiding them to enter the mainsteam of American life. Nonetheless, it is intrinsically undemocratic and is probably what lies at the bottom of some of the current hostility to higher education.

Increasingly, a major function of higher education in this country is simply to serve as a form of occupation for an ever-growing proportion of youth during the transitional years from adolescence into adulthood—a kind of *way station* on the trail of life. Many young people seem to be at college for no better reason than want of an acceptable alternative. If there were anything but deadend jobs available for them, or even jobs at all, or if there were interesting, productive forms of national service widely available, they might well prefer these alternatives. Lacking them, they drift into higher education.

This custodial function is clearly at odds with many of higher education's other functions. It consumes scarce resources, creates institutions of a size so massive they are virtually unmanageable, and creates conditions on campus which impede the progress of serious students. Nevertheless, the reluctant student with low motivation may gain considerable benefit from the experience, and perhaps society does too. A recent Carnegie Commission study, based on an analysis of data collected by social scientists over several decades, shows that people who have attended college are more tolerant in their attitudes toward other individuals and groups, more satisfied with their jobs, better paid and less subject to unemployment, more thoughtful and deliberate in their consumer expenditures, more likely to vote and to participate generally in community activities, and more informed about community, national, and world affairs. These are real benefits.

Although higher education has for many years, through its general extension programs and through part-time and evening study, offered *educational opportunities to adults*, this has certainly not been one of its most central functions. Nor have these activities enjoyed the prestige of undergraduate and graduate study by "regular" students. Attitudes are changing, however, both on and off the campus, and it now seems likely that the function of serving adults will assume much greater importance at a variety of institutions. It also seems likely that there will be a steadily growing demand by adults for the programs offered.

The provision of external degrees on a wide scale and lifelong entitlement to periods of study in a college or university are two new developments that may become quite general. Meeting the educational needs of adults is by no means inappropriate as a function of higher education, provided the activity is taken seriously and done well. Indeed, it may in the future be one of higher education's most important functions and one of the ways it brings greatest benefit to the nation.

In recent years most higher educational institutions have been obliged to offer work in two areas of liberal education, English and mathematics, that is frankly *remedial* and sometimes hardly even of secondary school level. A large part of this new function is associated with the extension of higher educational opportunity to able students with severely disadvantaged educational backgrounds. While this is a wholly laudable and defensible objective in today's circumstances, there can be little doubt the activity involved tends to be a drag on institutions and diminish their capacity to do genuine, college-level work.

A function of higher education which few of those who administer it care to recognize publicly is the role it has come to have as a major *purveyor of commercial entertainment*, principally through its football and basketball teams. Not only are intercollegiate contests in these sports themselves of wide public interest, being watched by millions on television, but college teams to a large degree serve as the training ground for professional teams. Not unsurprisingly, the enormous commercial importance of college sports leads to intense pressures toward their professionalization, pressures that are almost irresistible. Sometimes the resulting situation is rationalized on the grounds that having good teams helps maintain campus morale, gain legislative appropriations, win the support of alumni, or earn income for the support of other sports which do not have wide public appeal.

Substantial numbers of students are, however, beginning to question not only the ethics but also the appropriateness to higher education of "big time" college athletics. There seems to be a growing sensitivity about the exploitation of student athletes which may be involved and a new awareness that the values underlying this activity are probably inconsistent with the values of an academic campus. It is the perversion of it that has become increasingly troublesome.

Among these thirteen functions, several go back to the beginnings of higher education in this country (and well before that elsewhere), several date from the latter half of the last century, and several are quite new, or are older functions that have acquired such changed meaning in recent years as to have become virtually new. These new and refurbished functions both reflect and have contributed to significant new developments in American life—developments such as urbanization, population growth, affluence, scientific and technological advance, the communications revolution, ever-increasing specialization of knowledge, and the commitment to equal opportunity. Our colleges and universities have not stood apart from the transformation of the society brought on by these phenomena. They have helped cause it, and they have, in turn, been profoundly affected by it.

In the American context this interpenetration of campus and society seemed perfectly natural. Our instinct, time and again, was to turn to higher education whenever there was a new job to be done, and as a consequence both the functions of higher education and the varied activities these functions tended to spawn steadily multiplied, with little thought on anyone's part of the consequences, or of the alternatives.

In view of the formidable burden the nation has placed on its higher educational system, the astounding fact is how well it has succeeded, not how badly it has failed. It has performed its traditional functions well, on balance, and in some cases with high distinction. It has adjusted to the pressures of mass participation in a remarkable manner. It has provided a great range of services to the larger society, on the whole competently and at reasonable cost. The anomaly—the paradox—of the present situation is that a national institution which has risen magnificently to the challenges with which it has been confronted is now, by common agreement, in dire need of reform!

Approaches to Reform

There would seem to be three possible approaches to reform. The first is to retain the system of higher education essentially as it is but make such changes as are necessary on particular campuses to alleviate the worst strains resulting from the attempt to discharge partially incompatible functions. This involves transferring some activities to institutions where they can be more appropriately performed and curtailing or eliminating others. It is a process of moving toward greater differentiation of functions among different types of institutions and rationalization of activities within institutions. This approach has much to be said for it, and it is already well under way. But necessary as it is, it is likely to fall considerably short of what is required for the fundamental reform of higher education.

A second approach, which has its advocates in the academy, entails unilateral action by higher education to reduce its range of functions and activities sharply, thereby "purging" itself and reverting to the only "proper" pursuits—teaching and scholarly research. This approach makes for some good rhetoric, but it runs so contrary to the American concept of the role of higher education in society, especially public higher education, as to be quite unrealistic and impractical as a way of reforming the *system*, however attractive it may be to an occasional individual institution.

A third approach, and the one that seems now to be needed, assumes that all or nearly all of the present functions of higher education are likely to be continued but that substantial modifications should be made in the nature of the burden that performing these functions throws on higher education. This approach recognizes that the decisions made by governmental and other external agencies, acting for the larger society, as to what to ask of the campus are as important to reform as anything done on campus. It suggests a need to find alternative ways of accomplishing some of the tasks higher education now performs. It implies major changes in the structure of the higher educational system and very possibly the invention of some alternative kinds of social institutions.

This approach will not entirely eliminate the present confusion of purposes in higher education, because the roles we assign to it in this country will continue to be numerous and varied. If energetically pursued, however, such an approach should at least reduce the pressures on higher education to a manageable level and allow it to concentrate more, and with easier conscience, on its most central functions.

Reducing the Burden

Many of the kinds of specific measures that might be taken to lighten the burden on higher education have already been widely discussed. A substantial structural change proposed by the Carnegie Commission on Higher Education would be the reduction by a year of the normal undergraduate course. Such a step would recognize the better preparation and greater maturity of many college entrants today. It could also provide, without further capital investment, some of the additional capacity that must be found in the coming decade for expanding enrollments. Finally, it would reduce the cost of a college education to society and to the individual and enable higher education to use its limited resources to benefit more people.

A second measure, which has not been widely discussed, would be to cull out of higher education an extensive array of vocational courses it now offers to prepare students for medium-level occupations and subprofessions. While such a step might have great merit, it would necessitate the development of a network of new institutions for "further education" with their programs closely tied in, perhaps on a "sandwich" basis, to a variety of manufacturing and service industries. It might also imply the further development of educational activities within industry.

This course would immediately raise a major question about the role of junior and community colleges. At the moment they are considered part of higher education. Should they be, or should we move in the direction of splitting postsecondary education into "further" and "higher" education and make the two-year college part of the former and almost entirely vocational in character? There would be many advantages to so doing but also some distinct disadvantages. One would be the danger, so well illustrated in Britain, of creating a set of institutions which enjoyed a level of prestige so much lower than that accorded academic institutions as to be socially deeply divisive. Another would be destruction of the very important concept of wide availability of a full range of postsecondary education, including the liberal arts, close to home and at minimal cost.

A third way of reducing the responsibilities now placed on higher education would be to transfer some of the research now done in universities to independent research institutes, or government installations, especially where the research is of a type deemed less appropriate for an academic institution. In some cases new nonprofit institutes might have to be created for the purpose. This is the course currently being followed by one leading university, which is transferring to a new organization being set up for the purpose defense-related research and development programs running to many millions of dollars annually. While a step such as this can relieve an institution of a responsibility that has become awkward or burdensome to it, the costs in terms of overhead payments forfeited, in jeopardy to the quality of the research program, or in opportunities for graduate students foregone may be considerable.

In another area of functions, there is little question that some universities have made unwise decisions in agreeing to provide the administrative base for public service programs of a largely operational nature. Sometimes the administration of such a program is defensible as a research enterprise in itself, because it offers a practical milieu for student training, or simply because it is unavoidable as part of an institution's responsibility to the neighborhood in which it is situated. Nevertheless, academic institutions are not, on balance, well equipped to run large programs for the provision of services to the public, and unless there are powerful reasons for doing so, they could well leave the responsibility to others.

There is also reason to believe that the function performed by higher education of providing a talent pool for other institutions, principally government and industry, puts more of a burden on it than is generally recognized. Without by any means abolishing the function, universities could particularly at this time of faculty surplus, tighten up the administration of it so that it might better serve their interests.

Unquestionably the most important way that society could lighten the burden on higher education would be to find ways to relieve it of responsibility for the substantial numbers of young people who become students only because they feel they must avoid the stigma of *not* having attended college, or see no other way to spend the threshold years of adulthood that holds out any kind of promise to them.

This opens up the hard question of alternatives to higher education. What, indeed, can hundreds of thousands of eighteen to twenty-one year olds living in a highly urbanized, highly industrialized society do with their time? What kinds of maturing experiences can they have that will be constructive for the nation and for them, that will be sufficiently interesting to hold their attention, and will enable them to support themselves modestly, or at least contribute to their own support?

It is frequently suggested that the reluctant student would be better off out in the real world earning his living. But is this really possible? There are currently nearly fifteen million men and women in the eighteen to twenty-one age group, a number destined to rise to about seventeen million over the coming decade before beginning to decline gradually. Among the approximately nine million of this group in the labor force, which includes about two million also enrolled full- or part-time in higher education, the number unemployed is substantial. It is already well over a million and may well go higher. Furthermore, among those who are employed full-time, a great many hold jobs which offer little opportunity for the development of skills of more than a rudimentary kind.

The prospect, then, if hundreds of thousands of young men and women who are now, rather unwillingly, enrolled in higher education were to seek full-time employment instead, is that they would simply swell the ranks of the unemployed, or of those employed in deadend jobs, with all the negative social consequences that would entail.

There has also been a good deal of talk about national service programs for young people. Of these, the program most capable of absorbing additional young people in large numbers is military service. Such a course, however, whatever its merits or faults, would be widely unpopular, especially with the young people themselves. Nonmilitary service programs such as the Peace Corps and VISTA have been successful, but have obvious limitations in their capacity to absorb large numbers. Participation in them also requires a level of maturity which is by no means characteristic of all young people under twenty-one.

Moreover, there is the question of cost, a question which those who express concern over the tax burden of higher education would do well to remember. While the average annual real cost of having a student in college at the undergraduate level, including educational and general costs and board and lodging, is not more than $4000 (perhaps $6000 if foregone earnings are included), the cost of having the same person serve as a recruit in military service is $7500, as a Peace Corps volunteer nearly $10,000, and as a VISTA volunteer $7800. It should also be remembered that of the total annual expenditure on higher education only half comes from public tax sources, whereas in military and other national service programs the *entire* burden falls on the taxpayer.

A central task, then, if higher education is to be reformed through reduction of the pressures on it, is the invention of viable alternatives for some young people, alternatives that are at least as productive to society, as useful to the individual, and no more costly than going to college. This is no small assignment. It means the investment of huge sums of money to create new jobs with the potential for useful learning and personal satisfaction to those who hold them. It means the invention and financing of new low cost forms of national service. And perhaps it means some new ideas that no one has as yet even thought of.

If really viable alternatives can be invented and they prove attractive to some of our youth, not only will the burden on higher education be lightened but the role it plays in providing virtually the only means of social certification for middle class status in American life may also be diminished. Helpful in this regard also will be the many new nontraditional degree programs that are springing up today. To the person who decides to forego college immediately after high school they offer a second chance for higher education and the earning of a degree at a later date.

The Need for Leadership

In summary, it is apparent that the higher educational system in this country performs a very wide range of functions which, collectively, have enormous economic and social value. It is also obvious, both in relation to this value and to the economic and social costs of alternative ways for young people to occupy their time, that public expenditure on higher education is a national bargain and not the extravagance many people believe it to be. Finally, it is clear that reform, given the nature of the present national dependence on higher education, will have to involve the entire society and will entail the invention of ways to relieve higher education of some of its burdens and to lighten others. An understanding and acceptance of these three propositions would seem to be necessary to any concerted movement toward fundamental reform.

Although the national debate over the financing of higher education which has been taking place in the Congress, in state legislatures, and in the mind of the public is, understandably, focused on the question of institutional survival, one would like to see it enlarged to include the subject of reform—reform as delineated by the three propositions noted above. Reform and finance are inextricably linked. There can be no real reform which does not involve the major sources of finance, and, at bottom, it is unrealistic to debate the level of support for higher education without coming to grips with the question of what we expect of it.

Ultimately, there must and will be many parties to the debate on reform— the federal and state governments, private industry, private givers, the public and, not the least, the higher educational community itself. The debate, if it is to be constructive and result in measures that will be beneficial both to the campus and to the nation, will require informed, farsighted, and objective leadership. It is much in the interests of higher education not to let leadership of the reform movement pass by default to others but to assume this role itself. Higher education can do this, however, only by convincing the public that it can put the general interests of the nation ahead of its own special interests, and in the lead reform is unquestionably one of the greatest challenges facing the higher educational community today.

Revitalizing the Charitable Deduction

For more than half a century, almost as long as the United States has had a constitutionally valid income tax, the American taxpayer has had the right to reduce his taxable income by the amount he gives to charity. There was, apparently, little public or Congressional debate when this provision was first enacted in 1917; nor was there much in subsequent years. The deduction was simply accepted as something that was naturally good, both for the taxpayer and the country. Recently, however, this hitherto well-accepted feature of the Internal Revenue Code has become the object of some sharp questioning, to a point where its continued existence could be in doubt. While no legislation respecting the charitable deduction is presently under consideration or pending, the debate over it seems to be gathering momentum. Those who believe that this feature of the income tax represents sound public policy must look to its defense, or it may well be allowed to lapse in some future round of national tax reform.

Why has the charitable deduction suddenly become subject to doubt after so many years of public acceptance? There are probably two explanations. At the obvious level, there is the disenchantment of a growing body of citizens with the entire tax system because of its regressiveness and hence inequity toward lower income taxpayers. Given this situation and the fact that the great majority of low and moderate income taxpayers now make use of the standard deduction on their income tax forms, and are encouraged by government to do so, a special deduction for charitable giving is bound to seem to many taxpayers like a "loophole" designed principally to benefit the rich. The fact that the tax "savings" involved in charitable gifts stimulated by the charitable deduction go to the recipient institutions and not into the pockets of the donors is easily misunderstood.

At a deeper level, however, it is possible that public attitudes, not just toward the charitable deduction but toward charity itself, may have undergone a transformation. The time-honored concept of private benevolence for the public good, once widely respected in this country, may command less universal respect today than heretofore. To some Americans, charity has apparently become uncoupled from the notion of *public* benefit and tied to the idea of *private* advantage and privilege. To others, it is increasingly seen as anachronistic and even offensive in a society where the concept of citizens' rights to governmentally provided services is constantly expanding.

What is clear, certainly, is that there is considerable public ignorance of the role which the charitable sector plays in our national life and a kind of pervasive indifference to its fate. While it is true that private gifts to the institutions which make up this sector have increased substantially in recent years, these have been more than offset by inflation and rising costs, with the result that the financial position of the charitable sector has been seriously weakened in relative terms. The issue, however, is not just financial, important as that is. It is also moral and philosophical, having to do with the very nature of our society.

From another direction, the attack on the charitable deduction comes from a small but influential group of tax reformers, who are themselves specialists in tax law. Their indictment, as one analyst of the reform movement has put it, has three counts—"impropriety," "inefficiency," and "inequity." Impropriety stems from the view that charitable giving is actually no more than one form of consumption expenditure, equivalent, let us say, to going bowling, buying a boat, or taking a vacation. Why should the citizen who gets his pleasure from making donations to charity benefit over the one who prefers to spend his disposable income on some other form of "pleasure"? Assuming equal income, each should be taxed the same.

Inefficiency relates to the lack of firm evidence that the existence of the charitable deduction is, in fact, efficient in stimulating donations to charity beyond what the taxpayer would give anyway. The government is, therefore, seen as foregoing tax revenue without a proven equivalent benefit to charity.

The third count—inequity—has to do with the way the charitable deduction affects taxpayers with different levels of taxable income in differing ways. Because of the way the graduated bracket system operates, a low income taxpayer has little or no incentive to give and gains nothing or very little in tax "savings" from doing so. The middle income taxpayer has some incentive and gains some tax "savings," the upper income taxpayer has quite a bit of each, and the very rich taxpayer a great deal. Surely, say the reformers, it is illogical and unfair for the government to subsidize most heavily the charitable donations of those who can best afford to make them.

In addition to these specific criticisms of the charitable deductions, some of the tax reformers have a broad philosophical objection to Federal "tax expenditures" generally. They argue that all of the numerous features of the Internal Revenue Code which, for economic incentive and other reasons, permit corporations and individuals to escape taxation, must rightfully be regarded as expenditures under the Federal budget—expenditures, however, which are not subject to the discipline of Congressional review and appropriation.

A better system, they contend, would be one that achieved the same intended purposes by substituting for these tax expenditures direct appropriations, authorized under new legislation. In the case of the charitable deduction, the substitute might be direct Federal support of charitable institutions, except, of course, churches—grants to which would be clearly unconstitutional. Alternatively, some system of matching grants might be devised where the charity to which the taxpayer had made a donation would qualify for a grant from the Federal Government. The sum total of these matching grants would then have to be appropriated each year by Congress.

Implicit in this twin attack on the charitable deduction by populists, old and new, and by tax reformers seem to be several far-reaching, negative assumptions about the nature of charity and its role in American society. When stated explicitly, these assumptions are deeply disturbing.

The first assumption has been indicated, namely that the several prerogatives which charity enjoys under our present tax arrangements constitute a system of privilege, a system which benefits the rich at the expense of the poor and those of modest income.

The second assumption is that government has first claim on every citizen's income, and what it does not take from him is left as an act of grace. Permitting the deduction from taxable income of amounts given to charity is, therefore, no more than a demonstration of sheer generosity to the taxpayer by government. It could, and probably should, tax him on his full income, but as an act of *noblesse oblige* it chooses not to in this case.

The third assumption is that the government "portion" of a gift to charity, resulting from the charitable deduction, is actually a public subsidy to the recipient institution. By virtue of this subsidy, government has standing, that is, rights and responsibilities, in regard to that institution. No longer can it be seen as wholly private.

The fourth assumption is that decision making by legislative bodies which are "accountable" to the people at large is preferable to private choice when it comes to the channeling of funds to activities which are intended to be of public benefit. The charitable deduction is considered basically wrong because it rewards private initiative for the public good rather than stimulating government to take increased responsibility. In fairness, it should be noted that not all tax reformers share this point of view.

The Nature of Charity

Because "charity" is susceptible to various definitions in popular usage and, to many people, suggests the outdated and paternalistic notion of "Lady Bountiful," it may be useful to quote the Internal Revenue Code regulations defining the term. The regulations state that, for federal tax purposes, "charity," in general, comprises activities having educational, literary, religious, or scientific purposes. They go on to say, specifically, that "charitable" also includes:

> Relief of the poor and distressed or of the underprivileged; advancement of religion; advancement of education or science; erection or maintenance of public buildings, monuments, or works; lessening of the burdens of Government; and promotion of social welfare by organizations designed to accomplish any of the above purposes, or (i) to lessen neighborhood tensions; (ii) to eliminate prejudice and discrimination; (iii) to defend human and civil rights secured by law; or (iv) to combat community deterioration and juvenile delinquency.

Charity, it will be seen, covers a very broad range of activities carried out by a great variety of institutions, *all* of which are deemed to be of benefit to the community. The concept, which connotes both the act of giving and the institutions established for purposes recognized as charitable, is of course an ancient one, antedating by centuries the settlement of North America. In Britain, whence the concept came to the American Colonies, charity has a well-defined status in law, and a tax on the income of charity would be considered unconstitutional on the grounds that property, having been set aside for one "public" purpose, could not then be taken by government for another. In our own country charity has a constitutional position in the law of many of the states. Because it was considered a matter for the states to deal with, no mention of it was incorporated in the Federal Constitution. Indeed, issues affecting charity hardly arose at the Federal level until a national income tax was adopted, and it then seemed perfectly natural, so firmly was the concept established as being in the public interest, simply to exempt charity from the tax, and, shortly thereafter, to exclude gifts to charity from taxable income.

Given the historic and true character of charity—the gift of money or property for *public* benefit—there are certain self-evident propositions about it which stand out in sharp contrast to the assumptions underlying the current attack on the charitable deduction.

The first of these propositions is obvious—that charity, by its very nature, must serve the public welfare. It can have no other purpose. If it does, it simply is not charity.

The second is that private charitable action, while not intrinsically superior to governmental action, nonetheless provides certain qualities which are indispensable to the humane, enlightened, and free society, which is the American ideal. Charitable institutions can provide diversity, free choice and competition. They can experiment and they can set standards. They can enter fields too controversial for governmental bodies and can monitor governmental performance. They can fill vital gaps in publicly provided services. They can offer the means for participation by lay citizens in social action. They can help to safeguard intellectual and artistic freedom and civil liberties. And, finally, they can engage in the definition and preservation of the society's highest values, especially those of a spiritual and religious nature.

The third proposition is that since the purpose of government is to promote the general welfare, in the broadest sense of the term, it is as legitimate for government to encourage private charitable initiative for the public good as it is to legislate governmental programs to this end. Indeed, government has an obligation to pursue *both* courses.

The fourth proposition, which follows from the third, is that there are many ways for government to encourage charity. It can make charitable organizations exempt from taxation. It can create a stable legal framework within which charity can operate with assurance. It can regulate and supervise charity in such a way that the public has confidence in it. It can help create a favorable climate of public opinion by making clear in its actions and statements that it considers charity a public good. Finally, it can stimulate individuals, estates and corporations to contribute to charity through special arrangements in the tax system. Each of these forms of encouragement is entirely legitimate.

The Present Debate

There seem to be current today, then, two antithetical sets of views about the nature of charity, and beyond that about the nature of American society. The first set says that the tax benefits accorded charity are no more than a system of privilege for the wealthy; that government's failure to tax income given to charity is simply an act of grace on its part and, moreover, constitutes a public subsidy to the recipient private institutions, making them less than fully private; and, lastly, that governmental encouragement of charitable giving is wrong because it promotes private rather than public initiative for the public welfare.

The second set says that charity by its true, historical nature exists entirely for the public benefit and has no other nature or purpose; that charitable institutions provide certain qualities which are indispensable to the building and maintenance of a humane, enlightened, dynamic, and free society; that since government's most fundamental purpose is to promote the general welfare, it has an obligation to use every available means to this end, including the furthering of private charitable initiative for the public good; and that there are many legitimate ways to do this, among them provisions in the tax system which encourage gifts to charity.

While, admittedly, neither populists nor tax-reformers would claim to advocate the total abolition of charity at the present time, nor would those who defend it consider it to be above criticism, it seems clear that a major issue has been joined in the society which may come to a head in part in the next few years over the future of the charitable deduction. It is the issue of whether or not we believe private, charitable initiative for the public good is an essential feature of our way of life, and whether, therefore, we take public actions that strengthen it or weaken it.

Revitalizing Charity

While it is, perhaps, debatable whether antipathy or just ignorance and indifference is the more accurate way to characterize the current public mood toward charity, clearly the time has come when steps must be taken to rehabilitate and reinvigorate this basic concept in our national life. Wherever charity is misunderstood, efforts must be made to explain it. Wherever it is operating under a cloak of secrecy, it must be brought into the open. Wherever it is tainted by private self-interest, it must be purified. Wherever it is serving to perpetuate unwarranted privilege, it must be made more democratic. Wherever the arrangements of the tax system which help to support it can be made more equitable, this should be done. In short, if charity is to be uncoupled in the public mind from the idea of private advantage and privilege and reunited with its purpose of serving the general welfare—where it historically belongs—it must undergo further revisions and improvements and be brought closer to greater numbers of people.

Among possible revisions it would seem that none is more needed than changes in the charitable deduction—to make it more equitable to all taxpayers and to enable the support of charitable organizations and institutions to become a more democratic affair. No doubt there are a variety of ways to accomplish this. The following plan is put forward simply as one possibility, with no other purpose than to stimulate serious discussion and debate, and to generate other proposals as to how the charitable deduction might be substantially improved and its position thereby strengthened in our national life.

The Proposal

Under present law, any taxpayer who itemizes deductions on his federal income tax return is allowed to subtract from taxable income the amount of his charitable donations up to one half of his income. The marginal tax rate for individuals now ranges from a low of 14 percent to a high of 50 percent for income derived from salary and wages, and 70 percent for unearned income. Thus, the effect of the charitable deduction provision is to give the taxpayer a tax break of from 14 to 70 percent of the amount he gives to charity, depending on his tax bracket. Another way to portray this is to say that the government subsidizes 14 percent of a poor man's personal giving, 70 percent of a rich man's and somewhere in between for the others. For those not choosing to itemize deductions on their tax returns, an unspecified allowance for charitable donations is presumably included in the standard deduction.

What is proposed is simply that every taxpayer, whether or not he itemizes and whatever his tax bracket, be treated as if he were in the highest, or 50 percent, marginal bracket for salary and wage income for purposes of his charitable contributions. The effect of this, obviously, would be to give every taxpayer a 50 percent tax credit for his charitable donations. A person giving $200 would, for example, get $100 automatically knocked off his tax bill. For the sake of simplicity, this would be entered on the tax return as a tax credit after all other computations had been made, although in spirit it would remain a deduction and would have to be supported by the submission of an itemized list of contributions.

To ensure that this plan does not result in a reduction in charitable giving by those whose income is essentially unearned and who may be in a bracket higher than 50 percent, it is proposed that each taxpayer be given a choice either of filing under the present system or under the new 50 percent tax credit system, whichever benefits him most. Present ceilings on charitable contribution deductions as a proportion of taxable income would also be retained.

Possible Criticisms

One can readily foresee some of the criticisms that will be made of this proposal. Those who believe that any form of indirect public expenditure through tax deductions is bad policy will regard it simply as continuing down the wrong road. The difficulty with this criticism, however, is that although charitable institutions do receive public funds, under careful controls, through grants and contracts, no system for general, direct governmental subsidization of these institutions has ever been devised that does not threaten to compromise their autonomy. One can argue, therefore, that an absolutist approach to this issue is neither necessary nor right. Indirect public expenditure through tax deductions may be bad policy in regard to some objectives but is good policy in regard to the support of charity.

Other critics will emphasize the loss of revenue that the proposal would entail for the Federal Government—about $4 billion if it had been in operation for 1971. They will say it is not feasible unless compensated for by a general rise in tax rates (especially at the higher income levels) or a cut in the standard deduction, or both. This, of course, will be a powerful argument in a time of national budget deficits. The answer here lies in the realm of values. If one believes that private initiative for the public good is as fundamental to the American concept of a democratic society as governmental action, the "loss" on the governmental side of the ledger will be seen as a gain on the private side and of equal benefit to the general welfare. The "loss," therefore, does not have to be made good by a raising of tax rates. Some lower priority Federal budget item will simply have to be dropped in the interests of a step that helps to redress the overall balance between governmental and private initiative in the society.

Others will say that while the proposal goes some distance toward making the present system fairer, it does not go far enough. In particular, it does nothing for the person whose income is so low he pays no tax at all. This is true but hardly relevant. One must, after all, be a taxpayer at some level to be disadvantaged or discriminated against in relation to wealthier taxpayers who benefit most from the charitable deduction. These critics will also say that allowing the taxpayer with sufficient unearned income to place him in a tax bracket above 50 percent to continue to deduct according to the old system simply perpetuates a special privilege for the rich. This may be ture, but the proportion of taxpayers affected is minute and the revenue loss to government involved apparently only about $200 million, whereas the capacity of the very rich to make large capital donations, particularly to voluntary hospitals and private educational institutions, is a matter of the greatest social importance.

Others will point out that the feature of the proposal which requires those claiming a charitable deduction, in addition to the standard deduction, to itemize their gifts will further complicate administration of the income tax both for government and for the taxpayer. Again, this is true. But is it really much of an imposition on the taxpayer, in return for the advantages he gains, to set down on his tax form the names of the charities he has given to and the amounts? And as to "inconvenience" to the Internal Revenue Service, governmental bureaucracies exist to serve the public, not their own convenience. There is no reason to suppose that the IRS would see this otherwise, if the public benefit implied was sufficiently clear.

Still others will object that the proposal seems to provide an opportunity for a double deduction for the same charitable gifts by those who use the standard deduction, and since this now includes some 63 percent of taxpayers, the objection, it will be said, is of some consequence. It is impossible to assess fully the validity of this criticism because, under the present system, there is absolutely no way to determine whether any charitable donations are, in fact, made by those who take the standard deduction. The provision of the standard deduction assumes this but offers no incentive for it. Indeed, the government, in effect, tells the taxpayer it doesn't really care whether he gives to charity or not. It will give him the deduction anyway.

Nevertheless, if this criticism is considered a serious fault in the proposal, one possibility would be to amend it by reducing the standard deduction, for those who take advantage of the new tax credit plan, by the amount of their charitable contributions. This would not only prevent the double deduction but would reduce the revenue loss to government by about one billion dollars. The incentive for giving would, of course, also be somewhat reduced, but perhaps not seriously so, as the taxpayer would still benefit considerably over the present system. If, for example, he were in the 14 percent bracket and gave $400 to charity, he would be liable for $56 in tax on this amount but would receive a $200 credit, for a net advantage of $144. For a taxpayer in the 20 percent bracket the net advantage would be $120. Indeed, a taxpayer would have a net advantage until he reached the 50 percent bracket (presently $44,000 on joint returns).

Finally, some critics will argue that since there is no firm evidence that tax advantages do act as an incentive for charitable giving, except at very high income levels, there can be no assumption that the proposal will produce a significantly increased flow of funds to charity. The fault with this objection is that it is purely speculative. No one can predict what the response of taxpayers would be to a new plan such as this. Some would probably be stimulated to give more, some not. However, it seems quite possible that since the number of taxpayers benefiting from the new provision will be very large indeed, in fact more than 99 percent of all taxpayers, the aggregate return to charity would be quite considerable, perhaps several billion dollars annually. One would be banking here on the psychological impact of three factors: the effect on the average citizen of making the charitable deduction fairer, the visible attractiveness of a tax credit, and the strong reaffirmation of the government's approval of charitable giving inherent in its adoption of the new plan. Whatever the increase in annual giving proved to be, there would, it must be remembered, be an additional revenue loss to the U.S. Treasury of half that amount above the $4 billion loss in the present level of giving.

Advantages

The advantages in the new plan proposed here could be very considerable. Obviously, it would be a significant move toward making the charitable deduction provision fairer. Tax brackets would no longer make any difference in the tax liability of all taxpayers who made use of the new credit system, and, no matter what the level of income earned by taxpayers, government would be "matching" their charitable gifts equally. Not only would this increased equity be a worthwhile objective in itself, but it might also serve to reverse the present drift toward total abolition of the deduction, with its disastrous consequences for charitable institutions such as private colleges, voluntary hospitals, symphony orchestras, museums and certain welfare organizations. It might also as indicated above, increase the annual income of these organizations by a significant amount. In 1971 total donations to charity from all private sources came to about $21 billion, of which approximately $15 billion was given by individuals. If, therefore, the new plan stimulated, say, a 25 percent increase in individual giving, the additional income available for private charitable organizations would be about $3.75 billion.

At a deeper level, the reform, if adopted, might play a major role in helping to reinvigorate the role of charity in our national life by making it more democratic. Because the proposed tax credit would operate to the overwhelming advantage of lower and moderate income taxpayers, it would create in these sizeable groups a vast, new potential supporting constituency for charitable institutions, freeing the latter from the risk of undue dependence on the wealthy. These groups would, in effect, be a new community for private organizations and institutions to reach out to in their fund raising. Many of the possible new givers would, of course, be younger men and women on starting salaries, with a substantial potential for future giving. The value to charity generally of attracting not only the financial support but also the voluntary effort of young adults in its work cannot be overstated. In sum, the proposal's potential for widening and diversifying both the support and management of charity might go a long way in dispelling the unfortunate association that charity seems to have gained with privilege in the popular mind.

Most fundamentally, reform of the charitable deduction would be a step in the direction of decentralization of decision making in our society and the encouragement of diversity in the ways we achieve our social objectives. In short, both symbolically and in real terms, it would help to reaffirm the nation's long-standing tradition of private initiative for the public good. We are at a point in our history when the continued existence of that crucial idea is being seriously challenged. If it should continue to lose vitality and eventually disappear from the nation, much that is of the highest value, not just to the few, but to *all* Americans, will be lost with it.

Twenty Years in Retrospect:
A Personal View

Foundation work, by its very nature, is not likely to encourage retrospection. It tends to be engaged with the present and the future—and so it should be. There is, however, some mysterious quality about the end of a decade that tends to prompt most of us to take a long look into our past. Where were we ten, twenty, or thirty years ago? Were things better or worse then? What have we accomplished in those intervening years? What have we learned?

Reacting to such an urge, I have been reflecting lately about the two decades I have just completed at this foundation. I hope it will not be considered presumptuous if I share some of my observations on these years.

It is with a sense almost of incredulity that I realize twenty years have gone by here. I say this not because I have survived that long in this occupation, or that the occupation itself has survived, although there have been times when I wondered about both. No, the surprise lies in the speed with which the years have flown by, filled with an unending succession of stimulating people and demanding problems. There have been moments of exhilaration and satisfaction, and, of course, also of discouragement. But the days have never been dull, and therein, I suppose, lies the explanation of their swift transit.

Carnegie Corporation, I can see now more clearly than I might have earlier, has meant three quite different things to me. It has, most obviously been a place where I was initiated into the mysteries of being a foundation officer and, over time, became an old hand at the game, at first handling grant proposals within the Corporation's Commonwealth Program and later serving in an administrative capacity as vice president, acting president, and then president. Secondly, it has been a professional home to me, a congenial community within which I have enjoyed the companionship, support and intellectual stimulation of a remarkable set of staff and trustee colleagues. Lastly, it has been a base from which I have been able to reach out both here in this country and abroad, to pursue a variety of interests and public service activities: memberships on governmental and international commissions, advisory bodies and task forces, trusteeships of several universities and private organizations, participation in international conferences, and so on. Some of these pursuits have been directly related to the Corporation's program, some only tenuously so or not at all, but all, I believe, have enriched my life and, I hope, through me, the foundation.

Each of the things the foundation has been to me has exerted its special influence on my reflections, and together they have conjured up a quite personal vision of my years here, one which is unquestionably selective and probably warped as a result of the unconscious application of individual predilection and aversion to the process of memory. Certainly, my reflections cannot be thought to constitute anything like a comprehensive review of twenty years of Carnegie Corporation's history—far from it. That is another chronicle, and many important parts of it will be missing or have only glancing attention in this account.

Africa

Looking back over two decades here, it is clear that one great issue loomed larger than all others in absorbing my attention and interest during the initial years. This was the subject of African development, and its counterpart, emerging American relationships with Africa. Joining Carnegie Corporation in 1953 just after completing a five-month tour of British colonies in Africa as an administrator of the Fulbright Program in the United Kingdom, I brought to the foundation a keen interest in the continent and its peoples and, by American standards of the time, some knowledge of African problems and potential. Fresh from six years of residence in Britain, I was taken aback by the bumptiousness and naiveté of most American approaches of the day to Africa. On the other hand, I was painfully conscious of a pervasive and only thinly disguised British superciliousness toward many things American, especially American education, often based on sheer ignorance; and I was well aware of the determination of some, but by no means all, British officials to exclude American agencies from colonial affairs. Having made up their minds that their colonies in Africa and elsewhere should be prepared for independence—in ways and on a timetable determined in London—the British wanted no outside interference. My trip through Africa, however, had convinced me that independence was far closer than most British officials thought and the preparations for it had to be greatly accelerated, especially in the field of education. For this, American aid was urgently needed.

Since my interests and concerns were shared by Stephen Stackpole, the director of the Corporation's "British Dominions and Colonies Program," as it was then called, we moved ahead deliberately to develop a new program for the foundation in Africa. This had a number of strands to it: attempts to help the new British universities in places such as Nigeria, the Gold Coast and Uganda become less alien to their African environments; training of African educational leaders; assistance to university institutes and departments of education to enable them to aid the development of elementary and secondary education and teacher training; support for both short- and long-range planning in education; and, finally, a kind of private diplomacy aimed at building a spirit of Anglo-American-African tripartite cooperation in African educational development.

In retrospect—although I am, of course, a prejudiced witness—it seems to me that much was achieved in this new program as it unfolded in its initial decade and has evolved since. I think particularly of the establishment here in the United States of the Africa Liaison Committee of the American Council on Education (later changed to Overseas Liaison Committee) to serve as a counterpart to the Inter-University Council for Higher Education Overseas, in London. The Committee soon proved its value and has been immensely useful in helping to make the American educational effort in Africa, both governmental and private, more sophisticated, more productive and less abrasive. I think also of the Teachers for East Africa program, which stemmed from a Corporation-initiated conference, and of the Afro-Anglo-American Program in Teacher Education (involving African institutes of education, London University, and Teachers College, Columbia) which has now been transformed into the lively, Africa-based Association for Teacher Education in Africa. And then, among many other successful ventures, I recall the Commission on Post-School Certificate and Higher Education in Nigeria, the "Ashby Commission," in which three Nigerians, three Englishmen and three Americans, under a British chairman, together drew up a plan for future university development in that great African nation on the eve of its independence. All of these projects were based on the principle of tripartite cooperation.

Those ten years of deep involvement in Africa, a decade in which large parts of the continent achieved independence and in which faith in the power of education to promote social, political and economic development was almost unlimited, were an exciting period for me. That the faith proved to be unrealistically large and disappointment therefore became inevitable does not, in my view, diminish in the slightest the importance of education in Africa or the contributions Carnegie Corporation has been able to make to it. With the wisdom then which hindsight makes possible now, I would still have recommended very much the same bets for the foundation. Perhaps I would have had a somewhat more modest view of what universities can, by themselves, achieve in the promotion of national development in African countries, but I would certainly not have changed my view that they are essential to it.

The Study of Higher Education

A second activity that has a significant place in my reflections is my heavy involvement in recent years in the Corporation's concern for the welfare of higher education. The Carnegie Foundation for the Advancement of Teaching, the sister foundation of which I am also president, had been created in 1905 to give expression to Mr. Carnegie's concept of free pensions for virtually all college and university teachers of his day and to conduct educational studies. About 1965, however, the decrease in the pension load raised sharply the question of the Foundation's future. The issue was whether the trustees should end its life by merging it with Carnegie Corporation or preserve its independent character. The answer depended in good part on whether there was some purpose which the Foundation could serve that the Corporation could not, or which it might serve better.

As it happened, the Foundation possessed, in addition to an endowment fund of about $20 million, two unusual features among foundations generally: a charter binding its activities to the welfare of higher education and a board of trustees drawn almost entirely from the academic community. These were assets which were not lightly to be abandoned in the new era of "universal" higher education. After much thought and discussion, therefore, it was agreed that the Foundation would undertake a major project in higher education. The result was the establishment of the Carnegie Commission on Higher Education, which was financed over the ensuing six years at the rate of about $1 million per year primarily by the Corporation.

By 1971 the success of the Commission had become sufficiently clear to all concerned to demonstrate the wisdom of a continued existence for the Foundation. Two important steps accordingly were taken. By action of the trustees, the Foundation decided to devote its efforts exclusively in the future, beyond paying off the residue of its pension commitments, to the study of higher education, using its own resources for this purpose. By action of the Internal Revenue Service, its status as an "operating foundation" to carry out its new mission was confirmed under a provision of the Tax Reform Act of 1969. Thus, a prestigious but largely moribund organization, was, in the sixty-sixth year of its existence, infused with new life and a new sense of purpose: to analyze, study and make recommendations to the nation and to higher education itself respecting an enterprise which now enrolls over nine million students and spends some thirty billion dollars annually.

The creation of the Carnegie Commission of Higher Education and participation in its activities, the transformation of the Foundation and, more recently, planning for the next phase of its activity now that the Commission has completed its work have taken large amounts of my time over the past eight years, but I regret not one moment of it. I have no doubt that the Foundation has entered a new period of usefulness, and I believe that the Corporation's program in higher education has been clarified and strengthened as a result of the Foundation's activity. Beyond that, I am confident that the truly vast endeavor of the Carnegie Commission on Higher Education under the remarkable leadership of Clark Kerr—the largest, longest and most comprehensive review of a higher educational system ever undertaken, as far as we know anywhere in the world—

has already been of immense value to the nation and will continue to be for years to come. Again, I do not pretend to be a neutral witness, but as one who has followed the Commission's work in detail and participated in nearly all of its meetings, and who occupies a vantage point in two foundations from which to gain some degree of overview both of higher education and federal and state relationships with it, I perhaps have some credentials to make that claim. In any event, I shall make it!

It is true the Commission has been subject to criticism, principally from those who did not find in its work reaffirmation of their own special vision of undergraduate liberal education. While some of this criticism was, in my view, unjustified, it has nonetheless all been carefully noted and will be taken into consideration in the Foundation's future work.

Social Justice

A third topic which stands out clearly in my reflections is the development at the Corporation during the decade of the 1960s of a strong new commitment to the furtherance of social justice in our national life. Such a concern had not been totally lacking in earlier years, as evidenced by the foundation's initiation and support of the renowned Myrdal study of the American Negro. Nevertheless, from the end of the Second World War until the early 1960s other issues had commanded the Corporation's attention—matters such as the quest for excellence in education, the needs of the gifted student, and international research and training. A number of us on the staff, however, while we recognized that these were important questions, were becoming painfully aware of urgent problems of race, poverty and inequality of opportunity besetting this country. We proposed changes in the program, and gradually in the early 1960s the Corporation began to evince in its grants a concern for the disadvantaged. Since that time the commitment to a more equitable society has become steadily broader and stronger, and, during the past two or three years, has been augmented by a new interest in equal opportunity, especially educational opportunity, for women. This is a concern which grew naturally out of an earlier program at the foundation involving the continuing education of women.

The commitment to social justice, widely shared today by both trustees and staff, is a fundamental theme now running through all of the Corporation's programs and, indeed, through nearly every aspect of its work. Looking to the future, I see no prospect of this slacking off, at any rate not while I am in a position to have some influence on the Corporation's sense of direction. My own belief in the right of every human being to enjoy equal opportunity, equal respect and equal justice before the law is a deeply held conviction, and I could no longer be at ease in an organization not firmly committed to seeking these ends in American life. No foundation, perhaps, can feel wholly satisfied with its efforts in these fields, largely because of the immense difficulties involved, and I feel the same way about the Corporation's efforts. Nonetheless, we have tried to play a constructive role, and I am glad to say that the Corporation did not permit itself to be intimidated by the negative atmosphere surrounding the Tax Reform Act hearings in 1969 or to be deterred, by the "expenditure responsibility" requirements of the Act, from funding new organizations devoted to educational opportunities and rights for those who have been the victims of discrimination on account of their race, sex or economic circumstances.

Television, Children and Health

In addition to Africa, higher education and social justice, three other topics are so prominent in my reflections on the years here at the Corporation that they require at least brief mention. Chronologically, the first of these was the Carnegie Commission on Educational Television. This Commission, established in response to a request from the field of educational television and composed of a number of leading citizens, reported to the public in 1967 after more than a year's hard effort under the able chairmanship of James R. Killian, Jr. From the Commission's work emerged a vision of a new kind of television, *public television,* a structure for it, and a new quasi-public agency, the Corporation for Public Broadcasting, through which government could help finance it. Despite the controversy that has racked public television in recent years, the finding of the Carnegie Commission that the country needs both strong national programming centers and vigorous local stations remains essentially valid. In my view, public television has already come a long way, is here to stay, and will flourish in the future. We may one day even acquire the national maturity to have lively public affairs programming, politically independent of government though supported partially with federal funds through the CPB, as an essential part of it!

The Corporation's other major venture in the field of television has, of course, been the Children's Television Workshop. It was a former vice president of the foundation, Lloyd Morrisett, who conceived the idea of a study of children's television and had the inspiration to recruit Joan Ganz Cooney to carry it out. The study led directly to the founding of the Children's Television Workshop, with Joan Cooney as president. She and her colleagues, with additional financial support from the Ford Foundation, the United States Office of Education, the Corporation for Public Broadcasting and other sources, produced first *Sesame Street* and then a reading program, *The Electric Company,* both of which have been highly successful. Our intention in launching CTW was threefold: to help fill the void in good television entertainment for children, to assist early learning, and to help children from disadvantaged circumstances get off to a better start. What we never imagined, however, was the size of the potential audience for *Sesame Street* or its international appeal. It is now viewed regularly by nine million preschool youngsters here in the United States and is being shown in fifty-seven foreign countries to many additional millions. A Spanish language version for Latin America is produced in Mexico City, as well as a German version produced in Hamburg, and a Portuguese one in São Paulo. *The Electric Company* is watched regularly by three million grade school children in their classrooms and by another three million regularly in their homes.

A more recent initiative and one that is just now gathering its full momentum, is the Carnegie Council on Children, established in the summer of 1972 under the chairmanship of the imaginative and perceptive psychologist, Kenneth Keniston. This twelve-member body, with strong supporting staff in New Haven, is concentrating on American children in their years of most rapid physical, psychological and social growth, from conception to age nine. The Council is looking at the position of children in American life—public attitudes toward them and where they stand in the order of our national priorities—and is attempting to define their needs and determine whether these are being met by present public and private programs. Essentially, the Council is trying to examine all the major facets of child development and their interrelationships in order to try to answer the immensely difficult question: Are American children being given the start today that will equip them to live constructive, happy lives as adults in the twenty-first century?

Lastly, I must mention the Corporation's now discontinued program in health care. Entered into somewhat accidentally and opportunistically about eight years ago, it was, however, developed deliberately and with great care by Margaret Mahoney into an effective intervention into the problems of health care delivery. The program ended abruptly in 1972 when Ms. Mahoney became vice president of the Robert Wood Johnson Foundation and, by agreement between the two foundations, took the Corporation's interests and small staff with her to Princeton. While this was a responsible decision from every point of view, the Corporation's withdrawal from the health care field nonetheless saddened and disappointed me personally. Perhaps this was because I felt we had demonstrated that there was a place for a lay approach to health care delivery—the Corporation having had no medically-trained staff whatsoever. Perhaps it was because I found in the realities of health care some relief from the frustrations inherent in the necessarily abstract and theoretical nature of much of the Corporation's work in education. Perhaps I simply hated to lose a colleague who had joined the Corporation the same year as I and for whom I had the greatest respect and affection!

Some Lessons

It is no doubt presumptuous and perhaps foolhardy to discuss what lessons I believe I have learned as a foundation officer. This could easily seem self-serving and could also be somewhat meaningless. What may be lessons to one foundation will be irrelevant to another. Nonetheless, harking to the reader who may say, "surely he must have learned something about how to operate a foundation in all those years," I will have a try at it.

Above all other aspects of foundation work, I would put the human factor. I mean by this the attitudes and behavior of foundation staff members. If they are arrogant, self-important, dogmatic, conscious of power and status, or filled with a sense of their own omniscience—traits which the stewardship of money tends to bring out in some people—the foundation they serve cannot be a good one. If, on the other hand, they have genuine humility, are conscious of their own limitations, are aware that money does not confer wisdom, are humane, intellectually alive and curious people—men and women who above all else are eager to learn from others—the foundation they serve will probably be a good one. In short, the human qualities of its staff may in the end be far more important to what a foundation accomplishes than any other considerations.

A second lesson I believe I have learned is that not a great deal of wisdom is to be gained by foundation executives sitting in their offices in New York skyscrapers, or wherever else they may be, and letting the world come to them. It will at best be a limited part of the world they see, the part that has the inclination, time and money to visit them. Many of the best people the foundation should be supporting will never, in the ordinary course of events, come near its doors. Unless a foundation has a program severely restricted by geographic or other considerations, its officers must be willing to travel far and wide, and the foundation itself must be prepared to put substantial administrative funds into travel. There is simply no substitute for it.

Another lesson has to do with the definition of foundation programs. Few today would dispute the need for foundations to have defined areas within which they make their grants. "Scatteration" and superficiality are well identified sins in this business. Nevertheless, I have gradually reached the view that too rigid a definition of program can cause a foundation to become in-grown, stagnant and dull. To me a foundation's overall program should be a living organism. It should constantly be growing new cells and discarding old ones. New cells can be added by means of deliberate thought, study and debate by trustees and staff, and this is usually the case. Sometimes, however, it is a chance event or contact which produces an out-of-program proposal so interesting and important that it becomes the forerunner of a new program or subprogram. I see nothing to be ashamed of in this kind of opportunism; it goes naturally with an open, enquiring, undogmatic staff.

Flexibility of this kind also says something about the kinds of men and women a foundation hires for its program staff. If they are too deeply committed to a discipline, too much wrapped up in their own specialization, they may try to develop more of an emphasis on their field than the foundation wants to have. Conversely, they may be unwilling to learn about new fields or lack the openness of mind to recognize and seize new opportunities when these appear. Finally, they may have good analytical ability but not have the entrepreneurial instinct and administrative sense to ensure that something constructive really does happen when foundation money is spent. There are, in fact, few foundations that are large enough or have sufficiently narrow purposes to provide a home for the single-minded specialist. Most program officers must be jacks-of-all trades—and, to the very best of their ability, masters of several.

No discussion of lessons learned would be complete without some reference to the old and vexing issue of foundations and the "promotion of social change." More ill-informed and superficial comment has been expended on this question than on any other. The term, of course, is meaningless unless one states the object of the change. And, having done that, one can regard any particular movement as being forward, backward, or sideward depending on one's own bias. Critics, however, have generally had in mind "meddling" in the social and political system to promote ideologies unacceptable to the American people at large. While the overall record of foundations clearly and emphatically disproves such a charge, most of them supporting established charities and institutions, it nonetheless remains a hardy perennial, and whenever it reappears, someone always seems ready to listen to it. Why?

The answer I think lies in the very nature of foundation responsibility as many, though not by any means all, foundations see it. These foundations believe that as a consequence of their historic charitable status it is incumbent on them to be engaged either directly or indirectly through their beneficiaries with the great social problems of the day. In attacking the causes, rather than simply trying to alleviate the symptoms, of these problems, they have learned that what lies at the root of most social pathology is human *powerlessness*—the powerlessness of the poor, of the undernourished, of the uneducated, and of those who receive unequal treatment because of their race, color or sex—to claim a fair share of life's opportunities and rewards. Many foundation grants therefore have had as their ultimate objective helping those at the bottom of the social and economic ladder to become better educated, more skilled, better fed, healthier, less subject to discrimination, and more hopeful, so that they may be in a position to share in the decisions and control of events that affect their lives.

If one poses the social change issue slightly differently, as the question of whether or not a primary goal of foundations should be the promotion of greater social equity within our present economic and political systems, it is one that is real and faces almost every foundation. The questions this issue raises are many. By what right *does* a private organization not directly answerable to the people at large undertake to improve the lot of some people within the society at the possible expense of others? Is this a social objective consonant with charitable status, or is it really a political objective and hence not proper for a foundation? On the other hand, is it a responsible stance for a foundation *not* to be concerned about social equity? Does charitable status somehow imply such an obligation?

I have thought a good deal about these questions over the years, and especially in recent years. It is my belief that the promotion of social justice *should* be a concern of most foundations. I don't see how this can be otherwise as long as we have a society characterized by severe inequity. This is not to suggest, however, that other objectives, such as the advancement of knowledge, the training of leadership, the raising of aesthetic standards, and so on, are not meritorious, too. For inherent in the concept of charity is the principle that every charitable organization may pursue in its own way what it perceives to be the common good, provided of course, it adheres to its charter and conforms to the laws governing charity. The nation would be poorer if some kind of orthodoxy as to what is the best way to create the good society were ever to be imposed on foundations generally. Nevertheless, whatever set of goals a foundation may have, among them I would hope there would be some clear degree of commitment to making this a fairer and more just society.

The promotion of social justice, of course, is a tricky business for foundations, with many difficulties and dangers lying in wait for the unwary. From my experience I have found a few practical dicta to be useful in this arena. Some of these are: look carefully at the purposes, both immediate and longer range, to be served by a project and be sure both the proponent and the foundation are honest about them. Don't assume virtue greater than normal in people just because they are disadvantaged, poor, or of a different color. On the other hand, don't assume that they possess less intelligence, competence, or integrity than normal because of these characteristics. Don't be romantic. Projects will not succeed just because they are intended to help right some deep injustice. They must also be well-planned and well-administered. And, finally, don't be deterred by the first piece of criticism that comes along. The attainment of social justice is by definition controversial and one must expect criticism. For every critic of the foundation, though, there will be at least one enthusiastic supporter.

Perhaps the most difficult questions faced by a foundation in giving expression to a concern for social justice are those that relate to its investment policies. On the one hand, it has an obligation to invest its endowment funds in such a way as to produce maximum income for charitable distribution, adhering, of course, to the "prudent man" rule. On the other hand, it is illogical for a foundation to invest in the securities of corporations whose policies run counter to the ideals informing the foundation's grants program. In addition, the kinds of issues that have been selected for corporate proxy challenges in recent years have been so complex that a foundation, in deciding to vote for or against management, could not be certain it was acting fairly on the basis of complete information. To resolve this dilemma, Carnegie Corporation helped found a new, cooperative organization, the Investor Responsibility Research Center, to undertake detailed studies of proxy issues and provide non-partisan analytical information to its subscribers. On the basis of this information the Corporation is better able to make decisions as to how to vote its shares. The Corporation has also written letters to some companies in which it has stock, raising questions about management policies with respect to certain social functions. It is my belief that in some instances these letters have been moderately effective, along with actions taken by other groups, in encouraging to pursue more progressive policies.

The Challenge to Charity

Much of my time and attention in the past seven or eight years has gone to activities related to the foundation field at large, including at times its defense. In 1968 a few foundation executives and trustees began to sense that foundations had suffered a sharp loss of standing both in Congress and among the public at large, occasioned by certain real and some fancied instances of abuse in the foundation field. I wrote a piece for the Corporation's annual report that fall in which I called for the establishment of a special commission to study the field and noted that if foundations did not put their own house in order the government would surely do it for them.

Not long after this, in the course of the following spring, came the hearings on foundations before the Ways and Means Committee of the House of Representatives, in connection with the Tax Reform Act of 1969. Testifying at those hearings, I was shocked, as were other foundation representatives, at the antagonistic attitude displayed by some members of the Congress toward foundations. We were even more jolted by the harshness of the draft bill that emerged from the Committee and realized that the proposed restrictions would, if passed, severely limit the future usefulness of foundations in American life. Then began a hard, uphill battle to persuade the Senate to modify the bill. With the essential participation of a number of understanding senators, this battle reached its climax in the defeat on the Senate floor of a determined attempt to restrict the effective life of all foundations to forty years.

Although the Tax Reform Act, as finally passed, had some serious flaws in it, such as a 4 percent tax on foundation income (which in reality simply deprives recipients of grant funds), restrictions which greatly discourage the establishment of new foundations, and a mandatory payout requirement that is somewhat too high for prudent management of endowment funds, nevertheless it had many good features, such as new provisions against self-dealing, which, if properly enforced, will serve to protect those foundations which have always tried scrupulously to operate in the public interest.

For me personally the Tax Reform Act episode served to awaken a keen concern not only for foundations but for the field of charitable organizations generally. True, I had written about private organizations before but from a rather special point of view. I was interested then in what I called "quasi nongovernmental organizations," privately incorporated but largely governmentally financed agencies doing mainly government business but under private management and poised uneasily in a grey area somewhere between the public and private sectors. As the result of the events of 1969, however, I began to see that public support for charitable organizations of all kinds—whether educational, medical, welfare, cultural, or other—was beginning to erode and that one of this nation's most precious assets, the concept of private initiative for the public good, was in danger of serious decline. I expressed my concern as forcefully as possible in a personal essay called "The Jeopardy of Private Institutions" in the Corporation's 1970 annual report. In response to requests to the foundation, nearly fifty thousand copies of this essay have now been distributed. In another annual report essay in 1972 I proposed for discussion some changes in the charitable deduction that might help stimulate and democratize charitable giving.

Throughout the Tax Reform Act hearings and, subsequently, as I wrote on the subject of private organizations, attended countless meetings aimed at preserving and strengthening philanthropy, made speeches on the subject, and talked from time to time with representatives of the press, the question of why charity should be so much on the defensive continually puzzled and troubled me. Why, I wondered, should that centuries-old concept, so deeply embedded in Anglo-American tradition and law and so valuable to the nation throughout its history now seem to be the object of such widespread ignorance and indifference?

Several explanations seemed plausible: the increased availability of publicly provided social services had for many Americans undermined the notion of private responsibility for the general good; improved living standards for millions of citizens had put them in a position to bring into the open latent feelings of hostility toward private philanthropy as being, in their eyes, a condescending, paternalistic activity associated with great wealth and privilege; suspicion that charity was being abused for personal advantage had been mounting; there were young people who saw private institutions as indistinguishable from public ones in what they considered a generally unjust and corrupt social system in this country; and, finally, there was a growing feeling that charitable institutions were undemocratic and elitist in the composition of their boards of trustees and administrative staffs. If there was validity to these charges, then, it seemed to me, no time was to be lost in taking all necessary steps to modernize, purify and democratize charity in all its forms and in all aspects of its operations and simultaneously to reassert forcefully and explicitly its rightful claim to equal position with such concepts as free speech, a free press, an independent judiciary, and representative political institutions as a necessary part of our American vision of a democratic society.

In reasserting charity's role, two objectives seemed to be of paramount importance. The first was reeducating the public to an understanding of the simple truth that charity, by historical and legal definition, exists for the "benefit of the community"—with the great variety of meanings and points of view that phrase encompasses. The tax exemption granted to charity is, therefore, not a privilege enjoyed at the expense of the tax-paying public, as many today seem to think, but simply a logical feature of any activity designed to be of public benefit.

The second objective was a substantial improvement in the way the federal government relates to the field of charity. During the Tax Reform Act battle it had been borne in on me forcefully that there was simply no place within the vast range of the federal bureaucracy that had any responsibility to say a good word about foundations. even though most foundations had always acted in the public interest. More recently, I was one of several Americans who took part in an Anglo-American conference on charity, in which we learned a good deal about the workings of the British Charities Commission and were favorably impressed by it. As a result of these two experiences, I came to believe that a wholly new, independent federal agency is needed which would be solely concerned with the supervision and encouragement of charity, two activities which are really opposite sides of the same coin, if the supervisory function is carried out skillfully and sensitively.

The present system of regulation within the Internal Revenue Service has many faults. It confuses charitable organizations, where the benefit is to the community at large, with nineteen other forms of tax-exempt organizations where the benefit is to special, limited groups, often defined by membership. It has resulted over the years in inadequate auditing of charitable organizations, including foundations, the Service having had little incentive to spend its time on tax-exempt organizations when the auditing of individual and corporation returns can produce sizable additional government revenue. And, finally, there is little scope in the present system, being tied as it is to a tax collections agency, for the federal government to exercise its inherent responsibility to show a positive and constructive attitude toward any publicly beneficial activity. In September of 1973 three of us who took part in the Anglo-American meeting had the opportunity to propose a wholly new supervisory system for charity in hearings held by the Sub-Committee on Foundations of the Senate Finance Committee. We hope this testimony will have started a wide public discussion of the subject.

Although most of the time I have expended on the broad issue of the future of charity generally and of foundations specifically, including service as a director of The Foundation Center and of the Council on Foundations, has been external to Carnegie Corporation's immediate administration and program, the effort has by no means been irrelevant to the Corporation. Not only is the Corporation's future bound up with that of other foundations and with the future of charity at large, but some of the insights and perceptions I have gained have, I hope, been helpful in making the Corporation itself a more democratic, a more open and a more responsive institution.

A Final Word

This has been a piece about one person's view of his profession and his place within it. I could not close, however, without saying something about the two foundations for which I have worked. I have always considered them to be something quite special. They are, of course, the product of the men and women who have been their staffs and trustees over the years; yet in some mysterious way I have never quite fathomed they have always transcended these human beings and laid their own mark on those who have served them. Perhaps this is true of all great institutions. Perhaps, indeed, it is their distinguishing characteristic. In any event, I know that somewhere in that mystery lies my own deep sense of gratitude and privilege as I look back over my two decades here.

Foundations and
Public Policy Formation

Among the most difficult and important issues facing foundations is the question of the legitimacy and feasibility of their participation in public policy formation. In this function is to be found what is very possibly the most substantial opportunity foundations have today for service to the nation but also, perhaps, their greatest vulnerability.

Public policy is in essence the entire body of goals, plans, directives, and procedures, both domestic and foreign in their thrust, through which the common, or general, interest of the nation is advanced. The formal enactment of public policy, which of course takes place at all levels of government, is the responsibility of elected or appointed officials operating within a constitutional framework and accountable through representative political institutions. While it is expressed in a multiplicity of detailed laws, regulations, executive orders, judicial decisions and other forms, it rests ultimately on certain broad principles, most notably those expressed in the Declaration of Independence and the Constitution.

The processes which lead up to formal enactment of public policy in this country are extraordinarily complex. It is a deliberate part of our system that these processes are thrown open to wide citizen participation, involving input from, and interaction among, elected and appointed officials, political parties, the communications media, industry, trade associations, trade unions, professional associations, citizen action and many other groups, and, finally, the charitable sector with its wide range of private, nonprofit organizations. This intricate pre-enactment process serves not only as an instrument for the development of public policy but also as a means of mediating and reconciling the claims of conflicting interests in the society.

Foundations, as part of the charitable sector, have throughout their history in this country participated in the process of public policy formation. In general, almost anything a foundation does may in time affect some aspect of public policy. Under discussion here, however, is foundation action related to specific, identified issues, where the principal purpose has been to promote public discussion of an issue and shed light on it without respect to a specified outcome, or, less often, to advance a particular view of how public policy should develop.

Although the foundation role in such activity has a long and honorable history, the concept has always been controversial. While a few critics have claimed that foundations were not energetic and effective enough in helping shape public policy, most of their detractors have considered them too influential in this regard. From the populist left, particularly in an earlier era, has come the view that foundations, being closely associated with great industrial or financial wealth, power and privilege, have deliberately promoted conservative social and economic doctrines. The populist right, on the other hand, has made the charge that they are too liberal, even "communistic," in the causes they espouse.

The real nature of these concerns, whether expressed from the left or the right, is not always easy to understand fully, but at least two of its elements are reasonably clear. First, there is the notion that foundations are an organized, purposeful, secret and even sinister force, operating in an environment almost totally protected from any form of public oversight or supervision. Even middle-of-the-road observers have thought of them as having a considerable degree of homogeneity. Virtually all critics have attributed to them a position of power quite out of proportion to reality. While seeing nothing particularly wrong in a wide assortment of non-charitable, tax-exempt interest groups being permitted to influence the legislative process through direct lobbying, they have felt uncomfortable about the charitable sector, and especially foundations, doing this. Their doubts, moreover, have extended well beyond just lobbying to *any* foundation action which seems calculated to influence public policy, seeing this as *ipso facto* tantamount to "engaging in politics."

Secondly, there is a belief that the tax-exemption of foundations puts them in the special favored position of in effect spending public funds—funds that otherwise would "belong" to government—without being accountable to the people and their elected representatives. This principle, if ever fully established, would of course apply logically to *all* tax-exempt entities and make even churches answerable to public authority. Regardless of their lack of merit, these two elements of concern about foundation influence have had wide currency, leading many people to conclude that as a price for their privileged position, foundations should be quarantined from the mainstream controversies of the nation and prevented from infecting its body politic with their "pernicious" ideas!

Most of the time these fears have lain dormant just below the surface of the nation's political life, but periodically they have burst into the open, as in the Congressional investigations of foundations in 1915, 1952, 1953, and once again in 1969 in connection with the passage of the Tax Reform Act. This time Congress decided, after a good deal of deliberation, that it was *not* in the public interest to prohibit foundations from taking part in the broad and many-faceted process through which public policy is developed here in the United States. On the contrary, it specifically authorized them to "make available nonpartisan analysis, study and research" and to engage in discussion and comment on "policy problems, social and economic issues and other broad issues where such activities would be considered educational under existing law." Congress, it is true, did prohibit foundations from any direct lobbying (except in their own defense), either with legislators and other government officials or with the general public at the grass roots level in regard to specific pieces of legislation under current consideration, and it also ruled out any interference in political campaigns. But it definitely did not prohibit foundations from concerning themselves with policy issues just because these "might be expected to be dealt with ultimately by government."

The question, therefore, of whether foundations could legally engage in activities having a bearing on public policy development was definitely settled in 1969. However, the negative and even hostile atmosphere in which discussion of this issue took place in the Congress left just the opposite impression in the minds of many people in the Congress, in the press, in the interested public, and in foundations themselves. To them the Tax Reform Act, at least in spirit, was clearly intended to discourage foundation involvement in public policy matters. As a result, a paradoxical situation emerged, one that is still with us, in which foundations have been assured that they have every right to engage in such activities but at the same time have somehow been given a message that they would be unwise to do so.

In these circumstances there are many people involved in the management of foundations, as trustees or administrators, who believe the avoidance of anything even remotely controversial of a public policy nature is the only sensible course to follow. One can understand this position, especially when there are well-informed observers who assert it would take only one major, well-publicized mistake in the public policy area by a large foundation to cause the Congress to impose harsh new controls on the entire field. This cautious, fearful, keep-to-the-storm-cellar approach is defeatist, however, and if adhered to by many foundations must inevitably lead to a progressive decline of morale in the field and the eventual extinction of foundations as a significant constructive force in the nation's life.

An alternative and more persuasive view, which some foundation trustees and administrators hold just as strongly as the apostles of low-profile cautiousness hold theirs, is that the only ultimate protection for foundations is to remain relevant, necessary institutions—whatever the risks entailed. The best way for foundations to do this is to be constantly sensitive to public policy issues in the fields in which they operate and not be afraid to initiate or support activities that relate to these issues. Indeed, the greatest justification for foundations continuing to enjoy tax-exempt status lies in their making the maximum contribution they can, within their spheres of interest and competence and within the limits of the law, to the development of enlightened public policy for the nation.

This argument is firmly based because it is rooted in the nature of the American social and political system. In this country we have never thought of the concept of citizen participation in democratic self-government as being confined to the ballot box, essential as that is. We have always recognized a second important element, the right of citizens to advance what they conceive to be the common good through their own initiatives carried out by means of private organizations and associations. Indeed, this second string to the bow of American democracy is a good deal older than the first, since it was well established long before the nation achieved its independence.

Integral to this concept of democratic self-government has been the notion that the private side of American life not only should be permitted to contribute to the process of public policy formation but should be actively *encouraged* to do so. The charitable sector is an indispensible participant in the debate because the myriad institutions which comprise it constitute a rich storehouse of important knowledge and experience it would be foolish to overlook. Foundations, as part of this sector, have special responsibilities, sometimes as sources of expertise in themselves but more often as the funders of other charitable organizations capable of making a contribution. Were they to be debarred from engaging in the process of public policy formation, the role of the charitable sector at large would be seriously undermined. The end result could be not only an impoverishment of the debate on public policy but a weakening of the capacity of private citizens to challenge entrenched public authority.

Techniques and Procedures

The techniques that foundations can employ to play a part in public policy formation are many and varied. Those that have been well known through much of foundation history include the funding of: established institutions to conduct research; investigation or analysis with policy implications; conferences aimed at providing solutions to specific policy issues; specially created new organizations to work in particular policy areas: *ad hoc* commissions to study important issues and report to the nation; partnerships with governmental bodies in the launching of new policy-related ventures; information programs aimed at educating the public about policy issues; targeted programs to train individuals for special policy-making roles; and demonstration projects designed to try out experimental new policies on a scale large enough to test their suitability for general adoption by public authority.

Some newer techniques, evident principally in recent years, include the support of: preparatory work for litigation aimed at testing policy issues in the courts and validating new positions; the monitoring of governmental programs to assess their effectiveness and impact; new organizations created specifically to give a voice in policy issues to minorities, the poor and other groups previously excluded; and, lastly, projects designed to inform citizens of their constitutional right to register and vote.

Some of these techniques can entail direct action by a foundation itself, for example, the creation of a special commission to study a policy issue and report to the public, or the holding of a conference. Most techniques, however, involve a partnership between a foundation and an operating organization, in which the foundation provides money and sometimes counsel but leaves the doing of the job to its grant recipient. At a later stage the foundation can take on the additional function of helping give wide public dissemination to the results of the project. It is through the dissemination process, in fact, that foundations can sometimes have their greatest impact on the shaping of public policy. This, too, is an activity that can be furthered through a variety of techniques, such as the publication and distribution of books and other printed materials, press releases, press conferences, discussions with individual reporters and editors, conferences for policy makers and even the production of television programs. If a foundation wishes to maximize its effectiveness in the public policy arena, it must have an active and imaginative dissemination program.

Problems and Safeguards

Engaging in activities intended to help shape public policy has its problems for a foundation. With even a modicum of care it should not run afoul of the requirements of the Tax Reform Act, because there are many ways it can legitimately influence public policy without coming even close to doing anything illegal. The problems, rather, are ones that relate on the one hand to external perception of a foundation's position in society—its general reputation, its credibility with specific groups of citizens, and the view other foundations have of it—and, on the other hand, to its own internal perception of itself as an institution.

A frequently discussed problem connected with foundation participation in public policy formation is the one of objectivity—what this means and how far it must be honored. Stated another way, the issue is one of whether foundations, either consciously or unconsciously, do tend to bring a set of values into play in their program determination and in the making or withholding of grants, and, if so, to what extent the influence of these values is legitimate.

Values of course are of many kinds, ethical, religious, esthetic, philosophical, or political, and are extremely hard to define. What are values to one person are no more than unthinking prejudice and predilection to another. Values also are often in conflict with one another as, say, in the abortion issue or in the age-old conflict between liberty and justice which has its contemporary expression in the controversial issue of affirmative action.

There does, however, seem to be one broad set of values which all foundations in this country will probably share, the values embodied in what Gunnar Myrdal, in his brilliant study some years ago of the Negro in American life, called the American Creed. Briefly, this Creed encompasses a belief in the essential dignity of the individual human being, in the fundamental equality of all men and women, and in certain inalienable rights to freedom, justice and a fair opportunity. It has its origins in the philosophy of the Enlightenment, in the moral precepts common to the world's great religions, and in the English common law. If a foundation espouses such a set of values, it will have a broadly humanitarian outlook that is bound to affect the nature of its involvement in public policy issues, turning it instinctively toward those issues which have to do with bettering the condition of the least fortunate members of society. Application of this set of values can be regarded as a departure from "objectivity" so deep and broadly endorsed by the culture as to be inescapable. As a people, we cannot claim neutrality with respect to these values without divesting ourselves of our history, our origins as a nation, and, indeed, our very identity.

No foundation, therefore, any more than any other institution, can be totally "objective," because the human beings who manage it have values that shape their judgments and hence the foundation's collective judgment. To ask that a foundation have no identifiable values as a condition of its engagement in public policy matters is therefore asking the impossible.

Even so, how far foundations should go in allowing the personal values of trustees and officers to influence their public policy activities is a difficult question to answer and one that has bothered every thoughtful person who has ever worked for a foundation. There is a point at which generalized values pushed into ever deeper levels of specificity may somehow turn into particular political and social biases. At this point, those who manage foundations have begun to ride personal hobbyhorses, in violation of the foundation's public trust.

The challenge, then, is to find the dividing line between the legitimate application of values and nonlegitimate partisanship in behalf of a cause. It can be argued that the very choice of a grant recipient can represent a crossing of that line where the agency involved has stated purposes that tend to give it a particular point of view. To withhold support solely for this reason would, however, be both unnecessary and unfair and is certainly not required by the tax law.

Unquestionably this is treacherous ground. There are no rulebooks or manuals to supply easy reference answers to the almost infinite variety of situations that will be encountered. Answers, if there are any, can ultimately be found only in experience, common sense, and, most importantly, in a willingness on the part of foundation officers to be honest about their own motives and those of the proposed grant recipient.

110

There are, however, some practical safeguards a foundation can employ to minimize its risks. When a foundation takes an action it believes will affect public policy, it has a duty to inform itself as fully as it can about the policy area in question, to seek competent advice, and to weigh most carefully the consequences of its action. Only on the basis of the most thorough, penetrating, and deliberate staff work is it justified in going ahead. Specifically, the foundation can check with the greatest care to find out the kind of record an organization it proposes to support and the people running it have established in the past. Is there evidence that the organization, within its frame of reference and stated purposes, has been reasonably objective in what it has done? Has it, for example, employed qualified researchers or other personnel in its work? Has it shown itself willing to publish all its findings, contrary as well as favorable? Has it ever used broadly-based advisory committees in its projects? Does it have a reputation for fairness?

Alternatively, has the organization left behind it a trail of militant partisanship, in which ends have clearly been used to justify means? Has it, under the guise of publishing the results of research, disseminated what is little more than propaganda or unsupported opinion? Has it used research simply to "prove" an already established case?

A foundation can test its own integrity by asking itself whether it would be willing to publicize fully the purposes and circumstances of a proposed grant and later report openly to the public on the outcome. If such a prospect makes it uncomfortable, the chances are that it suspects, but has been unwilling to recognize overtly, that its proposed grant recipient has a hidden agenda of politically partisan activity.

Beyond these practical approaches to the problem, probably the only protection available to a foundation lies in having a diversified board of trustees and staff in which a reasonably wide variety of *experience* in the nation's life is represented. If there is too much homogeneity in a foundation's management— homogeneity of occupational or professional background, economic status or interest, social perspective, or political persuasion—there is likely to be no one involved at the critical moment of decision to challenge the assumptions underlying a proposed course of action.

Allied with the issues of values and objectivity is the ancient question that has always troubled mankind: How is truth to be known? In contemporary terms, what is good public policy and how can it be discovered? Can a foundation tell whether it is acting in the best interests of the nation when it follows a given course? Can it be sure it is not doing more harm than good? How can it know whether its actions will be of any lasting benefit to those it seeks to help?

There are, of course, no final, convincing responses to these questions, and if one were to worry about them too much, total paralysis would be the inevitable result. Nevertheless, it is a serious matter—one that cannot be dismissed with the cavalier comment that what "seems right" at the moment of decision is justification enough for plunging ahead.

Although the problem of how to divine what is helpful and what is harmful in the search for beneficial public policy plagues all policy areas, nowhere is it more difficult than in the complex, loosely-defined area known as social justice. Among the myriad issues in this field that foundations have wrestled with are such matters as rectifying the results of historical discrimination against women and blacks and other minorities, protecting the rights of children, school integration, open housing, bilingualism in education, school decentralization and a host of others. These are immensely complicated issues, fraught with many previous public policy failures, bedeviled by ambiguities, moral dilemmas, shifting currents of thought, and constant new problems, and, finally, exacerbated by the militancy of many of the people foundations must work with, stemming from their understandable feelings of rage and frustration at the slow pace with which society has dealt with their concerns. Although the need to seek social justice is an imperative that arises from the American Creed, the path to it is often obscure. The possibility that foundations will make mistakes in this area, however skillfully and conscientiously they go about their business, cannot be avoided—a risk to which governmental bodies, be it said, are equally prone. Nonetheless, among all public policy areas needing foundation attention, the case for social justice is probably most compelling.

A third problem for foundations which feel a responsibility to be involved in the illumination of public policy issues is that of reconciling the desirability of a flexible openness of mind, so that opportunities can be seized wherever and however they appear, with the equal desirability of sticking to established program areas where the foundation can operate sure-footedly and in the knowledge that it is furthering agreed program goals. There are good arguments to be made on both sides. The answer, perhaps, is to lean toward program restrictiveness in order not to end up with a hodge-podge of superficial, widely-scattered and non-mutually-supporting initiatives, but to be open to an occasional opportunity for public policy service in other areas where the need is great and the chances of success substantial. One of the most important contributions Carnegie Corporation ever made, for example, was in its response to a suggestion out of the blue that it create a national commission on educational television, an area in which it had no program and only the sketchiest of experience.

One of the most baffling problems faced by foundations when they engage in the process of public policy formation is explaining to the public the inherent limits of their "accountability." Foundations are accountable—and strictly accountable—to the Internal Revenue Service and to state authorities for the integrity of their financial dealings and for their adherence to the laws governing charitable organizations. Beyond this, many foundations, including Carnegie Corporation, have always felt a sense of accountability directly to the public arising out of their charitable mission to serve the public good. As part of this broader sense of accountability, they have recognized an obligation to inform the public about what they are doing and, therefore, have issued comprehensive annual reports, press releases and other publications which they have made widely available.

When, however, a foundation becomes involved in the business of helping to develop public policy, especially in a controversial realm such as social justice, many people seem to assume that it has taken on responsibility for a third level of accountability—accountability for the *results* of the work it has financed. A foundation, however, by the very character of its relationship to grant recipients, in which their independence and freedom of expression must be respected, cannot take responsibility for the validity of the ultimate product. It can take responsibility only for its own initial judgments with respect to the quality and integrity of those whom it decided to support. This position is partially modified, of course, when a foundation deliberately decides to help in the dissemination process, for such a decision in itself says that the product is at least considered worthy of public attention, whether the foundation fully endorses it or not. Nonetheless, the product remains someone else's and is not directly the foundation's.

From the foundation point of view, this seems an entirely reasonable posture, conforming as it does to the canons of academic freedom and to the right to independence of private organizations. To some public officials, members of the press and to much of the public, however, such a disclaimer is hard to understand, and may seem disingenuous or even evasive. If a foundation isn't willing to accept responsibility for what its grant recipients do when this clearly affects the formation of public policy, it should not make such grants, these critics would contend. Alternatively, they seem to imply that the foundation should somehow find a way to control or "discipline" its grantees. Such views are particularly strongly held when the organization supported by the foundation is assumed, because of its very purposes, to have a commitment to one side or another of a public policy issue, although freedom from such a commitment is by no means a requirement of charitable status.

The chances that a foundation will be held accountable for the results of policy-related work it supports are no doubt increased by the difficulty which the press, news magazines and other media sometimes face in reporting such findings. Frequently these findings are complex, subject to important qualifications, and heavily dependent for comprehensibility on full exposition of a surrounding context. Thus they do not always lend themselves to the requirements for brevity and newsworthiness of the media. There is simply a basic misfit in some instances between the media and the nature of scholarly communication, which is neither's fault. But the attempt to reconcile this difference does sometimes lead to misinterpretation of findings and subsequent public misunderstanding, which, once established, is very hard to correct.

Although a foundation can and must take every opportunity to explain to the public why it cannot be held responsible for the ultimate results of the work it supports, as distinct from the quality of its original decision-making in respect to a grant, this is an area where there will always be a potential for public misunderstanding. When controversy develops and certain groups become emotionally aroused, the human need to find someone or something to blame seems to be overpowering. In such situations, whatever their disclaimers, foundations will come in for a certain amount of criticism, and however unjustified this may be, it perhaps isn't altogether a bad thing as a reminder to them that in an open society they can never expect to occupy a totally protected position immune from the give-and-take of everyday life.

In Summary

Whatever is said about the right of foundations to engage in activities designed to influence the development of public policy for the nation, there will be some, both inside and outside the foundation field, who remain skeptical. They may still have a vague feeling of uneasiness about such activity, perhaps resulting from the antipathy to foundations aroused in 1969, or perhaps from the slightly anomalous position foundations seem to occupy in our society.

People of this outlook should in fairness weigh several considerations. First, foundations generally were reminded during the painful proceedings of 1969 of some long-standing rules of good foundation practice, especially the importance of meticulous staff work and the need to be well informed about the actions of grant recipients. They also had cause to consider, perhaps more deeply than ever before, the question of what distinguishes the legitimate application of values in grant-making from using grants improperly to advance partisan causes.

Secondly, it must be recognized that there are real, built-in limitations to the degree of influence which foundations, even large ones, or, for that matter, groups of foundations working together, can exercise. Among all the many private sector groups which play a part in the complex process of public policy formation, foundations are only one voice. In comparison with the prestige and financial power of government agencies and the political power of private pressure groups, their capabilities are small indeed. Ultimately, whatever they do is subject to the harsh rule of the market place. Their products enjoy no automatically privileged status because they have a foundation label on them, and they are certainly not immune from criticism. They have to complete, along with rival products put forward by others, in a kind of public opinion bazaar, to find favor with the public and make their way into new or improved public policy, or to be rejected and go onto the scrap heap. Although laws which restrict direct foundation interference in the legislative process are considered necessary by some people, it is the discipline of this open, competitive process in this country which provides the best, and probably only truly necessary, guarantee against a foundation becoming too influential.

Finally, there remains the spectre that the entire foundation field, with its 30,000 or more members, might unite to use its collective strength to influence public policy on some important national issue. Such a thought is really quite ludicrous, so insignificant are most of this number in size and so wide is the diversity among foundations in their interests and in their philosophical outlook. Indeed, on almost any issue one could think of, people connected with foundations would almost certainly be found on each side of it, reflecting the division of opinion on the issue in the nation at large.

One can conclude that foundations do have a legitimate—indeed essential—role to play in public policy formation, although no one should doubt there are some real risks involved. Nevertheless, if the role is played conscientiously and is informed at every stage by candor, openness and integrity, it seems likely there will be a sufficient degree of overall public tolerance, perhaps even regard, for foundations to ensure their continued independence. Certainly the alternative, which is for them to operate with such cautiousness that they transform themselves gradually into quaint, anachronistic, and ultimately irrelevant, appendages of American society, must be regarded both as a clear denial of the public interest that inheres in all foundations and a violation of the public trust which those who manage them have unquestionably accepted.

Higher Education in the Nation's Consciousness

Like many other institutions these days, higher education has become the object of widespread skepticism. After an era of unprecedented growth, affluence and exalted status in the 1960's, it stands very much on the defensive. No longer is it assured of the unquestioning public regard and financial support it once enjoyed. Increasingly, doubts are being voiced as to whether its benefits are not outweighed by its costs and burdens.

Some of these doubts are well-intentioned and well-informed. Others seem prejudiced and even tinged with vindictiveness. Still others appear to be part of a new journalistic fad of disparaging the value of college attendance. Whatever the nature of the skepticism, whether justified or unfair, it consitutes a clear danger and a challenge to the academic community to set about regaining the public's confidence as rapidly as possible.

The causes of the present disenchantment are many and complex, and range widely across the political and social spectrums of our national life. They include lingering public reaction against the excesses of student unrest in the late sixties, the disaffection of young people themselves from higher education because of the impersonal nature and tradition-bound rigidities of many campuses, the ideologically-based hostility toward intellectual, "liberal," institutions generally fomented during the Nixon administration, and, finally, the ever-increasing costs of attending college.

More recently, public disenchantment with higher education may have been associated with a broad sense of alienation felt by many Americans from their leading social and political institutions, based on a gnawing consciousness of the nation's mistakes and failures in Southeast Asia, its seeming powerlessness to solve its most serious social problems, and its inability to achieve a stable economy.

Where these misgivings have affected the academic world, they have taken the form of a sharp reaction to the inflated and overconfident claims that were earlier made in its behalf. Higher education, it is now being said, was overbuilt and oversold during its golden age of the sixties. The notion that a more educated populace would produce a more enlightened, more progressive and more just society was a delusion. The university's claim to a special capacity to solve great social, economic and technological problems was overblown. Going to college is *not* the certain path to greater income and higher social standing it was represented to be.

Given this general litany of disillusionment, it was almost inevitable that questions would begin to be raised about the priority higher education should be assigned in the allocation of scarce resources. Higher education has, of course, always had to compete with other public needs for its share of the tax dollar, and even in its heyday of greatest affluence could make a case that it was underfunded. Today, however, when the nation is still in the throes of the most prolonged and deepest economic recession in many decades, the issue of where the campus should stand in public funding priorities is infinitely more accute than at any time in recent memory. Indeed, it is probably higher education's greatest cause for concern today. Public officials all over the country as well as in Washington are now asking themselves whether it is morally right to be spending so much money on higher education when the cities are in a state of fiscal crisis, mass transit facilities in most places are badly underfunded, crime is rampant and unemployment at its highest level since the great depression of the thirties.

Still another doubt concerning higher education has become evident in the last few months that seems to have caught the public fancy. This is the assertion, made confidently in many quarters now, that a college degree is no longer worth a young person's investment in it because of its declining economic return.

It stands to reason, of course, that indefinite expansion of the numbers of degrees awarded throughout the nation would sooner or later bring about a decline in their monetary value to the recipients. And some widely publicized recent research does seem to confirm that there has been a substantial drop in the starting salaries of new graduates relative to the earnings of their co-workers, though more so for white males than for women and minorities. It also indicates that recent graduates have had to take jobs for which the were "overqualified," have landed in fields for which they were not trained, or have found no employment at all. The important issue, however, is not this finding, per se, but what one makes of it.

The researchers themselves conclude that the apparent decline in economic value of a degree represents a serious threat to the financial viability of colleges and universities in the years ahead since it will lead to sharply falling enrollments. In fact, they say, it already has. During the past five years it has caused a severe drop—from 44 to 33 percent—in the proportion of 18-19 year old males enrolled in college.

But this conclusion does not take into account other factors that may explain the falling enrollment rate for young males, such as changes in the draft after 1969, rising tuition, and the liberalization of admissions policies that had made deferred entry to college a popular alternative.

One must remember too that *overall* enrollments in higher education have continued to rise steadily because of the growing size of the college-age cohort, increased enrollment by women and adults, and the temporary effects of the recession that have made higher education, at least for the time being, a more attractive alternative than employment. Finally, there is the point that, whatever the cost of going to college today, the cost of not going, if one wants a white collar job, is prohibitive as long as college is virtually the only route to such employment.

It is therefore not all clear that the declining economic return of a degree to the individual is going to be the financial disaster for higher education at large that some people think.

Far more disturbing than the conclusion by the researchers, however, is the mischievous implication in the present spate of popular books and articles on the subject that the declining economic value of a degree is somehow indicative of failure on the part of higher education and is yet another reason for losing confidence in it. Such a verdict rests on three utterly fallacious assumptions.

The first of these assumptions is that because the relative economic value of a degree to the individual is declining, the general economic value of higher education to society at large is also declining. A moment's thought will show how erroneous this assumption is. The economic value of higher education to the nation lies, of course, in its research and service capabilities and in the trained manpower it produces; it is only marginally related over the long term to questions of the relative earnings of graduates and non-graduates. Only if the earnings of the former in certain fields essential to the economy, such as engineering, fell to a point where there was little incentive for anyone to enroll would there be a connection between individual and societal economic returns. And it would not be long before the unsatisfied demand for engineers forced the relative earnings of graduates in this field up again, thereby stimulating increased enrollments. In short, market forces would quickly take over.

The second assumption is equally dubious, namely that the value of going to college is to be measured principally in economic terms. One cannot blame young people for thinking this since college has often been sold to them on the basis of such a tawdry and selfish rationale. The appeal to them should, of course, have been made on the much more legitimate grounds that higher education helps individuals develop intellectual abilities, humanistic understandings and aesthetic sensitivities that will enable them to enjoy life more fully and contribute more effectively to the general welfare of mankind.

The third false assumption is that the decline in the relative economic returns of higher education to the individual is necessarily a bad thing. It stands to reason there should be some monetary reward for personal investment in higher education in addition to the many non-pecuniary rewards, but this need not be as great as it has been in the past to provide adequate incentive for attending college—provided the true value of the experience is explained to young people. In fact, if the economic rewards do prove to be smaller, higher education is likely to be less a determinant of class status and less socially divisive than it has been in the past. This is good both intrinsically and for the welfare of higher education, since the latter's continued viability must depend on the support of the entire populace, not just those citizens who have reaped its benefits in their own personal lives.

In sum, while it may be true that a degree, in relative terms, is worth less money now than it used to be, it is utterly wrong to conclude from this that higher education is of less value to the nation and therefore deserves less support, or that its future is necessarily in jeopardy, or that it is a poor way for the individual to spend his money. Conclusions such as these are totally unwarranted.

The present popularity of the economic returns argument is, nonetheless, dangerous. On the one hand, by confusing individual economic benefit with economic benefit to the society at large, it gives public officials who are looking for a rationale to assign to higher education a lower funding priority just the excuse they are seeking. On the other hand, it may discourage young people from going to college who would profit greatly in other ways from the experience.

The Case for Higher Education

Clearly, in view of the widespread loss of public confidence in higher education, those who understand its importance and continue to put their faith in it must be prepared to reargue the case for it. In doing so, however, they face some awkward difficulties, in particular the appearance of seeming blindly to defend a past which is by no means wholly defensible. They must start therefore with a candid admission that during its great period of expansion the academic community did acquire some unattractive faults. For all its great achievements it became somewhat arrogant and pretentious, lax in its intellectual and moral standards, and insensitive to the needs of the individual student. It came, furthermore, to perceive success more in terms of enrollment growth, number of degrees granted, the construction of ever finer new buildings, and the continuous expansion of functions than in the enhancement of academic quality—which made inevitable a sharp loss of self-confidence and a psychological sense of failure when criteria such as these for measuring progress became bankrupt.

Nevertheless, having acknowledged higher education's evident faults and the demonstrable case for wide-reaching reform—reform, incidentally, that is now under way in many places—there is much that one can say in support of the academic enterprise. Many voices can now be heard attacking it and discounting its value; others are badly needed to defend it now, before the present wave of disenchantment goes so far that irreparable damage is done. Such a defense can best start with a reminder of the ways in which higher eduction's varied functions affect virtually every aspect of the nation's welfare. They may be roughly grouped under three headings: educational, cultural, and socio-economic.

Educational

The educational functions are obvious and should need little defense. They include higher intellectual development, professional and occupational training, the development of research capability and, most importantly, cultivation in students of a breadth, flexibility and autonomy of mind, and a questioning, even skeptical spirit, that will best prepare them to meet the demanding responsibilities of democratic citizenship in a rapidly changing nation and world. One would think that the importance of these functions would be obvious to all, yet many of our fellow citizens, including some who should know better, act as though they consider them of little significance. Suffice it to say that if higher education did not perform these functions, the nation's industrial, financial, educational, medical, scientific, and governmental systems, to name only the most obvious, simply could not operate at the level of sophistication and effectiveness required to meet our domestic and international needs in the world of today.

Less understood is the degree to which colleges and universities these days devote their attention to remedial work—making good the deficiencies of secondary and even elementary education. Higher education should not, of course, have to perform this function and should shed it as quickly as it possibly can. The provision of remedial education has been one of the inevitable consequences of the effort to promote equality of opportunity in higher education, but it is not entirely associated with that phenomenon: many traditional types of students also go to college with weaknesses in their academic preparation that reflect no credit in the schools they previously attended.

Cultural

Cultural functions are threefold. First, the American concept of a democratic society has come to assume the right of all to share in the comprehension, enjoyment and preservation of our immensely rich and varied cultural heritage. It has become higher education's responsibility, under the heading of liberal education, to keep alive this heritage by providing an opportunity to understand it to large numbers of young people. It is hard to believe that as a people we are not the stronger for it. There is a popular book out entitled *The Case Against College*. The democratic case *for* it must never be forgotten.

Closely associated with this function is the role higher education plays as the actual conservator, custodian and developer of the cultural heritage through its great libraries and museums and through the continuous illumination and reinterpretation of that heritage by a handful of truly great scholars. The number of academic institutions capable of performing this function at its highest level is relatively limited, and it is simply impossible to overstate their value to the nation.

A third function under this heading is the one most colleges and universities perform in serving as cultural centers for the surrounding community. The enjoyment and informal education which the public gains—at very moderate cost—from campus art exhibitions, musical and dramatic performances, special lectures and other events, is significant in many areas of the country.

Socio-economic

Socio-economic functions are many. One of the most significant of these is the role higher education plays as the principal device for channeling literally millions of Americans into a wide variety of professions and higher level occupations. It does this not only by training them and helping them find jobs but also by providing evidence of their qualifications to potential employers. This channeling and credentialing function has been much criticized, especially by those who would "deschool" society, but whatever its faults it meets a tremendous national need, and it is difficult to imagine just what we would do without it. It is certainly preferable to the alternative found in authoritarian societies of simply assigning trained people to jobs according to a national manpower plan—whether they like it or not.

A second immensely important socio-economic function concerns the discovery of new knowledge. High-level research is not a monopoly of the academy and should not be, but much pure research, unrelated at the time it is conducted to any purpose other than enlargement of the boundaries of knowledge, would never be done elsewhere. Sometimes this research is of only esoteric interest, but over time it frequently proves to be of enormous practical significance to the nation's economy, to its security and to the quality of life of its people. No element of the rampant anti-intellectualism of recent years has been more foolish, more indulgent of the emotions at the expense of reason, and ultimately more dangerous, than the negative attitude toward maintaining and strengthening the academic community's research capacity—especially in the basic sciences. We will surely pay for this in years to come.

Not unrelated to high education's role in preserving and extending knowledge is the capacity of the campus to provide a protected environment or base for dispassionate criticism of the larger society. This is a function that has sometimes been abused, when the criticism has amounted to little more than unsupported political or social opinion, or when individual scholars have allowed themselves to become paid spokesmen for special interests. Nonetheless, where criticism is, as it should be, based on professional competence and hard evidence derived from objective study and research, the function is of critical importance to the maintenance of a free society and deserves strong support.

Two other socio-economic functions are closely related to one another. One is higher education's service role, in which it provides the administrative base and intellectual resources for externally-financed technical assistance programs in a variety of areas. The other is its role as the permanent home for a large pool of highly trained faculty talent available on an individual consulting basis to government, industry and non-profit organizations. Although, as indicated, the university's claim to a special problem-solving capacity became vastly exaggerated, and although faculty consulting too frequently has taken the form of self-seeking absenteeism from the campus, higher education's technical assistance capability, nonetheless, is of real value of the nation.

Perhaps the socio-economic function of higher education with which the public is most familiar is its role as the principal agent of social mobility and certifier of class status in the society, albeit with less assurance of success today than in the past. Much of the controversy surrounding higher education relates to this function. On the one hand, the opportunity to go to college has offered to many Americans just about their *only* chance to rise to middle and upper middle-class status, and they have seized it avidly. On the other, as more and more people have gone to college, increasingly those who have not have been implicitly, and of course, unfairly, stigmatized as failures. The blame for this dilemma should be assigned not to higher education alone but to the society at large, for its failure to create viable alternative paths to economic success and social approbation.

Closely associated is higher education's function as the principal agency for the induction of youth into adulthood. This has both its positive and negative aspects. Viewing youth as a social and psychological stage of life during which some young people feel the need to pause for a few years of personal development before making an irrevocable commitment to the adult world, the campus provides just this opportunity, and usefully so. However, as virtually the only large-scale institution organized to meet the needs of young people between roughly the ages of 18 and 22, higher education tends to attract some students who profit little from it and would probably, given desirable alternatives, prefer not to be there. If greatly expanded open-entry apprenticeship opportunities, or substantial volunteer or low-paid service programs, or secure employment leading to productive careers were available for young people, higher education would not be called on to play this "warehousing" role.

Still another socio-economic function and one which is rapidly gaining in significance is the opportunity higher education offers to adults, primarily through part-time study, for intellectual stimulation, career advancement and personal growth. As the proportion of older people in the population increases steadily in the years ahead, following predictable demographic trends, this phenomenon will undoubtedly grow, to a point where some institutions may find that they have as many people over 40 enrolled, at least part-time, as they do under 20.

What Must Be Done

Looking over this wide range of educational, cultural and socio-economic functions, one cannot help but be impressed by the extraordinarily influential role higher education plays in this nation. Without qualification it affects the lives of all Americans—their economic well-being, their health, the environment they live in, their security in an increasingly dangerous world and many other facets of their existence. An enterprise that was once of marginal value to the nation has become central to its strengths, and this will ever be so. There is no possibility now of turning back from that reality.

Loss of public confidence in higher education is therefore nothing short of a national tragedy, for it is ourselves we are hurting, not a group of meaningless institutions appended to society but not intrinsic to it. The damage already done is extensive and it will be catastrophic if public estrangement from the campus is allowed to continue. The nation's fund of high-level intellectual capital, on which it is now so dependent, is far from being a permanent asset. Once acquired, it wastes rapidly if its replenishment is neglected. This replenishment consists not only of support for the great libraries, laboratories and museums, the research that goes on in them, and the identification and advanced training of particularly talented students. It also consists of maintaining and strengthening the academic community's capacity to train the millions of managers, professionals and technicians who are needed in a complementary role if the nation is to make effective use of its high-level intellectual capital. We owe it to future generations never to let this precious fund and the wider structure that must undergird it atrophy and deteriorate.

As we look toward the end of this century, we see two possible futures for higher education. The first is a strong, diversified system of academic institutions, ranging from world class universities to locally oriented two-year colleges, all reaching a high degree of excellence in their varied missions, flexible enough to accommodate a pluralistic American population. The other is an array of stagnant institutions, plagued by low morale, unable to meet the demands of society, with few, if any, commanding international respect. The outcome can be the former or the latter according to what we determine it will be. Unfortunately, the process of making that decision—by default—in favor of a negative vision of the future is already under way. It will only be reversed if a new consensus can be developed in regard to the position higher education should occupy in our scale of national priorities and values.

It is hard to see how such a consensus is to be attained without strong leadership from Washington. We are presently in what might be called a period of modest thaw after the long freeze in White House relations with the academic world, in which the President has made visits to several campuses. These conciliatory gestures are most welcome, but they are hardly enough. What is needed now is a clear demonstration by the nation's highest political leadership, both in Congress and in the administration, of its awareness of higher education's importance to all Americans and a strong avowal of confidence in it.

The framework of a sensible federal program for the support of higher education is largely in place as a result of steps that have been taken over past years, although some parts of it are seriously underfunded and in other places supplemental actions and modifications are needed. The Carnegie Council on Policy Studies in Higher Education has recently made a series of proposals for such changes in a statement entitled *The Federal Role in Post-Secondary Education, Unfinished Business 1975-1980.*

Approaching the matter in a way that differs only slightly from that taken by the Council, one can list seven priorities for federal aid. These are:

— A generous program of support for graduate students.
— The support of advanced research, on a basis of competitive quality.
— Special grants for major research libraries and museums, both those that are university related and those that are independent.
— The support of medical and other health-related training.
— Strengthening of higher education's international dimension through the support of special language and area studies programs, research and educational exchange.
— Maintenance of the existing special fund for assistance to experimental undertakings within higher education.
— Provision of the funds necessary to make equality of opportunity in higher education a reality.

Also highly desirable would be the program of tuition-equalization grants proposed by the Carnegie Council as a form of basic assistance to private institutions.

The principal responsibility for higher education, however, continues to lie with the states. They have an enormous stake in it as the source of the trained people needed to maintain healthy economies and to provide necessary governmental and social services to their residents. On balance, the states have done a good job with higher education and until recently their support of it has held up extremely well. Nowhere, however, does the negative attitude toward higher education seem to be greater today than among some elected state officials. The harshness of the criticisms one hears from them, especially in reference to the faculty, can be quite shocking. In certain states there seems to be an outright determination by legislators to reduce their great public universities from hard-won national and international ranking back to the status of purely local or, at best, regional institutions.

Nothing could be more short-sighted than this kind of negativism, yet turning it around will not be easy, so pervasive is it and so deeply is it now entrenched.

A positive new attitude from Washington could, as indicated, make a considerable difference but may not be enough. Ways may also have to be found in particular states to arouse public opinion, perhaps through the creation of voluntary citizen movements. Those state officials who do continue to support higher education will also have to exert more leadership.

The same kind of negativism that characterizes many public officials is also evident in the business community. There one finds a deep resentment at what is considered to be a prevailing bias among faculty members and students against the corporate world, indeed against the "free enterprise system." For their part, many members of the academic community believe that recent disclosures of illegal or improper corporate activities do give them good cause to be suspicious of business, and some faculty and students unquestionably do have basic doubts about the capacity of the present economic system to produce a just society. Nevertheless, on neither side is the perception of the other wholly justified. There is, in fact, a wide range of economic and political opinion within the academic community, and of course many corporations have certainly not been guilty of any wrongdoing and have, indeed, demonstrated a clear sense of social responsibility. A certain amount of tension between the business and academic communities is understandable and not necessarily a bad thing. The estrangement may, however, have reached a point today where it is injurious to the welfare of both parties and contrary to the national interest. On its side, business is heavily dependent on higher education for the research and trained manpower it produces, whereas higher education badly needs the business community's moral and financial support.

Forging a New Consensus

If a new consensus regarding the position of higher education in American life is to emerge, there is much that academic institutions themselves can do to assist.

First, they must stop trying to sell higher education to potential students on the grounds primarily of its economic benefits. This simply plays into the hands of those who are saying that the economic returns are no longer worth the investment. Colleges and universities should instead be stressing to students the many non-pecuniary benefits of the experience. To the public they must do a much better job of explaining the wide variety of functions performed by higher education. The more effective they can be in demonstrating the broad public interest in what they are about the less they will be in the unhappy position of always seeming to plead a special self-interest.

Secondly, higher educational institutions must continue to press ahead with the administrative and educational reforms on which they are now embarked. Every effort must be made to pare away unnecessary expense. Unproductive activities must be dropped. Existing resources must, in some cases, be diverted from their present uses to meet newly identified public needs. In this kind of restructuring, however, the liberal arts, which are the very heart of higher education, must be neither jettisoned nor deemphasized. There may well be fewer students who feel that it is in their interest to graduate with majors in certain disciplines, but it ought to be mandatory for all students, whatever their majors, to include a generous portion of liberal education in meeting the requirements for their degrees. We dare not turn out narrowly trained graduates who lack the breadth and flexibility of mind that will be required for intelligent decision-making in a rapidly changing world.

The most important task ahead for the academic community is to cut costs while at the same time preserving or even improving quality. Cost-cutting should not be designed just to save institutional expense but to effect real savings for students, parents and taxpayers. One way to accomplish this, although it does not help institutional budgets unless enrollments are increased, is to reduce the length of time required to gain degrees by better articulation of secondary, undergraduate and graduate education as well as by improved organization of degree courses. The savings, if this new policy were to become general, would be considerable. A number of experiments are being carried out now in various parts of the country to see how the time required to gain degrees can be reduced without depreciating—and perhaps even enhancing—their value. Successful efforts to cut the cost of higher education by shortening its duration may prove to be one of the most helpful steps the academic community can take to regain public approbation and support. Two cautions, however, must always be kept in mind if this movement grows: time-shortened degrees are by no means appropriate for all students, and they should never be achieved at the expense of reducing or abandoning the breadth of study necessary to produce a truly educated person.

Another area for consideration is that of faculty productivity. Some of the complaints being heard about low teaching loads are grossly distorted and unfair. Nonetheless, evidence from a recent national survey of faculty indicates that the great majority of scholarly research and publication is done by a small minority of the professoriate. Clearly this raises the awkward question of whether some faculty members should have their teaching loads set on the assumption that they are doing research and writing they never have done and probably never will do.

Finally, higher education should review every aspect of its operations—its governance, administration, teaching, research, student life and external service—to be certain that in a moral sense it really does qualify for public trust and approval. For trustees and regents this means individual attention to the best interests of the institutions they are supposed to be serving and the elimination of self-interest in all its varied and subtle forms. For administrators it means constant alertness to see that the highest ethical standards are adhered to in every facet of institutional life. For faculty it means a greater devotion of the welfare of the institutions that employ them and to the best interests of students, as well as increased attention to moral values and ethical issues in their teaching. For students it means greater tolerance for the opinions and mores of other groups in the society. One cannot stress too heavily this need to strengthen the moral dimension of academic life, for renewal and growth in this realm is the very heart of the reform higher education must undergo if it is to regain wide public regard.

The building of a new consensus about the place of higher education in our national life, and reversal of the present negativism toward it, is an enormous task, involving public officials, leading citizens, young people, the general public and, most of all, academic institutions themselves. No one can promise that this urgent undertaking will succeed. If it does not, however, it will not be higher education alone but the entire nation that will be at risk, for what is at stake is no less than this.

Women Working:
Toward a New Society

Recent times have seen dramatic changes in American family life, in male-female relationships, in expectations about sex roles, and in our social attitudes and behavior. While the fresh currents of thought and emerging new social conventions are by no means acceptable to everyone, their existence is undeniable, and their impact on American society can be easily observed. Despite this, important governmental and private-sector policies that intimately affect the family, not to mention our individual lives, are still in the main geared to earlier value systems and beliefs. Social policies have not yet caught up with changing social practice.

Nowhere is this disparity between reality and myth as the foundation for social policy more evident than in regard to the large-scale movement of women into the labor force—a phenomenon that could have consequences of immense magnitude for the nation. Its effects on the economy, on the labor market, on family welfare, and on community life are already apparent. It has become both an aspect of change and a prime mover for further change. Yet, in our failure to take account of this occurrence may lie the cause of hardship and inequity for increasing numbers of people, and the potential for considerable social unrest.

Women have always contributed to the nation's economy. In addition to meeting their domestic responsibilities, they have, especially in earlier times, earned income for their families by producing goods at home for sale in the market. What is new in the twentieth century, however, is the increasing proportion of women working away from their homes. In 1920, 20 percent of all women 16 years and over were in the work force. Their labor force participation has risen steadily since then, accelerating during the 1960's and reaching 43 percent in 1970. By the end of 1976, nearly half of all women were working or looking for work, making up approximately 41 percent of the labor force. This shows a cumulative change in degree sufficient to constitute a change in kind.

Although the pace may slow somewhat, there are no signs that the trend will be reversed. On the contrary, since women outnumber men in the population by seven million, and since the labor force participation rate of males has been slowly declining with the trend toward earlier retirement, it may not be too long before one out of every two American workers is a woman. Certainly, projections to the year 1990 indicate a situation in which adults born during the post-World War II "baby boom" will have been fully absorbed into the labor force, and there will be 1.3 million fewer young workers than there are today. Assuming the jobs will be there, labor demand for women should intensify.

The fact is, women are being drawn into the labor force today not, as in World War II, by a temporary crisis but by powerful economic, demographic, and social forces and far-reaching attitudinal changes. It is pointless, therefore, to try to judge, on moral, social, economic or any other grounds, whether women working is harmful to the nation or not. Women must work, they want to work, and their labor is needed. Recognition of these realities should help us to institute new policies that not only make appropriate accommodations but spur wide-ranging reforms in many areas of life. Indeed, the large-scale movement of women into the work force opens up the exciting possibility of creating a much improved society for all Americans.

Characteristics of the Working Woman

Who are these working women? Most of them, in contrast to earlier times, are married and living with their husbands and are likely to have school-age children. By last year, in approximately 46 million intact marriages in the nation, over 21 million of the wives were working full or part time.

As may be expected, the second largest category of female workers, now totaling more than 15 million, is composed of individuals who are single, separated, widowed, or divorced, with divorced women showing the highest participation rates. A large proportion of this group, furthermore, has young children, reflecting the startling fact that over the past decade families headed by women on their own have grown ten times as fast as two-parent families. In the short period from 1970 to 1973, the number of female-headed families with children rose by over a million. As of March 1975, they totaled 7.2 million—one out of every eight families in the country.

Although the presence of children is thought to inhibit women's labor force participation, in 1975 nearly 28 million children under the age of 18 had working mothers; of these, six and a half million were under the age of six. Mothers of almost half the children in the nation, therefore, were at work earning, or helping to earn, the family's living.

Some of the forces encouraging women into the labor force are clear enough.

Among economic factors are the need to be self-supporting, unemployment of husbands, the effects of inflation on family budgets, changing notions of what constitutes a decent standard of living, and accelerated demand for female labor through the growth of service and technical jobs where women have been traditionally employed. Strongly associated with women's rising labor force participation are drastically lowered fertility rates. With a longer life span and two children increasingly the norm, many women are spending a shorter period of their lives raising children and thus have time available for other endeavors. More opportunities for postsecondary education have raised women's expectations and their qualifications for employment. Other factors are advances in household technologies, improved family health, and new legislation promoting equality of opportunity in education and in employment.

One cannot discount the impact of diminishing social prejudice against the idea of women moving out of the home into areas of public life. Credit must go to the women's movement for helping to generate a more positive climate for these changes, for giving moral support to women who do work, and for inspiring them to fight for more equal treatment in the work place.

There has undoubtedly been a marked change of attitude about work on the part of younger women. Many still go through adolescence and their early twenties thinking that their future economic security will be largely dependent on the marriages they make. Increasingly, however, women of this new generation are growing up believing that whatever their fate, be it a stable marriage, divorce, or remaining single, they must expect to be all or partly self-supporting, and to provide for any children they may have. This very anticipation of working is impelling more women into the labor force.

Finally, women work not only for income but, like men, because of their desire for achievement and the satisfaction that comes from using their skills and being recognized for it. This tends to be overlooked in the emphasis on economic motivation.

Consequences

The accelerated movement of women into the work force is allied to changes of major consequence for the nation as well as for the family and for individual lives. First, while some strong rearguard actions are being fought, more and more Americans are beginning to see the full employment of women's abilities as a social and political imperative. Not only is it a national moral obligation stemming from our country's basic principles, but, more pragmatically, we are beginning to realize that the safety and prosperity of the nation will increasingly depend on the maximum use of our entire stock of human talent.

In the national economy we are seeing, with the emergence of the two-worker family, a fundamental change in the manner in which families provide for their economic welfare. The median income of a two-worker family in 1975 was $17,237,

131

compared with $12,750 for a family with only one member employed. With their extra income, families in which both the husband and wife work have been better able to keep pace with inflation and in some cases to increase their consumer buying power substantially. Double incomes in addition have provided some families with their only hope of meeting the cost of educating children. Interestingly, wives are more likely to work if their husband's income is already in the middle range than if it is either very high or very low. This pattern has served to narrow the disparity between the wealthy and the average American family.

To discover the full effects of the shift to the two-worker family, however, one needs to look beyond the economic indicators. We can assume, for example, that once they are employed, many women achieve new dimensions of self-confidence and a sense of pride in their ability to support themselves or contribute to the support of a family. For some, the environment of work makes their lives more interesting and broadens their horizons. For others, the work itself provides a sense of accomplishment or fulfillment that care of the home alone has left unsatisfied. Although outside employment may in some instances lead to role conflicts and add strains in a woman's relationship with her husband and children, in others, it may actually serve to strengthen these ties by establishing the relationship on a more equalitarian basis. For the single woman, work can become the most important element in her existence, giving her not only the means of support but human companionship and the security of a recognized position in the community.

With more women working, age-old mores about the distinctive roles of the sexes and appropriate relationships between them are being questioned, notably by younger couples but also by others. There is now an assumption by such people that women will work and, hence, acknowledgment of the fact that household maintenance and child care must be shared by both marriage partners. Other effects on social norms and life styles are just beginning to be studied, and while they may not yet extend throughout the society, they are nonetheless profound.

In the work place, many employers, increasingly concerned about job satisfaction and productivity, and also responding to pressures to recognize the dual responsibilities of women workers for home and job, have begun to experiment with more part-time work or with arrangements that provide flexibility in the hours of the work day or the work week. Some firms have shortened the work week by lengthening the work day, or they have instituted flexible starting and finishing times and staggered work schedules for individual employees. The result is, at the very least, no decline in work performance. Employees of both sexes report a better balance between work and private life, and improved morale and loyalty to employers.

Businesses, in addition, are facing changing outlooks toward work in male employees who have working wives. Men in this position are less willing to transfer from one location to another, and their unemployment rates have been higher during the recession than those of male heads of households generally. There are some indications also that men are showing a preference for shorter or more flexible work hours. We may one day see a time when considerable numbers of men and women, whether by choice or necessity, will be nearly alike in their attitudes toward work.

Working women's organizations and other women's interest groups have been exerting more pressure on employers and government to implement equal employment opportunity and equal pay laws and to remedy the effects of past inequities through affirmative action. Awareness of the role of education in preparing women for the world of work has led to extensive legislation promoting equal educational opportunity. In 1977, to mention only one change, educational institutions will be required to initiate programs to overcome sex discrimination and sex stereotyping in vocational education programs and to make all courses accessible to everyone. The entry barriers to many traditionally sex-related jobs have been crumbling, allowing a certain number of women to enter male-dominated occupations. Some employers are making sincere efforts to recruit and promote women into positions men have held in the past. Evidence shows the impact of the changes. Since 1960, the rate of increase of women in the skilled crafts has exceeded that of men. The greatest advances, however, have been made in the professions by highly educated women. Graduate and professional schools are reporting rapid rises in enrollments among women; the employment of women lawyers, physicians, and dentists more than doubled between 1960 and 1970 and is still rising. Clearly, some improvement has already occurred in women's employment status in the last decade or so, not all of it reflected in existing statistics.

While maternity leaves, pension and other benefit programs, and social security policies are a burning issue for women's organizations, progress has been made in these areas to reduce discrimination against women. Such progress is based on recognition of the existence of the working wife and elimination of the presumption of female dependency. Part-time workers, however, the majority of whom are women, are still denied major benefits because they are not considered a permanent part of the work force. The recent decision of the U.S. Supreme Court permitting the exclusion of pregnancy disabilities from an employer's disability compensation plan, and the New York State Supreme Court ruling that such exclusion is unconstitutional point up, if nothing else, the need for the country to establish a coherent set of policies that reflect emerging realities and recognize the interdependence of work and family life.

Despite some favorable omens associated with women working, problems, already existing but hidden, or resulting from failure of social policy to make accommodations, have become evident. In the first place, while the addition of a wife's earnings has helped middle-income families fight inflation, and even improve their living standard, those intact families which have only one income earner, or single men or women with children, are comparatively worse off. Particularly disadvantaged is the family headed by a woman on her own. Women's earnings in the aggregate are three-fifths those of men for full-time year-round work; overall, their median earned income in 1975 was only two-fifths that of men, partly because of their predominance in part-time work. The earning capacity of a female head of family is further limited because her educational attainment tends to be low. Relatively poor skills and the presence of children often make it impossible for such women to work at all. One in three female-headed families, in fact, has an income below the poverty level. Indeed, the hardship faced by these families, whether the mother is working or is on welfare, is one of the greatest social problems the nation has today.

Second, research shows that the greatest increase recently of mental depression in the American populace has been among young, poor women who are single parents and young married mothers who work in low-level jobs. Stress and a sense that they lack the power to improve their circumstances seem to be the chief causes of low morale.

Third is the immense physical and emotional burden that dual responsibilities for home and job place on both married women and single women heading families. One survey suggests that the average employed woman puts at least 26 hours per week into household duties in addition to her job, making a 66-hour working week, plus travel time. Obviously such a schedule leaves little time or energy for organized recreation or even for simple relaxation. Role conflicts in addition can leave working women feeling guilty. While husbands are beginning to help with housework and child care, sharing of these responsibilities is still not general because of the persistence on the part of both men and women of traditional ideas about appropriate sex roles, because of force of habit, and because the demands of some kinds of jobs held by men bring them home exhausted, too.

A fourth and crucial problem associated with women working in increased numbers is that of what happens to their children. Families today get by with various child care arrangements—hiring baby-sitters, placing their preschool youngsters in publicly supported or private daycare facilities, or leaving them with relatives, friends, or women who look after small groups of children in their homes. Older children are in school part of the day, but the availability of after-school care is extremely limited. Working parents often have no alternative but to give their children the house key and hope for the best. Taken together, these measures, all of which, except possibly the last, are adequate for some families in some circumstances, fall short of constituting a national solution to the problem. For too many, the unavailability of good, affordable child care remains a chronic problem, causing anguish to parents and in some cases having a direct bearing on whether women can work at all.

We have not yet learned the full effects of all these pressures on the family, but we do know that they are most severe for lower-income wives and mothers, who are also the women with the least access to services and opportunities that might ameliorate their condition.

Finally, there are the economic consequences arising from the changing size and composition of the work force. The question is whether the large-scale entry of women—coming just at a time when the pool of potential new workers among the nation's youth is swollen as a result of the post-war baby boom and, further, when minority-group unemployment continues at about 13 percent— has greatly diminished any prospect that the country will ever achieve full employment. An apparent paradox of the past two years has been the expanding number of jobs filled at a time when unemployment has also been at its highest level since the Great Depression. At present, more than 88 million Americans actually hold jobs and about 7.9 million are officially unemployed, making a civilian labor force of about 96 million. If one adds to this a considerable number of "discouraged job seekers," we have a national labor force at the present time approaching 100 million, not counting the category of potential workers who are, at present, essentially unemployable because they lack the necessary skills.

Manpower economists on the whole agree that young people and adult women trying to enter the labor market do not compete with each other directly for the same jobs—aside from the obvious competition between younger and older women for certain kinds of positions, especially for part-time work. Nevertheless, the only hope that considerable numbers of young people, minority-group members, and women have of working is in those relatively unskilled jobs that permit substitution of one type of worker for another. There is therefore at least theoretical competition among them, in which it would seem that the addition of ever-greater numbers of women to the labor force—some 1.5 million just in the past year—cannot but be a complicating factor. This could become an important question for the future as we move toward greater occupational integration.

The long and the short of it is that more Americans than ever before want to work, but we have not developed the means to provide them with jobs. Whether the problem is regarded as structural or economic or both, any solution we devise will unquestionably have to reckon with the reality that women in large numbers are in the labor force to stay. The answer will not come about by inducing women to leave their jobs and stay at home "where they belong"— as if this could just be mandated or as if the majority of women and their families really had a choice under present conditions.

Laws prohibiting discrimination, promoting equal opportunity, and requiring employers to take "affirmative action" where inequalities are found are on the books, but there has been a mounting outcry among women's and civil rights organizations about the slow progress being made to give these laws full effect. A major hindrance, even when employers make sincere efforts to comply with the law, seems to be the long-standing problem of occupational segregation of men and women. Many employers traditionally limit hiring for certain job categories to one sex. Such sex-typing discourages male entry into such challenging fields as nursing or teaching, but the preponderant effect is to deny women training, job opportunities, and wages commensurate with those of men. A high proportion of the jobs that are open to women are in the marginal, low-paid, low-status areas generally lacking in opportunities for advancement. And while more women are entering male-dominated occupations, their numbers remain relatively small, and limitations on their upward mobility are still prevalent.

The areas of greatest job expansion for women continue to be in certain kinds of technical and professional occupations and in clerical and service jobs. This employment is mainly in government at all levels, particularly in educational, health, and welfare services, and in banking and insurance. Most women go into white-collar jobs, more than one-third of them in bookkeeping, secretarial, typing, and clerical work. The rest are in blue-collar factory and farm jobs (18 percent) and in service work (21 percent).

A high proportion of the women holding jobs in these areas do not receive wages commensurate with the level of responsibility or skill demanded of them. This widespread undervaluation of their work goes far to explain why women earn only three-fifths as much as men.

Other reasons for women's lower earnings may have to do with employers' complaints that women are less skilled than men or are less motivated to try for those jobs that lead to advancement. This is a question more of public attitudes and the educational system, they say, than of anything that goes on in the work place. There is also the prevailing belief among employers that women's work attachment is intermittent, making it a poor investment to train them for greater responsibility. Many women do drop out of the labor force temporarily to have children, or they find that their home responsibilities allow them to work only part time. Nevertheless, their total time in the labor force has risen dramatically—from an average of 6 years in 1900 to 22.9 years today (compared with 40.1 years for men). In spite of this, the myth of women's work instability has helped to keep them in those low-earning, dead-end jobs that seem structured to fulfill the very prophecy that provides employers the excuse not to train them for better positions.

Incredible as it may seem, the average wage differential between men and women is wider today than it was 20 years ago, even though the educational attainment of working women has reached that of men, women's work-life expectancy has risen greatly, and more women are securing higher-level and better-paying positions. Beyond the continuation of some outright discrimination, one can only speculate on the causes. One reason may be that a larger proportion of female than male workers are working at, or near, entry levels of pay. Another may be that, as more women work or look for work in the traditional "female" fields, the more they come into direct competition with one another, allowing employers to pay them less. It must be remembered that, despite women's rush into the labor force, their unemployment rate is still higher than that of men.

All of these factors serve to restrict severely women's chances of upward mobility in employment and hence increased earnings—a situation that is particularly unfair to the substantial, and growing, proportion of women who do remain in the labor force full time from entry until retirement.

Another consequence of the increasing labor force participation of women is a decline in the number of women available for traditional community voluntary activities—in schools, health care facilities, churches, and welfare organizations. Women and men who have reached retirement age, are still in good health, and want to remain contributing members of society will possibly make up the difference. Some successful experiments with retirees suggest this will not be too hard to do, but it will take time.

To sum up, on the favorable side there are signs that American society is accepting the philosophical, legal, and pragmatic rationales for the full employment of women's talents in the work place. The rights of women are specifically protected by legislation and by Presidential executive orders, and will be further reinforced by passage of the Equal Rights Amendment. Women have made some advances in their employment status, and the benefits to the nation are evident—in added family income, in a stronger national economy, and in improved service to the public. There is also evidence that greater equality at home and in the work place is giving women increased confidence and a greater sense of efficacy. Finally, there are indications that institutions are beginning to recognize the special problems of the working woman and to make some needed adjustments.

There are other aspects of women working, however, attributable mainly to society's failure to accommodate rapidly enough to their needs, that are cause for concern. Women frequently are the victims at work of occupational segregation the law seems powerless to affect, suffer from low earnings, and have limited opportunity for advancement. A large proportion of women heading families live in poverty, with virtually no chance to improve their circumstances. The heavy burden implicit in women's dual responsibility for home and job has not been sufficiently eased by a sharing of housework and child care on the part of men. The unavailability of child care during working hours of parents remains a major problem.

In a more speculative vein, new stresses in the lives of women with children, caused by divided loyalties to family and career, may be giving rise to physical and emotional problems and adding strains to family life. The kinds of studies necessary to understand these problems fully have not yet been done and should be given high priority in the future.

Finally, although the ultimate consequence of women working in such large numbers should be beneficial both to the economy and the nature of American society, there are likely, in the shorter run, to be disturbances and special problems in the labor market before employment generally adjusts to the new phenomenon.

Two Possible Futures

If, as it seems, the conclusion is valid that the working woman is now a fixture in American life, two possible futures can be envisioned. The most realistic suggests that the present situation will simply be allowed to drift on. In time, after decades have elapsed, a new generation has reached maturity, much additional hardship has been suffered, and a good deal of militant social action by women has taken place, the nation, in both its public and private sectors, will perhaps yield to the pressures and make fundamental changes.

An alternative future, designed to avoid the hardship and social unrest the first course would cause, envisages the nation setting out now to remedy the defects of the present situation and, in the process, to work toward the creation of a new type of society. This would entail looking at the reality of the working woman as the opening wedge for broad social reform. It would require study of the entire structure of work and family life as it affects women, men, and children, and then active planning for change. Such a future is unquestionably optimistic and idealistic, but it is not beyond the realm of the possible if we have the national will to press for it.

What would be the chief characteristics of such a new society? It would be informed by four basic principles: the right to a job for anyone who needs to or wants to work; equal opportunity and fair rewards for everyone in all sectors of employment; development and utilization of the abilities of every citizen; and maximum flexibility for each person in the organization of his or her own pattern of life.

The new society would have the aim of greater occupational equality and freedom of choice for men and women in the work place. It would assume cooperation between men and women in the sharing of family responsibilities. It would entail better articulation than now exists between work and home life and between work and education. It would permit flexibilities in the amount of time an individual might allocate to education, work, family life, and leisure at any age during the course of a lifetime.

Interrelated and interdependent, these goals, if they were achieved, would lead to a fundamental reordering of the values underlying American life—in which the objectives of greater choice for the individual and improved quality of life would for the first time be equated with our traditional concern for productivity.

To meet these goals, broad changes will be needed in six major areas: in employment, in family life and child care, in welfare and tax policy, in education, in sex roles, and in the phasing of stages of the life cycle. Some of the required steps would be quite new and speculative; others have been tried on a small scale and would now have to be given wider application; and still others would constitute an intensification of major trends already under way. All would require cooperation among educational institutions, employers, government, and the community.

In the area of employment, the first and most obvious need is for vigorous new measures to reduce unemployment. Not only must additional job opportunities and training be created, but flexibility must be introduced into the work structure to permit more people to be absorbed into the labor force. This could include the encouragement of "flextime," work sharing, shorter work days or weeks, part-time jobs, and work-study arrangements in which employees would interrupt work to pursue further education. Work exchanges—that is, shifting jobs within firms—would also broaden horizons, extend skills, and introduce flexibility into employees' career patterns.

Second, employers, policy-makers, and organizations representing the interests of women must continue to press for compliance with laws that prohibit discrimination against women in the work force and mandate affirmative action to remedy the effects of past discrimination. Recognition of the child-rearing responsibilities of men and women should be built into employment policies. For too long women have been penalized for their reproductive role, with no choice but to adapt to a rigid work structure or drop out. Any weakening of present provisions guaranteeing women's right to equal treatment in employment must be resisted.

There is much that management within a large firm or organization can do to assist both the advancement of women and their entry into occupations traditionally considered appropriate only for men. It is true, of course, that if unemployment is high in the jobs in which men predominate, and if the seniority system is well entrenched, the chances of women moving into these areas may be virtually nonexistent. Nevertheless, a chief executive officer personally committed to equal opportunity can bring about considerable progress.

Most of the measures that can be taken to advance women are well known and include the appointment of women to boards of directors, vigorous recruitment of women into an organization, with concomitant training and promotional opportunity, the advancement of existing female employees into management positions, and programs to build a supportive environment for women in new kinds of jobs.

The opening up of opportunities for women in large organizations, whether governmental or private enterprise, will help but will not alone solve the issue of occupational segregation, since our social, legal, educational, and economic systems all interact to perpetuate this employment pattern. A full answer will be found only in basic changes in the labor market demand for women and in new societal values. Such changes will not come painlessly, but they must come. Useful here would be a broad educational effort aimed at altering public attitudes as to what are "proper" kinds of employment for the respective sexes, both in the home and in the market. The broadcast media, especially television, could be particularly helpful in presenting men and women in nontraditional roles and in publicizing the entry of men and women into fields conventionally associated with the opposite sex.

Whatever progress is made in giving women's work a higher value and in promoting greater occupational integration will necessarily depend on the individual initiative and determination of women themselves, and on their willingness to work together to press for recognition and reward for what they do and to achieve power over decisions that affect their lives. The responsibility that women must take upon themselves to accomplish these objectives cannot be overstated.

Another priority must be the provision—for all families which need them—of adequate daycare and after-school care arrangements for children. Related to the provision of child care is the creation of an income support system for families. A number of proposals, including the negative income tax, a system of family allowances, or a combination of the two, have been made that would achieve this purpose. All of them contemplate elimination of the present program of aid to families with dependent children, which appears to drive potential male contributors to child support out of the home and to lock women who might well become self-sufficient workers into being permanent welfare recipients.

The point is to achieve a condition in which those with incomes well below the national median can be assured a decent standard of living without the indignities of the present welfare system. Whatever policy is adopted, it must be so designed that it expressly meets the needs of the single parent with dependent children, most of whom will be women. This means that it must enable those who prefer to stay at home caring for their children to do so while not penalizing those who want to work.

What is really needed is a comprehensive family support system which provides direct financial assistance to those families that need it and makes available to all families a wide range of services. American society expects a great deal of its families, but it does not provide sufficient help to enable them to give their children the best possible start in life.

Naturally, a combination of measures to provide jobs for more people, to ensure a decent guaranteed income for all, and to make possible the provision and funding of an adequate family support system will cost a great deal of money. It should be possible, however, to offset these costs by elimination of public expenditure for families with dependent children (AFDC), a reduction of other types of welfare costs, and a lessening of the very heavy burden of unemployment compensation. Growth in the economy resulting from expanded employment could also be expected to produce higher tax revenues to government.

It seems doubtful that public opinion in this country is yet ready to accept something like the Swedish experiment in "parental insurance." Under this program, supported jointly by government and employers, husbands whose wives have just given birth are allowed up to seven months leave at 95 percent of salary to stay at home helping with care of the baby and housework. If both parents work, they can divide the leave between them. Sweden, however, is a nation that puts a far higher value on the family and children in its scale of national priorities than does the United States.

In the educational realm a large number of changes can be made that will have an influence on equal opportunity for women in the world of work. These measures would affect every level of education, from preschool to graduate training. They include a continuing attack on sex-stereotyping in curricula and in educational materials, new efforts to interest girls in mathematics and science during their high school years, attention in counseling at both the high school and college level to the relationship between course selection and later occupational choice, new programs at community colleges to encourage women to enter male-dominated occupations where the prospects for advancement and high pay are good, particular efforts by college placement officers to help women find jobs in areas where they are not well represented, and, finally, the expansion of opportunities at colleges and universities for adults to earn degrees or otherwise add to their qualifications through part-time or external study.

The educational world must also move vigorously to put its own house in order on the employment front by making every effort to overcome the effects of past discrimination against women. In public education all over the country, there are still very few female principals, at least at the high-school level, and female superintendents are all but unknown. In higher education, relatively few women have been appointed to senior administrative positions, and the same is true in regard to tenured faculty positions. The fact that little growth is taking place at any level of the educational system today of course makes the advancement of women exceptionally difficult. Nonetheless, the problem is not totally intractable, if effort and good will are applied to it.

Higher educational institutions must of course maintain equality of opportunity for women in both undergraduate and graduate enrollments and equal treatment of women on the campus. Of particular importance is the granting of undergraduate financial aid and the award of fellowships for graduate or professional study on a nondiscriminatory basis.

In the area of relationships between the sexes there will have to be substantial changes as we move toward a new society. Most importantly, the traditional assumption of female dependency, on which so much of our social and economic structure rests, will have to disappear. New women's rights laws have already made illegal many types of discrimination that assumed women's inferior status and dependency on men, but public opinion still predominantly holds to the traditional position. One can, nevertheless, envisage a gradual erosion of old beliefs and practices and the coming of a time when the governing relationship

141

between the sexes will be one of mutual respect based on the full autonomy, independence, and freedom of choice for both men and women. Establishment of this new relationship will be fundamental to true equality for women—as much so for those who choose the responsibilities of home or of home and volunteer work as their mode of life as for those who opt for outside paid employment.

Finally, there is the intriguing possibility of major alterations in the traditional stages of the life cycle. At present, for most people, the pattern is inflexible. The educational phase of their lives usually ends somewhere between the ages of 16 and 22. This is followed by an unbroken stretch of from 40 to 50 years of work, which in turn is followed by retirement.

In practice, this normal progression is modified for some people through involuntary periods of unemployment. Others modify it deliberately by interrupting the work phase of their lives with a period of full-time study aimed at gaining higher qualifications. Many women leave the labor force for several years to have children, sometimes taking the time to engage in volunteer work and further education or training before reentering paid employment. They can, however, pay heavily for this "irregularity" by having to start all over again at beginning entry levels, forfeiting seniority and hence opportunity for advancement both in position and in earnings, and losing the chance to compete for more interesting jobs.

One could imagine a new, flexible arrangement, however, in which it would be normal for most people—women and men—to alternate periods of study, employment, and work in the home and to plan their lives accordingly. While this would require major changes in present administrative structures and financial arrangements, the idea of making new life patterns possible for those who want them should not be out of the question in a nation as rich as the United States. Proposals such as two free years of study "in the bank" for everyone, available at any time one chooses, have indeed already received wide discussion.

The gains to be expected from greater flexibility in life patterns are many. If, for example, it were to become normal practice for both men and women to withdraw temporarily from the labor force, for periods of study, to retrain for new careers, to care for children, or just to pursue special interests, intermittent employment would have to be accorded society's official sanction, and the special onus now placed on women would be removed. For both men and women, periodic interruptions in the long grind of employment would certainly refresh their spirits, increase personal satisfaction, enhance loyalty to employers, and possibly increase productivity. It might, furthermore, enable more people to be absorbed into the labor force.

Most importantly, in making these changes, the nation would be confirming a belief in individual development and self-fulfillment and in the need to give higher priority to the quality of human life. It would not for a moment be to

142

suggest that work is not important. Rather, it would be a declaration that other things are also important and that the major portion of a lifetime given to work should have many compensations to it beyond simply economic reward.

Finally, it would permit the growth of a new societal attitude in which education would be seen not just as preparation for life but as part of life itself, to be enjoyed simply as recreation or for its ability to enhance human understanding and capability over the entire life cycle.

In Conclusion

It is possible therefore to regard the new phenomenon of women's large-scale entry into the labor force as an unprecedented opportunity for building a better nation. The new society would be moral, pragmatic, and humane. It would be moral because it would be founded on a belief that the worth and dignity of the individual and his or her right to be respected are more important than the claims of corporate structures or of the state. It would be pragmatic because it would release presently suppressed human abilities to the nation's creative and productive processes. It would be humane because it would have the flexibility to allow for the free expression of individual differences and would recognize that when these differences become disadvantages in the quest for job equality, as in the case of the female capacity for bearing children, society must make adjustments.

Realistically, of course, implementation of these ideas faces some severe constraints. We have to recognize that traditional beliefs about the respective roles of the sexes, though changing, are deep-rooted and persistent. We must also recognize that without a strong and growing economy, new public policies of the kind envisaged will be difficult to achieve. Nevertheless, even with these constraints, much progress toward the new society can be achieved if we but have the will to press for it. The alternative is to incur the immeasurable cost of doing nothing—of allowing the drift in our national policy to continue.

If we pass up this opportunity to use accommodation to the new reality of large numbers of women working as a spearhead for much broader change, we will not only be inflicting needless hardship on numbers of our fellow citizens but also denying to all of us the chance of living in a more humane and equitable society. We must have the courage and imagination to seize the opportunity that lies open to us—for the rewards can be great indeed.

Black Progress:
Achievement, Failure, and an
Uncertain Future

The measurement of social change in its many aspects is an imprecise art, especially in the realm of attitudes and beliefs. Nevertheless, it is important at this time to try to assess the progress toward racial equality that black Americans have and *have not* made in recent decades, because there is a growing perception among white Americans that black advancement has now become self-sustaining and needs no further impetus or assistance.

Indeed, there are many today who believe that the nation's debt to black people for past injustice has been so fully paid that whites themselves are becoming the victims of reverse discrimination. In their view, few if any inequalities between the races still exist, and those which do can be laid to "deficiencies" in the motivation, character, or intellect of individual blacks.

The spread of these disturbing ideas understandably is increasing fears among blacks that progress has come to a halt and that some of their hard-won gains may be lost. Some blacks think that an era of retrogression has already set in as they contemplate the implications of the *Bakke* case for education and jobs and of other reverse discrimination suits in the field of employment. Everywhere they look they see evidence of white backlash and a retreat from the civil rights convictions of the 1960's.

More than 35 years have elapsed since Gunnar Myrdal, the Swedish social scientist, was commissioned by Carnegie Corporation to investigate and record, however painful the story, the condition of the black minority in the United States. His monumental book, entitled *An American Dilemma: The Negro Problem and American Democracy*, still stands as a benchmark for assessing progress toward racial equality and the fulfillment of the American creed. Now, another important book on race relations sponsored by the foundation is about to be published. Called *Protest, Politics, and Prosperity: Black Americans and White Institutions, 1940-75*, it was written by Dorothy Newman and associates,* who were asked to describe changes in the status of blacks over the past three-and-a-half decades and the causes thereof.

Between Myrdal and Newman, then, lies a span of time which should allow us to sketch the main trends in race relations and to see where blacks stand today in this centrally important aspect of the nation's existence. It is a period that witnessed almost unimaginable changes in the world and national scene, including seven presidencies, three wars, a nearly doubled U.S. population, several economic booms and recessions, and enormous social and technological transformations. Not least was the civil rights activism of the 1960's, which so profoundly affected the status and attitudes of blacks that it seems, for many of us, hard to believe what life was like for most black people only a short while ago. In the early 1940's, writes Newman,

> three out of four black Americans still lived in the South, but North or South, virtually the only jobs open to them were the most menial; over half of all black workers were employed in agriculture or personal service. How much education a black man or woman might have meant little; skilled jobs involving contact with white workers were simply not available. Such jobs as blacks could get paid scarcely human wages: long days at stoop labor sometimes brought $3.00 or less a week, sunup to sundown; domestic work little more. Black children went to schools that were open fewer days each year (to free them up for field work during picking seasons), and black adults could still expect to be beaten or fired from their jobs for attempting to register to vote. Ordinary life was conditioned by discrimination: separate parks, separate water fountains, separate sections of the bus or train. One wartime munitions factory in St. Louis went so far as to build a separate factory for black workers; elsewhere, places that did hire black secretaries or clerks hid them behind partitions.

> "No colored need apply." "Whites only." "Negroes served in back." America had its own version of apartheid in those days. In the South the signs were everywhere and a matter of law; in the North they were not common except in want ads, and a matter of custom rather than law, but the effect was similar. Black and white everywhere shared the same geographical space while living in different worlds. Black accident victims would bleed to death before white hospitals would treat them. White restaurants would serve German prisoners-of-war inside, while black American soldiers were made to stay, unfed, outside. . . . To be black was tantamount to being marked for victimization. It is little wonder that black people were more often disabled, more often sick, more often dead in what should have been the prime of life.

---

*Nancy J. Amidei, Barbara L. Carter, Dawn Day, William J. Kruvant, Jack S. Russell.

These were the conditions that Gunnar Myrdal also discovered and chronicled, in the years between 1938 and 1942. But more than simply describing what he found, he probed deeper to uncover the sociological, psychological, economic, and political causes. He illuminated every nook and cranny of what he called "the Negro problem," noting ironically that, "When we say there is a Negro *problem* in America, what we mean is that Americans are worried about it."

Our great national dilemma, wrote Myrdal, was the stark contradiction between our fundamental beliefs as a people in freedom, equality, and justice, and the actuality of society's treatment of the Negro. So indefensible was this contradiction that it constituted a gigantic flaw in the fabric of American democracy, a flaw which Myrdal predicted would become ever more insupportable to the conscience of the white majority and lead inevitably to improvement in the lot of black people. Thus, he saw the slow movement toward equality as inexorable and the moral conscience of whites as the driving wheel of change.

While Newman's book, with the advantage of hindsight, contends that black protest, rather than white guilt, provided the main catalyst for change, there can be no dispute that the country has made great strides toward an equalitarian society. In the area of constitutional rights, blacks can now vote without legal impediment, equal access to public accommodations is guaranteed, and discrimination in employment and education is illegal. Indeed, the entire, elaborate panoply of legalized discrimination has been swept away.

Few would disagree that it is in educational attainment that blacks have made their most impressive gains. In 1940 the proportion of blacks completing high school was only 7.3 percent; today 75.3 percent of black youngsters complete high school, lower than the rate of 85.1 percent for whites but still a spectacular improvement. Blacks are now taking part in post-secondary education in vastly increasing numbers. In 1940 total black enrollment was less than 50,000, over 95 percent of it in the traditionally Negro colleges. By 1976 the number of blacks in colleges and universities had risen dramatically, to 1,062,000, including part-time enrollment. Although enrollment at the graduate-level and in graduate professional schools remains low compared with white enrollment, more and more blacks are completing advanced training and are making their way into the managerial, professional, and technical ranks of the labor force.

We have also seen tremendous improvement in other key aspects of life for black Americans. For example, the infant mortality rate for non-white persons (mainly blacks) dropped from 74 per thousand live births to 25 between 1940 and 1974—still, of course, appreciably above the 15 per thousand rate for whites. Life expectancy for blacks and other minorities at birth increased from 63 to 66, and maternal death in childbirth decreased from 7.7 per thousand live births to 3.2. Blacks, too, are experiencing improved access to justice in the courts, and we see black elected officials sitting in both houses of Congress, in state legislatures, on city councils, on school boards, and as members of other official

147

bodies. We see them as mayors of some of the nation's largest cities, as members of the Cabinet, and representing us at the United Nations. Moreover, the power of the black vote was felt as never before in the last presidential election.

Minority entrepreneurship has grown from essentially a few family stores, mostly in rural communities in the South, to the point in 1976 where the 100 largest black companies recorded gross sales of $775 million from such enterprises as insurance, magazine and music publishing, electronics manufacturing and auto sales and service. Black families are living in formerly all-white suburbs and attending previously all-white schools. There is wide integration in sports, entertainment, and the arts.

Such accomplishments and the desire of American blacks to recognize and take pride in their heritage undoubtedly account for the rising respect accorded blacks by whites and for the greater self-confidence and sense of efficacy felt by blacks themselves.

To the casual observer, then, the "Negro problem" would seem to have disappeared, since blacks, apparently, no longer suffer discrimination or other external barriers to advancement in American society. The gains they make from here on would appear to be strictly up to them.

While there has indeed been a vast social transformation of American life, most of it taking place during the past 15 years, it is impossible to speak of it without uttering a distinct *but*. Progress for blacks yes, but also extensive failure measured against the nation's highest ideals and against the national self-interest. Scrutiny of field after field reveals that blacks are still materially much worse off than whites, that racial prejudice and discrimination are still pervasive, and that new, more subtle barriers to further progress are being erected. The disparities are illustrated most graphically in the income of blacks, in their employment opportunities, in their housing, and in the quality of their educational experience. We have come some distance along the road to a just society, but we are far, far from the goal of true racial equality. On the contrary, there is the danger that we might turn back, unless we can find new reserves of energy and new strategies to sustain the momentum for change.

Income

Nowhere is evidence of the continued inequality between blacks and whites more obvious than it is in regard to income. Since 1940 the standard of living for most Americans has risen markedly, and both races have in the aggregate made real economic gains. What would have been considered luxuries three or four decades ago are today classed as necessities by both white and black families. Even so, the relative position of the masses of blacks has scarcely improved. From 1947 to 1975 the ratio of income earned by blacks to that earned by whites narrowed by only 11 points, from 51 to 62 percent. Today the average earnings of black families have receded to only 59 percent that of whites.

The economic situation of the black poor has clearly deteriorated—not only relative to that of whites but to that of the growing black middle class. There are indications that the movement of blacks from lower-paying into higher-paying jobs has slowed considerably during the 1970's. The steady decrease between 1959 and 1968 in the proportion of black families of low income came to a halt in 1969 and has not improved since then. In fact, blacks, while accounting for only 11 percent of the population in 1974, constituted one-third of all Americans living below the official "poverty line" of just over $5,000 for a non-farm family of four. The proportion of poor familes headed by a black woman increased markedly in the early 1970's, and by 1975 three-quarters of these families were receiving some or all of their income from public assistance. In total, four out of ten black children were being raised in poverty in that year, while only one out of ten white children was classified as poor. The situation today would not be appreciably different.

One would suppose that the greater economic vulnerability of blacks during the 1940-77 period qualified them to benefit proportionately from such public income transfer programs as social security, unemployment compensation, Aid to Families with Dependent Children (AFDC), and food stamps. However, this has not been the case. Although 95 percent of the aged who were white received social security benefits in 1975, only 87 percent of elderly blacks qualified. In 1970 only 67 percent of black and other non-white workers were covered by unemployment insurance as against 74 percent of whites. In 1973 the average monthly benefit of retired nonwhite workers was just 80 percent that of whites. One reason for these differences of course is that many blacks have had to take jobs that are "off the books," such as domestic work, and the wages earned are not reported for social security or tax purposes.

Jobs

During World War II blacks and other minorities made great gains in employment. Since 1948, however, their unemployment rate has been consistently worse than that of whites. In 1958 minority unemployment was 12.6 percent, and it remained over 10 percent until the Vietnam war. Even in the mid-sixties the rate was 7.4 percent while that of whites fell to under 4 percent. Black unemployment since 1975 has fluctuated between 12 and 14 percent. In November 1977 it was 13.8 percent.

While it is clear that blacks have made substantial gains during boom periods, especially those associated with war efforts, it is equally clear that they have lost more heavily during economic recessions. In the labor market they were, until quite recently, virtually excluded from the manufacturing and building trades. Occupational segregation, *de facto* job ceilings, discrimination in hiring, and lack of job seniority have continued to limit employment opportunities for them. Blacks are still found disproportionately in the dirtiest, least desirable occupations and in the lowest levels of the employment pyramid. And while increasing numbers have made it into craft, technical, and even management jobs, few are in positions of real influence in the power structure of the nation's economy.

It should be apparent from the experience of recent decades that we can never count on the "normal" functioning of the economy to equalize economic opportunity for blacks. Such equality can only come about through full compliance with equal opportunity laws and regulations in employment, the removal of job ceilings, and intensive programs of job training and placement for skilled, desirable jobs—all backed up by a serious commitment by government to full employment.

Even so, measures such as these will probably not solve the chronic problem of jobless black youth. The unemployment rate for black teenagers, officially an alarming 39 percent in November 1977, is in reality very much higher because "discouraged workers" are not counted. Poorly educated, untrained, heavily concentrated in urban slums, and ostensibly ill-suited for steady employment, the several hundred thousand youngsters who make up this group are an alienated, crime-prone element in our communities. Today the unemployment rate for black youth is two-and-a-half times that for white youth, and their labor force participation is only 75 percent that of whites.

The reasons for this upsurge in unemployment among black youth are varied and complex. During a slowing economy job opportunities have not been commensurate with the rising educational level of blacks, so that young people with a high school credential no longer necessarily "qualify" for entry into skilled occupations. Many low-level jobs traditionally available to blacks are now disdained by those who feel they deserve more from their education and whose self-image will not permit them to do what they regard as menial labor. For their part, employers, compelled to pay a rising minimum wage, may be reluctant to hire young people with low skills—especially if they are black. Moreover, young blacks who in the 1960's benefitted from targeted, federally-financed training and employment programs, even though these programs did not always lead to permanent employment, have received much less attention in the 1970's. In recent years neither government nor industry has been responding effectively to their needs.

Beyond these factors, however, some serious structural problems have developed that have simply eliminated many jobs for which blacks of all ages might otherwise have qualified. These include the rapid growth of highly competitive, labor-intensive industries in other countries (for example in the needle trades and in the electronics field), the migration of industry from inner cities to suburbs that are inaccessible by public transportation, and the introduction of new technologies that have reduced the need for labor in both manufacturing and service industries.

Looking down the road, it seems likely that the problem of unemployment among young blacks will, if anything, get worse rather than better, thereby further diminishing the already slim prospect these young people have of making a successful transition from youth to a productive adulthood.

Housing

Directly related to the economic disadvantage suffered by blacks is their poor housing. Three-fifths of all blacks inhabit the declining centers of large cities, crowded into decaying structures that frequently lack adequate heat and sanitary facilities. Often these homes are far distant from the places where jobs are now to be found.

It is true that some black families have been able, with the help of fair-housing provisions of the 1968 Civil Rights Act, to break the color bar in previously all-white suburbs, but the numbers involved are relatively small. The majority of blacks still live in run-down, segregated inner cities, because this is the best they can afford and because of fierce opposition to low-income housing projects by residents of the suburbs. Furthermore, the denial of mortgage money and insurance protection for homes and small businesses in "declining" areas—known as "redlining," or more euphemistically "geographic disinvestment"—has helped cause the rapid deterioration and eventually the virtual destruction of some neighborhoods heavily populated by blacks.

At least 80 percent of all American families today live in segregated neighborhoods, white or black. *De facto*, the United States is still two nations.

Effectiveness of Schools in Promoting Equality

From roughly 1960 onwards much attention has been focused on the fact that black pupils generally perform less well in school than do whites, as measured by classroom performance, scores on standardized aptitude and achievement tests, and years of school completed. The rationale behind some of the Great Society programs of the mid-sixties was that the poorer school performance and lower educational attainment of blacks largely accounted for their depressed socio-economic position in adult life.

In a new book sponsored by the Carnegie Council on Children, called *Minority Education and Caste: The American System in Cross-Cultural Perspective*, John Ogbu, a Nigerian social anthropologist who has done many years of research in this country, examines the phenomenon of black school failure and reviews various theories advanced in recent years to explain it. One theory held that black children suffered from "cultural deprivation" in their home backgrounds. Another theory held that the conflict between the dominant white, middle-class culture of the public schools and the different culture of the black world, with its own values and even its own dialect, produced severe learning handicaps for the black child. A third theory emphasized the notion of institutional deficiency—that in myriad ways schools are organized to favor white, middle-class children at the expense of black children. Examples cited were hostile attitudes of white teachers, their insensitivity toward black children and their expectations that they would fail, educational "tracking," over-dependence on standardized tests in which blacks do poorly, and so on. A fourth theory put blame on the failure of the schools to ensure meaningful educational equality by instituting effective remedial programs to counteract the negative influences of home and community. A final, highly controversial and generally discredited theory attributed the lower school performance of black children to their allegedly inferior genetic capacity to learn certain kinds of cognitive skills.

Ogbu then examined the two principal strategies employed since the early sixties to overcome black school failure: compensatory programs, such as Head Start and Title I, and school integration. Although he agreed that both these strategies are justified because they serve important moral and social objectives, neither, he found, has been particularly successful in equalizing black school performance. The reason is that, like the theories on which they rest, they focus their attention on what are essentially symptoms of the pathology of black failure rather than on its root cause. This root cause, which lies not in black but in white America, is the systematic relegation of blacks over many centuries to an inferior, caste-like status in our national life, with devastating consequences for their motivation and skills.

Ogbu argues that blacks occupy inferior social and occupational positions in society not because they lack educational qualifications for anything higher. Rather, he says, they are in this situation because the institutions of society exclude them by a system of racial stratification that virtually assures their low status in adult life. The evidence is abundant, he goes on, that blacks with the requisite education and credentials do not have access to occupational and social roles commensurate with their abilities. And as long as this remains the case, black progress will be thwarted.

One must, however, introduce two qualifying comments to Ogbu's thesis—generally persuasive as it is. First, although the hope of later success in the labor market is clearly important to the stimulation of educational motivation, we cannot deny that the quality of education available is also relevant. We know that many blacks, when they have been exposed to good schools, whether segregated or integrated, have become highly motivated and have performed well in their studies, completing high school and going on to college.

Second, while it is true there is no body of convincing evidence to indicate that school integration improves the educational performance of black children, it must be recognized that a large proportion of black youngsters still attend schools that are not integrated. In fact, real integration is still very much more a hope (or fear) than a reality in most areas of the country because of the almost irresistible impact of residential segregation. We simply do not know, therefore, what the effect of true integration, practiced over several generations, would be on the school performance of black children. Certainly, in these circumstances, it would seem that a total discounting of the *educational* value of integration to blacks is premature.

An Uncertain Future

Whether one attributes the perpetuation of racial inequality to caste or class barriers, or elements of both, most observers agree that the problem at times seems almost intractable. Active white resistance, lack of the political commitment and will to break up these barriers, the self-interest of those who benefit disproportionately from the *status quo*, all combine to continue the lag between promise and reality. The rise of increasing numbers of blacks to the social, economic, and political ranks of the middle class does not change this dismal fact. What improvement there has been in the status of most black people has, as Ogbu points out, taken place only in times of national crisis, when their labor has been in demand, or in direct response to the civil rights initiatives of blacks and their white supporters. Obviously, we cannot rely on national crises to make the difference. Thus, the most effective course, in Ogbu's view, is pressure by blacks for priorities and preferential treatment as a compensation for generations of discrimination and exclusion. Such pressure "will have to increase before the white power structure will design and implement a comprehensive policy for total elimination of the caste barriers. . . ."

Taking a similar position in *Protest, Politics, and Prosperity*, Dorothy Newman and her associates conclude without hesitation that "the cutting edge" of progress for black Americans has been black protest. They write:

> Our findings are unequivocal that vigilant, aggressive protest is necessary at all times . . . to maintain gains, to prevent losses, and to make progress. The gains by black Americans since 1940 have been truly theirs, with relatively few champions who have spent a lifetime in their struggle. If "the Lord helps those who help themselves," black Americans would long since have achieved equality with white Americans. Intense effort has been an integral part of their lives. That even so persistent and creative an effort has not yet achieved its goal is testimony to the power and influence of the white majority. This is not only because of their wealth, or because of the ordinary restrictions societies impose on minorities; it is also because black and white minorities still live out their lives in separate social worlds. . . .
> The separate social worlds of black and white Americans is only one manifestation of how racism has become institutionalized in America. We have seen how blacks are denied employment regardless of merit; denied housing regardless of credit worthiness; and receive less from income security systems regardless of characteristics similar to white fellow citizens. Institutionalized racism, that which is built into organizations' ways of proceeding, eases the burden of personal guilt, and so is readily perpetuated.
>
> Our predominantly white institutions—public and private—and the indi-

viduals in them do not take it on themselves to remove barriers or to act forcefully on behalf of black Americans without pressure being brought to bear. The managing white world continues to be ingenious in finding ways to resist change even under the restraints of law. Only persistent protest, using equally ingenious ways of carrying on the struggle, has been an equally powerful way of meeting and overcoming that resistance.

As we have seen, Gunnar Myrdal, writing nearly four decades ago, predicted great changes in the relationship between blacks and whites in the United States, based on his belief that the conflict between the nation's highest ideals and its daily practices would become so insupportable to the conscience of whites that change would be inevitable. He did not rule out the significance of black protest, but he assigned it a lesser role in the generation of black progress. While not entirely dismissing the importance of white conscience, Dorothy Newman *et al* are firm in their belief that black protest has been the prime mover of change.

Looking back over the years since 1940, one can find much to agree with in the conclusions of Myrdal, Newman, and Ogbu. Although they differ in their emphases on the roots of social inequality between blacks and whites and in the reasons for the gains blacks *have* made in their struggle for full participation in society, their messages are not necessarily antithetical. On balance, the idea that black protest has been the single most important element in black progress seems valid. Certainly this was the case in the 1960's when the emotions stirred by the inspiration of Martin Luther King, Jr., and other leaders, by student protest, by the rise of "black power," and, one must admit, by urban rioting, caused white America to make major concessions to blacks in meeting their claims to equal treatment. Nor can one deny that for more than three centuries blacks were relegated to a caste-like status in this country, leaving an enormous legacy of social wreckage for blacks and whites alike that will take many more decades fully to clear up.

At the same time, one cannot discount the role of white conscience as a force for change. While it is true that institutionalized racism served to ease the burden of personal guilt, many white Americans felt deep qualms of conscience over the historic wrong done to blacks and supported public and private action to compensate. The leadership of President Johnson in transforming the principles of the civil rights movement into national law was centrally important, and this accomplishment can never be denied him.

In the past few years, however, we seem to have arrived at a moment in our history when both protest and conscience are dormant. True, the voices of some black leaders have been raised sharply against the disgracefully high unemployment rate of blacks. True, some whites have maintained their concern about racial injustice. Nonetheless, there seems to be no one today, black or white, capable of evoking anew the nation's latent sense of conscience and mobilizing it into action.

The reasons for this are difficult to pinpoint. Certainly, we have had two administrations that assigned black progress a low priority, and we have one now whose effectiveness in promoting the interests of blacks has yet to be demonstrated. Furthermore, a certain complacency may have set in in the leadership group of the black community after the dramatic gains of the 1960's. The folly of such a relaxation of vigilance has come home to them as they confront the possibility that some of the hard-won opportunities now open to blacks in the all-important fields of employment and education may soon be restricted.

Another reason for the let-up in pressure may be the phenomenon of increasing class differentiation among blacks, as those who have broken through the barriers and gained a foothold on the ladder of success find their interests diverging from those they have left behind. A faltering economy, of course, has always heavily penalized those on the margins of power and affluence, where blacks are to be found in disproportionate numbers. Furthermore, whereas blacks had the almost exclusive attention of the nation's conscience in the 1960's, other groups—the Spanish-speaking and Native American minorities, women, children, the elderly and the handicapped—are now competing for a share of that attention.

Most important, it must be recognized that many of the gains made by blacks in the 1960's were in securing things that whites already had, such as voting rights, access to public accommodations and educational opportunity, and hence did not come at the *expense* of whites. Today, however, the advances being sought by blacks are of a kind that, given the nation's conservative mood and a sluggish economy, put them in direct competition with whites. For this reason it may well be fruitless for black leaders to continue to make their appeal to white conscience on racial grounds alone. Rather, they should be putting their effort into building a broad coalition of all who have interests in common—those who suffer from discrimination, poverty, unemployment, poor housing, poor education, and inadequate health care—and seeking gains for blacks within this context. The success of this approach will then depend as much on the amount of political and organizational power such a coalition can generate as on the stirring of the nation's conscience.

In spite of the many uncertainties of the moment, there do seem to be grounds for cautious optimism. The very fact that the nation has come as far as it has in the past decades is astounding. The fact that discrimination, despite frequent circumventions of the law, is illegal has created a solid basis for further progress. And, it is a source of hope that there are ever greater numbers of well-educated, confident black citizens, for it is from this group that a cadre of able black leaders is emerging, visible in every sphere of our national life but especially in political office.

What we must now revive and bring up-to-date is the philosophical and moral vision of the 1960's, and the practical recognition that it is in our national self-interest to convert this vision into reality. We must hope that an observer, writing as many years in the future as Gunnar Myrdal wrote in the past, will be able to record that the United States of this day committed itself unreservedly to true racial equality and hence to the realization of its highest ideals. If that should happen, then Myrdal's classic "American dilemma" will at long last have been solved.

Perceptions of
Childhood and Youth

Virtually every age and society has had certain perceptions of the meaning and place of childhood and youth in the social order. Such views, although often considered sacrosanct, have in fact varied widely according to cultural context and have changed over time in response to new demographic, social, and economic currents.

Children have, for example, been seen as economic assets or liabilities to their families; as objects of societal "investment" or as simply part of the general populace needing no special recognition; as fully adult beings at puberty or as young people whose immaturity continues well past adolescence; as the "possessions" of adults or as young citizens endowed with active rights of their own; and, finally, as innocent creatures deserving of unqualified love and compassion or as inherently sinful "demons" whose will must be broken. All of these perceptions can exist simultaneously in a society, giving rise to much of the ambivalence that adults may feel toward the young.

As recent years have, indisputably, been ones of deep and far-reaching change in American society, it is instructive and important to consider how this period of major social upheaval is affecting our attitudes toward young people, and what the consequences may be for their future and, through them, for the nation generally—however tentative such speculations may be.

Nowhere has change been more arresting than in the area of demography. Fifteen years of a very low birthrate, following two decades of unusually high fertility, and increased longevity have considerably distorted the age composition of the population. Ours has become an aging society, with relatively few children, a plethora of young adults, and mounting numbers of elderly.

To illustrate the situation more graphically, about 29 percent of today's population is under the age of 18, in contrast to 34 percent in 1970. Just since that year, the number of children under 15 has dropped by 6.4 million, or 4.5 percent, while the 25-to-34 year old group has swelled by 7.9 million—a 32 percent gain, and the number of those 65 and older has increased by 3.4 million, a 17 percent gain. Annual births in that time have declined from 4.3 to 3.3 million, and the median age of the population has risen from 27.9 to 29.4 years. In its highest year, 1957, the fertility rate was 3.7; today it has shrunk to 1.799.

The startling fact is that only 38 percent of American households today actually have any children living in them. The overwhelming trend is toward later marriage and childbearing. Two decades ago, 28 percent of women in the 20 to 24 age group were single, as against 45 percent today. In the same period, the average age at which a woman has her first child has risen from 21.8 to 22.7. An increasing number of couples are choosing to have no children at all.

This has also been a period of great change in the economic realm. High inflation, sluggish growth, increased energy costs, and troublesome balance-of-payments problems have undermined confidence in the economy and made many Americans fearful of the future. Pressure has grown on most families as real income has declined. This in turn has been a major cause of increased participation in the labor force by women, including large numbers with small children. Two-worker families have thus become the norm, widening drastically the income disparity between this group and single-parent families. Since 1969, all of the increase in the numbers of families living in poverty has been in families headed by women. At the same time, the cost of raising children has risen sharply, to the point today that a family with an annual income of $10,000 must spend more than $50,000 to raise a child to the age of 18, not including savings put aside for higher education.

Paralleling these trends have come striking alterations in the social position of women and in established family patterns. The latter include an extraordinarily high divorce rate, numerous unmarried couples living together, an increasing percentage of children born to unmarried women, and such a growth in single-parent families headed by women that they now comprise more than one out of every five families. The traditional nuclear family, composed of father as breadwinner, mother as homemaker and one or more children, meanwhile has declined to less than one third of all families.

Finally, accompanying all of these trends, there has been a radical shift in social values and conventions, including the appearance of self-centered, inward-turning attitudes among the more affluent and a growing tendency among Americans generally to live for the present, rather than to defer immediate gratification in the hopes of ensuring a better future for themselves and their children. One writer calls this movement the "epidemic of obsession with ego or self."

How will these developments alter, if at all, our view of the young? What will be the role of children and youth in an aging society and in an increasingly childless one? Will children, particularly those most in need, get better or worse schooling and services as their numbers diminish, and when an unstable economy may mean limited resources for everyone? Will parents and taxpayers be more caring toward the fewer children there are, or will the needs of the young increasingly be seen to conflict with adult goals for economic security and self-fulfillment?

And what will the prospects for the present crop of children after they have reached adulthood? Will their small numbers prove to be a boon to them or a liability? Will it turn out that they have been born in the best of times or the worst?

Toward a Demographic Day of Reckoning

It is no doubt possible that the transitions we are now experiencing will produce at least some favorable dividends for the young. One leading demographer, at any rate, takes a rosy view of it. It is his contention that, as the smaller cohorts of children today start entering the job market in the mid-1980s, the reduced competition among them for entry-level jobs will so increase their market value, employment, and earnings, it will give them a sense of confidence about the future. With improved earnings and prospects, they will marry earlier and produce more children, the divorce rate will slow down, crime, suicide and other anti-social or self-destructive behavior among the young will decline, and college enrollments will rise.

One could extrapolate from this prognosis the further possibility that, in due course, rising fertility rates will produce an improved climate of opinion toward children and a bettering of their condition, since, as in the 1950s, there will be a built-in lobby in their behalf.

This outlook for the later 1980s and early 1990s is intriguing but not very convincing on the face of it. The prediction assumes that young women, influenced by the improved economic position of young males, will go back to early marriage and start having babies at the rate their counterparts did in the 1950s. Such an assumption ignores the nature of the revolution that has taken place in the last decade in the aspirations and education of women and in the labor force demand for their talents. All evidence, in fact, seems to point to a continued desire, and need, on their part to combine careers or jobs with marriage and to defer childbearing until they have gained a secure foothold in the work world— behavior that militates against having more than one or two children, if any.

In addition, if the experience of some European countries is any lesson to us, it seems doubtful that any explicit pronatalist policies we might initiate will result in an increased birthrate. It would appear, therefore, that a sharp upturn in childbearing is highly improbable and that we would be unwise to count on it. (There will of course be some increase in the actual numbers of children being born as the baby-boom generation starts families, but this will be a temporary phenomenon in the long-term decline in childbearing.)

A more likely outlook for the period ahead is that young workers, after they have been absorbed into entry-level jobs, will be frustrated by the lack of promotional opportunity, since the better jobs will already be occupied by the numerous members of the baby-boom cohorts on the ladder just above them, who will not approach retirement age until after the turn of the century. Thus, it by no means follows that the short-term prospects of young workers will be so bright that their expectations will stimulate a general sense of optimism about the future. In fact, young people can probably look forward to relatively static income and a rivalry with older workers for some period of time.

Conflict of another kind between age groups could intensify as the ever-growing numbers of older people, with their mounting voting strength, press their concerns, at the expense of the very young. Few people realize the extent of the massive shift that has already taken place in the allocation of public spending toward the elderly, principally through increases in Social Security payments and Medicare. Indeed, the substantial portion of the federal budget now going to the elderly represents the largest income redistribution scheme in the nation's history. According to one recent study, the economic status of old people has, since 1960, improved considerably more than the economic status of children. The reason for this, the study suggests, is simply that the people who make the laws are old, and there are more organized elderly people fighting for their own interests today.

Although, in the latter half of the 1990s, today's children should find themselves beginning to advance quite rapidly, they will be taking on a very heavy burden. Indeed, for them it will be a time of unprecedented opportunity combined with maximum responsibility. It will be the job of this relatively small group not only to produce the nation's cadres of professional, administrative, technical, and skilled workers but to ensure the well-being of the generation behind it as well as provide assistance to the 15 to 20 percent of the population of elderly people that the nation will have by then.

Compared with today, more of this responsibility will fall upon members of minority groups, whose fertility rates are higher than the national level. In 1976, the rate for whites was 1.679 but for blacks was 2.23. Currently, blacks constitute about 11 percent of the population and number some 24 million persons, three-quarters of whom are resident in major metropolitan areas. Their median age, understandably, is lower than that of whites.

Although the Census Bureau does not compile separate birth statistics for Hispanics, there is abundant evidence that their fertility rate is extremely high by national standards. Officially, they make up only 5 percent of the population and number about 11 million. However, if persons of Spanish origin living here illegally were included, the proportion would perhaps be as much as 8 percent and the numbers as many as 17 million people. By the end of the century, if not sooner, Hispanics may well be the nation's largest minority. Close to one-half of them are under the age of 18. They too are heavily urbanized, some four-fifths living in major metropolitan areas.

In short, while in the opening decades of the next century the number of prime-age workers will be relatively small, a far larger proportion of this group will be black or Hispanic than is true today, especially in the cities and in certain regions of the country.

The conclusion to be drawn from these figures is clear. Every child alive today or born in the years just ahead, whether male, female, black, white, Hispanic or otherwise, will be a scarce resource and a precious asset as an adult in the early part of the next century. At that time, the nation's standard of living, its capacity to defend itself—perhaps its very viability as a nation—will be almost wholly dependent on the small contingent of men and women who are today's children.

The Liabilities of Childhood

Given the inexorable nature of this march toward a demographic day of reckoning, common sense would seem to dictate that we start now making the welfare of children, especially those who are most in need of special help, our highest priority.

Surely it is true that most of today's young children will grow up to be strong and capable, healthy and whole adults. For a substantial number, however, the prospects for such a future are clouded. Nationally, three million arrests were made for juvenile crimes last year; millions of children and adolescents suffer from drug and alcohol abuse; one million teenage girls become pregnant each year; a million youngsters run away from home; suicide has become the highest killer of teenagers after accidents. We know that the abuse and neglect of children have reached shocking proportions, that hundreds of thousands of children lead miserable lives in institutions, that millions are physically, mentally, or emotionally disabled, that half a million are in foster care, that well over a million under the age of 15 are not in school, that the national school dropout rate is 15 percent, and that upwards of 500,000 children age 16 and under, most of them from migrant families, are working in the fields because of loopholes in the child labor laws, while the real unemployment rate for urban black youths is believed to be over 50 percent.

One would think that, in the face of the steady decline in the numbers of young people being born today, we would be more favorably disposed to do our best by those we have. The irony is that the opposite seems to be the case: as the numbers have declined, public attitudes have turned to indifference or even outright antagonism. Evidence of this can be found in the widespread exclusion of families with children from rental housing, in the growth of single life styles, in the reluctance of many parents to stint themselves in behalf of children, and in mounting taxpayer opposition to spending on the schools and on aid to families with dependent children.

Added to these difficulties, there is the problem of widespread disillusionment today with the great social programs of the 1960s, so many of which were designed to benefit children, either directly or indirectly. While many of these programs are still alive and have been shown to work well, the political base for them has largely withered away.

A further inhibition on the search for solutions to the problems of children is what has been called the "collapse of the children's cause." The coalition of child and youth advocates had rallied around the Child and Family Services Act of 1971, which was to provide for federal support of day care, but when it was vetoed by President Nixon as anti-family, the organizations went their own way. Since then, no similar national coalition has formed.

The Carter Administration came to Washington pledged to a strong pro-family policy. Although there have been a few initiatives and some successes, it seems unlikely the Administration will be able to push more than piecemeal reforms. Moreover, some of the strongest children's advocates in the Congress have turned their attention to other responsibilities and interests. Whether any new advocates will be found to take their places is an open question.

Reducing the Lag between Changing Family Patterns and Social Policy

A focal point of such concern as does exist about children today is the single-parent family, usually headed by a woman, often of minority background, and almost always poor. Children raised in such circumstances are liable to be the most at risk of any in the nation. Virtually every misfortune one can imagine can lie in store for them—and then for their children after them. The cumulative cost to society of those casualties over their lifetimes will be many times the cost of investing in programs for children now to try to prevent failure.

The need for welfare reform is obvious. For too long, the society has tolerated a system that humiliates and demoralizes the so-called beneficiaries yet penalizes their efforts and dulls their desire to work themselves out of their predicament.

There are, furthermore, those single-parent or single-worker families which do not live below the official poverty line but which, nonetheless, cannot afford certain necessities such as decent housing, adequate health care, and a nutritious diet. They are, indeed, almost as badly off as families receiving public assistance. For families headed by single women the problem is heightened by the system of occupational segregation that prevents many qualified women from gaining access to the better-paying jobs with more opportunity for advancement—jobs that traditionally have been available only to men. Efforts to break down the sex division of labor, matched by vocational training opportunities for nontraditional jobs, must be accelerated.

Two-parent families with children, where the mother as well as the father works outside the home, are also under heavy stress today. True, the fact that the wife and mother is working produces much-needed income, enabling many families to keep up with inflation or stay out of poverty. Furthermore, employment outside the home can broaden the horizons of women, make their lives more interesting, give them additional self-confidence and a new sense of efficacy about themselves, and, in so doing, enable children to play a useful role in family life as well as provide them with new perceptions about the role of the female sex in society. In some cases it can strengthen marriages, increasing husbands' respect for their wives; in others it gives women the financial independence to extricate themselves and their children from totally destructive situations.

On the other hand, the fact that both parents are obliged, or choose, to work outside the home can, through the fault of neither parent, add new emotional and physical strains to marriage and family life. Where adequate child care is unattainable, it can result in serious neglect of children. A recent survey conducted to find out how children are taken care of when the mother is at work found that 30 percent under the age of 13 were left alone or were left with older brothers and sisters in the afternoon hours. Relatively few of the mothers surveyed felt that the child care they were able to arrange was adequate.

It should be pointed out that there is no scientifically verifiable body of evidence to indicate that women working outside the home is of itself harmful to children. The problem lies in the lack of high-quality alternative care for them, including the unwillingness or inability of fathers to accept their share of responsibility. And since the clock will probably not turn back, the nation's institutions, from government to employers to the family itself, simply have to recognize the fact of the permanently changed circumstances under which children are growing up today, and make the necessary adjustments.

The issue, in short, is not whether women should work but how to make this possible with the least harmful consequences for children. Pressure for widespread provision of preschool and after-school care of the young is bound to increase as women continue to find it necessary to work. There will also be growing demands for a better articulation between home life and the work place and greater accommodation by *institutions* of all kinds to the schedules of working parents.

Finally, there must be renewed efforts and reforms aimed at raising the school achievement levels of children who are educationally disadvantaged and at keeping them in school. No longer can the educational system be allowed to function as if substantial numbers of youngsters can be considered expendable.

Of course, it cannot be proven that a loving family environment, good preschool and after-school care, effective public education, high-quality health care, proper nutrition, and the availability of wholesome recreation necessarily inoculate children against the failures and hardships of adult life. On the other hand, it can be proven that a lack of these qualities in the lives of children can so impair their development that millions of them will become crippled adults who make little or no contribution to society, and who become expensive liabilities to the community. This is a double burden that any nation can ill afford but one that will be catastrophic for ours in the early decades of the next century because of the skewed age composition of the population.

What More Can Be Done

Given the negative or indifferent climate of opinion toward children and youth today, any thought that they are suddenly going to be accorded the priority attention they deserve seems naively optimistic. This is especially true of children from disadvantaged backgrounds. As the conservative mood of the nation deepens, appeals for attention to the needs of young people will no doubt increasingly go unheard, and negative perceptions of them will probably thrive— if for no other reason than that these perceptions serve as a convenient rationalization for failure of conscience and compassion. Young people will probably continue to be seen as economic burdens rather than as assets, their problems will go unrecognized or be subordinated to the claims of older groups, they will be given little chance to play a constructive role in the nation, and they will be regarded essentially as a threat to the comfort and security of adults.

If there is hope that this pessimistic prediction will prove false, it may, somewhat paradoxically, lie in the continued surge of women with children into the labor force. These women, joined by their husbands, might, if they were to organize and gain political power, become a potent force for change. In pressing for reforms that would ease their particular family situations—good publicly supported preschool and after-school care for children, the introduction of flexible work scheduling, wider provision of paid matenity leave for both wives *and* husbands, and an end to the prevalent occupational segregation that is keeping the average level of women's earning so low—they could go a long way toward solving some of the problems of children that are caused by anachronistic assumptions about the nature of family life today.

Hope may lie, further, in the institution of permanent mechanisms for monitoring the impact of social and economic trends on the condition of children and youth. Without such mechanisms, new problems could be developing for them of which the nation is largely unaware. The task of such analysis and reporting should be both a public and private responsibility. The recently completed work of the Carnegie Council on Children was one such effort in the private realm.

Beyond this possibility, those who are concerned about children may have to place less emphasis on an appeal to the nation's finer instincts—the perception of young people as a special part of humanity deserving of adult love, protection, and nurturing—and more emphasis on a frank appeal to adult self-interest based on demographic considerations. Such an approach would say that we must invest in children now to assure our *own* well-being as elderly people a few decades hence. This can be a powerful argument, and it is one that has yet to be adequately made. If the argument seems cynical and unworthy of us as a people with a great humanitarian tradition, if it seems to take a wholly instrumental view of children, so be it, provided it directs public attention back to the needs of children and serves thereby to make their lives happier and more fruitful.

No nation, and especially not this one at this stage in its history, can afford to neglect its children. Whatever importance we attach as a people to expenditure on armaments, to programs for older Americans, to maintaining high levels of consumption and to a hundred other purposes, the welfare of children has to be our highest priority. Not only are they our future security, but their dreams and ideals can provide a much-needed renaissance of spirit in what is becoming an aging, tired, and disillusioned society. In the end the *only* thing we have is our young people. If we fail them, all else is in vain.

Bilingual Education and
the Hispanic Challenge

In retrospect, the 1970's will certainly be seen as a period of reassessment of the great federal social programs of the previous decade. While a review of the achievements of these programs was not in itself inappropriate, many of the specific evaluations that comprised it are now known to have been poorly conceived or politically inspired. Among the programs reviewed, the experiments designed to help ensure equality of educational opportunity for disadvantaged children came in for particularly heavy attack. Most have managed to survive, but the broad public base of support for them has largely eroded, and those who advocate continuation of such programs face a constant uphill battle to maintain funding levels.

The latest federally supported educational program to come under public scrutiny is bilingual education.

Bilingual education is an instructional tool that has developed quietly over the past decade and a half to help students whose first language is not English overcome their linguistic and academic difficulties and, it is hoped, perform as well as their English-speaking peers in school. While the particular approaches used vary widely, the term usually refers to programs that employ a child's native tongue as a medium of instruction while he or she is being helped to learn English. The theory is that, by enabling students to master cognitive skills in the language they know best before making the transition to English, bilingual classes will prevent academic retardation. Often, a secondary aim is to enhance and maintain a child's proficiency in the home language. Classes also frequently draw on a child's heritage and culture as a means of building self-esteem and increasing comprehension and motivation to learn.

There are an estimated 3.6 million pupils in the country judged to be in need

167

of some form of special language assistance to enable them to cope with the regular school curriculum.

The federal government began funding demonstration programs in bilingual education in the late 1960's and has steadily expanded its support since then, from $7.5 million in 1969, affecting some 76 projects reaching about 26,000 children, to $107 million in 1980, for about 575 projects reaching roughly 315,000 children. Meanwhile, under the stimulus of federal and court action, state and local governments have expanded their support for bilingual education, too, so that together they now more than match annual federal funding.

It is safe to say that the total amount of money spent in the field, although not insignificant, would scarcely make a dent in the national budget for compensatory education programs. Over $3 billion, for example, was appropriated in 1980 just for Title I, the largest of such federally supported programs of special assistance to "educationally deprived children in low-income areas."

Nonetheless, despite the fact that expenditures for bilingual education are comparatively low and that it reaches only a fraction of eligible pupils, the program has become highly controversial. Indeed, few other educational experiments in recent years have managed to arouse such passionate debate—so much so, in fact, that the future of this promising pedagogical tool is uncertain.

The reasons for this are complex and probably only a matter of speculation. One source of the controversy, surely, is to be found in public perceptions about the record of accomplishment in bilingual education thus far. Generalizations are unwise at this stage: the few evaluation studies that have been done are not considered a fair assessment of bilingual education's potential. But indications are that many bilingual programs were launched hastily, with little empirical evidence of "what works," without adequate diagnosis of children's varying linguistic needs, without properly trained teachers or appropriate curricular materials, and often without the strong support of school administrators. Today, evidence of many good programs, according to such measures as improved academic performance, higher school retention rates, and enhanced self-concept among affected children, is beginning to emerge, the results of basic and operational research are at last being fed into the design of programs, and enough time has passed to begin producing a new cadre of qualified teachers. But the widespread impression has already been given that bilingual education has not been very effective, leading critics to conclude that the concept itself, as opposed to its implementation, is unsound.

Another source of controversy lies in the apparent departure of bilingual education from the traditional language policy of the schools. Immigrant groups have always been free to keep alive their native languages and heritage through private efforts, but this has not, by and large, been considered the responsibility of the schools. On the contrary, public education in the 20th century has been employed as the chief means of assimilating children of foreign-language backgrounds into the English-speaking mainstream. Since the First World War,

English has been the sole medium of instruction in the early grades. To many Americans, a belief in the appropriateness of such a policy, in which they cooperated, often at the price of the cultural heritage they brought with them, has formed a deep and abiding part of their national identity and consciousness. With the introduction of native languages in the classroom, however, this policy seems to have been reversed, and many people wonder what it all means. Some see it as but the first step on the road to official recognition of multilingualism, extending from the schools to other public institutions in the society. Already the concept of language *rights* has been established, the Voting Rights Act mandates bilingual election materials, interpreters are now required in courts of law, and languages other than English are increasingly being used in the delivery of social services in areas where there are large concentrations of non-English speakers. Bilingual education therefore seems to be challenging some of our traditional assumptions and practices regarding cultural assimilation.

But perhaps no one of these concerns would be as great if bilingual education were not associated in the minds of large segments of society with Hispanic Americans. Currently, although the federal government funds programs using 74 languages, more than 65 percent of the money goes for Spanish-English bilingual education. The programs have been strongly promoted by Hispanic organizations, and the educational, political, and administrative leadership for bilingual education has been mainly Hispanic. Indeed, bilingual education, as a vehicle for heightening respect and recognition of native languages and culture, for fighting discrimination against non-English speaking groups, and for obtaining jobs and political leverage, has become the preeminent civil rights issue within Hispanic communities. This development, coupled with the fact that Hispanics, through natural increase and immigration, are growing rapidly in numbers, has made the issue more visible and politicized than it might otherwise have been. Bilingual education is no longer regarded strictly as an educational measure but also as a strategy for realizing the social, political, and economic aspirations of Hispanic peoples.

These three sets of concerns interlock, so that it is virtually impossible to discuss bilingual education without reference to the broader context in which it has evolved. At the same time, its very vulnerability to criticism on political grounds makes it especially incumbent upon this experiment to justify itself educationally. Nothing less will do justice to the needs of children from linguistic minorities and to the meaning of equal educational opportunity. This will be the major challenge of its supporters over the next few years.

The Development of Bilingual Education

Contrary to popular belief, instruction in two languages is not new in American education. Its use began in the 19th century within private schools and some public schools in communities settled by German, Scandinavian, and French immigrants. Between 1840 and 1917, schools in Cincinnati offered classes in German to pupils who understood no English, and from time to time New York City schools resorted to Yiddish, German, Italian, and Chinese to educate new waves of foreign-born children. Then, around the First World War, when anti-German sentiment swept the country and speaking English became a kind of index of political loyalty and "adequacy" as a citizen, bilingual education was stamped out. In many states all use of foreign languages below the eighth grade was forbidden in the schools. The policy of Americanization, the cornerstone of which was instruction solely in English, then began in earnest.

A few educators at that time argued that submersion in the English-language curriculum was an unnecessarily harsh approach and that a gentler transition from the mother tongue was better for the children and their families. They also called for schools to respect and help keep alive the heritage these children brought with them. Their protests went unheeded, however, and the English-only policy remained throughout the succeeding decades (although many private or community-supported schools continued to offer dual-language instruction).

The modern revival of public bilingual education began in the early 1960's when schools in the Miami area, faced with a sudden influx of refugee Cuban students, responded by offering instruction in Spanish until the children were able to learn in English. The technique also began to be employed elsewhere—in New Mexico and in Texas, for example.

The concept received fresh impetus in the wake of the civil rights movement and a new national interest in ethnicity and cultural pluralism, which allowed minority groups to take a more outspoken pride in their heritage and their contributions to American life.

Federal attention to the educational problems of "linguistically different" children began in 1968 with the signing of the Bilingual Education Act, added as Title VII to the Elementary and Secondary Education Act of 1965, and brought about by a coalition of community leaders, educators, and legislators as well as some senior federal officials. It was clear to them that masses of children whose first language was not English were failing academically and that dropout rates for them were inordinately high. If they were receiving any special assistance in learning English, it was usually in the form of ESL (English as a Second Language) courses, requiring them to be taken out of regular classes for periods of the day, so that while they did indeed learn English, they lost the content and fell behind in their schoolwork.

The original aim of Title VII was modest enough: to give seed money to local educational agencies for new and innovative elementary and secondary programs designed to meet the "special educational needs of children of limited English-speaking ability in schools having a high concentration of such children from families . . . with incomes below $3,000 per year."

Then, in 1974, the U. S. Supreme Court handed down a unanimous decision on a lawsuit that changed the way in which bilingual education has been regarded ever since. The case, called *Lau vs. Nichols*, involved non-English-speaking Chinese students, who had accused the San Francisco Unified School District in 1970 of language discrimination because they were receiving instruction only in English, a language they could not understand and were not being helped to learn. They claimed that the absence of programs designed to meet their special needs violated both Title VI of the 1964 Civil Rights Act, which contained a provision forbidding discrimination on the basis of national origin, and the equal protection clause of the 14th Amendment to the Constitution.

The Court agreed on the charge of language discrimination, basing its decision not on the Constitution but on Title VI as interpreted by existing Department of Health, Education, and Welfare (HEW) guidelines to the schools. These guidelines stated that, "Where inability to speak and understand the English language excludes national-origin minority-group children from effective participation in the educational program offered by a school district, the district must take affirmative steps to rectify the language deficiency in order to open its instructional program to these students."

The import of *Lau* was enormous. The Bilingual Education Act had already given federal validation to the voluntary use of native languages in the classroom. Now, for the first time, language rights were recognized as a civil right. Federally aided schools henceforth were legally obligated to provide special assistance to students with limited English-speaking ability in overcoming their language difficulties. Furthermore, schools were told that children must not be denied full participation in the educational process while they were learning English. The Court left it to the states and the educators to decide how this should be done, but because its decision relied on existing federal legislation and administrative intent, it left the way open for federal determination of what "affirmative steps" were acceptable under Title VI.

Following the *Lau* ruling the Office of Civil Rights of HEW issued informal guidelines, called "*Lau* remedies," which schools might take to provide equal educational opportunity for students of limited English-speaking ability. While the remedies did not mandate bilingual education, they specifically rejected the sole use of ESL at the elementary level as an instructional technique for students who spoke either little or no English. This was tantamount to requiring that bilingual programs be established, with ESL as a component, unless the schools could produce an equally acceptable alternative.

The Court's decision and the *Lau* remedies provided the underpinning for lawsuits brought by organizations speaking for the rights of children from linguistic minorities, resulting in a number of court-mandated bilingual programs. In addition, under the influence of *Lau*, the Bilingual Education Act, when it was reauthorized in 1974, minimized the compensatory aspects of the program and stated that the aim of the Act was to "establish equal educational opportunity for all children."

In other ways *Lau* had far-reaching effects. It spurred the passage of many state bilingual education laws, overturning the prohibition against foreign-language teaching in the lower grades that had been in effect since World War I. And it stimulated, along with the federal Bilingual Education Act, activity around the country in linguistic, educational, social science, and legal research, in curriculum and materials development, and in teacher training, in the process giving rise to a whole new educational movement.

The Hispanic Involvement in Bilingual Education

Of all linguistic minority groups, Hispanic Americans, by virtue of their numbers in the population if for no other reason, would seem to have the most at stake in the survival of bilingual education. Most of the advocacy work in the field has been conducted by Hispanic parent groups and by organizations such as the National Association of Bilingual Education, the Mexican American Legal Defense and Educational Fund, the Puerto Rican Legal Defense and Education Fund, the Chicano Education Project, and Aspira of New York. Many see bilingual education as the single most effective mechanism at their disposal for focusing public attention on the educational plight of Hispanic children, for seeking redress for decades of discrimination against them by the schools, and for preparing them to succeed in the mainstream while promoting respect for their native language and cultural identity.

Estimates of the population of Hispanics in the United States are various. Difficulties stem from the failure of earlier censuses to make a full count of Spanish-surnamed residents and the impossibility of knowing how many un-documented workers of Hispanic origin are in the country at any given time. Nevertheless, assuming that there are possibly 3-to-6 million of the latter, the total number of persons of Hispanic background on the mainland is probably not less than 16 million, making up approximately 7 percent of the total pop-ulation. A recent Congressional study of immigration has noted that more than one-third of all illegal immigrants entering the country since 1965 have been Hispanic; the highest rate of unauthorized entry is also among this group. These and other demographic trends suggest that Hispanics may well be the nation's largest minority group by the end of the decade.

The term Hispanic applies, of course, to several distinct subgroups within the larger community. Nearly 60 percent, or some 7.3 million persons, are Mexican American. While perhaps as much as a third of the Mexican-American population is descended from citizens living in Mexican territory annexed in 1848, the majority appears to stem from later immigration, especially that which took place after 1920, following the Mexican revolution. The latest wave of immigration began in the late 1950's. Traditionally resident in the border states and other parts of the Southwest, Mexican Americans are also found in increasing numbers in the Midwest and Northwest.

The second largest subgroup is composed of people whose origins lie on the island of Puerto Rico. Some 1.7 million Puerto Ricans now reside on the mainland. Concentrated in the Northeast, more than a million live in New York City alone, although Chicago and Miami have growing Puerto Rican communities as well.

A third subgroup is the Cubans, most of whom came here in the early 1960's following the Communist revolution in their country. Living mainly in the Miami area, they now number close to 800,000.

A fourth subgroup, in addition to those descended from older stock originating in Spain, includes a rapidly growing new community of immigrants from the Caribbean and now Central and South American countries (other than Cuba and Mexico) such as the Dominican Republic, Ecuador, and Colombia. This group is believed to number around 2.2 million and, like the Puerto Rican community, is largely resident in the Northeast.

Hispanics, then, are an exceedingly heterogeneous population. What they have in common, however, far outweighs the differences among them, and this is a broad sense of ethnic identity based on allegiance to a shared mother language and culture. This sense of Hispanic identity is constantly being reinvigorated with persistent high rates of immigration and by the continual circulation of Hispanic peoples, especially Puerto Ricans and those of Mexican descent, to their homelands and back.

The very size and dominance of one linguistic and cultural group stands to have profound implications for educational policy in the United States. School enrollments of Hispanic children in some of our major cities alone tell a vivid story: In New York City, they currently comprise 30 percent of the school population; in Los Angeles 45 percent; in San Antonio 52 percent; in Miami 32 percent; in Denver 31 percent; in Hartford 35 percent. In the face of these figures, the question of how best to meet the educational needs of the children, a large proportion of whom speak only Spanish or are not sufficiently proficient in either English or Spanish, becomes one of paramount importance for the country in the years ahead.

Unfortunately, Hispanic children as a whole have not fared well in the public education system. Typically they are two to three grade levels behind other students. A mere 30 percent manage to complete high school. Nationwide, in urban ghetto areas, the school dropout rate for Hispanics reaches as high as 85 percent. Less than 7 percent have completed college. In 1975–1976, Hispanics received only 2.8 percent of the B.A. degrees awarded, 2 percent of the masters degrees, 2.6 percent of the law degrees, 2.3 percent of the medical degrees, and 1.2 percent of all doctorates.

Not surprisingly, the income figures for Hispanics are very low. In 1978, Hispanic Americans in general had a median annual family income of $12,600, compared with $17,600 for the nation as a whole. Puerto Ricans were the worst off, with a median family income of only $8,300 and 30 percent living in poverty. At the next level were Mexican Americans, with a median family income of

173

$12,800 and 12 percent in poverty. Even the Cubans, who brought with them a professional class and benefited from substantial aid by the U. S. government, had a median family income of only $15,300 with 10 percent in poverty. Only 8 percent of Hispanics held professional and technical positions, compared with 16 percent of nonHispanics. Most were found in low-paying jobs in the service and manufacturing industries and in agriculture.

To be sure, the schools cannot alone be blamed for the dismal record of academic and economic achievement among Hispanics. Many Hispanic newcomers have tended to be poor, uneducated, and untrained for skilled jobs when they came here. They have been hindered in economic advancement by the language barrier, by their congregation into rural, suburban, and urban barrios, and by the cultural differences that have served to isolate them from the American mainstream and perpetuate their low social status.

But whatever weight may properly be given to the background of Hispanics themselves, the factor of discrimination must surely assume a major share of the responsibility for the academic problems of Hispanic students. Schools, as transmitters of society's values, in a variety of ways have made a signal contribution to the school performance rates of Hispanics—by shunting Spanish-speaking children from poor families into educational tracks designed for low achievers, by classifying them as mentally retarded or emotionally disturbed, by denigrating their Hispanic heritage, by giving them the message that they cannot, or are not expected to succeed. In short, the public education system as a whole has neither welcomed Hispanic children nor been willing to deal with their learning problems in any effective way.

Since, however, there is a clear correlation in this country between educational achievement and socioeconomic status, and since a high percentage of the Hispanic population is young—42 percent are under age 25—Hispanic parents and leaders, despite the past record of the public schools, place great hopes for the future of their communities on the schools' ability to educate their children. A principal tool they have chosen in order to achieve this is bilingual education.

The Record to Date

How, then, has bilingual education served Hispanic children under the impact of federal legislative, judicial, and administrative action?

The answer is a mixed one. The bilingual education movement has unquestionably shown remarkable growth and energy over the past 12 years, propelled along by Hispanic leaders and some educators and policy makers. But its proponents have had reason to despair over the many problems of implementing it effectively on a broad scale. In this regard the recent history of bilingual education is probably not too different from that of Head Start, Follow-Through, and other educational inventions of the Great Society intended to help disadvantaged children. Similarly, bilingual education now finds itself on the defensive. Three years remain before the Bilingual Education Act comes up for reauthorization, and in that time, all those who believe in it will be under obligation to prove its worth to an increasingly skeptical public.

The federal effort in bilingual education was originally seen by its sponsors almost exclusively as a means of correcting English-language deficiencies in primary-school children, with the rationale that it could help them make the transition from the mother tongue to English and promote assimilation into mainstream education. It has therefore been viewed largely as a compensatory measure for students who have fallen behind or who are likely to do so. It has *not* had as its central aim the fostering and maintaining of competence in two languages, although some federal monies have in fact been used for what have turned out to be "maintenance" programs, and school districts are free to implement two-language instruction through all grade levels if they choose.

Little, however, has been known about the exact nature of such programs and their progress in achieving their academic and linguistic goals, and much of the fault, it appears, can be laid to laxity in federal planning and supervision. As one researcher pointed out, before 1978 less than .25 percent of Title VII funds were spent for basic and operational research on bilingual education; a good deal of the existing evaluation research, moreover, has been judged worthless. The first Bilingual Education Act included no funds for research at all. The emphasis, it seems, was on immediate action, without much prior understanding of what measures should be taken with children showing varying degrees of proficiency in speaking, reading, writing, and comprehending English.

In fact funding for research has greatly expanded recently. The federal government spent $2 million for research in 1979; $4.6 million is being spent in 1980; and appropriations total $6 million for 1981. Additionally, evidence is mounting that, in favorable circumstances, programs of high quality do meet the goal of providing equal educational opportunity for students of non-English-speaking backgrounds. A 1978 review of program evaluations by the Center for Applied Linguistics found at least 12 programs in which bilingual education students performed as well (or better) on tests of reading, writing, math concepts, and social science, and other measures as comparable groups in regular classes. Attendance figures for bilingual students were in general higher than would otherwise have been the case, and there were indications that many students showed a positive attitude toward the programs and their academic capabilities.

A study of evaluation reports of bilingual programs in Colorado showed that such programs had been generally effective in improving the English reading skills of students as well as improving school attendance and dropout rates. They also helped bring about greater parental involvement in school programs.

Other long-term studies suggest that bilingual instruction may have a cumulative effect, with results that may not show up in short-term, one-year-at-a-time evaluations. This is a critical point, which suggests that bilingual education, as with other special programs for educationally disadvantaged students, must be given a longer time to work than had been thought.

Perhaps the most interesting research, which may have a bearing on the American experience, is a study of Finnish immigrant children in Sweden. These children were more likely to approach the norms of Swedish students when they emigrated to Sweden around the age of 10 or 12, *after* they had five or six years of education in their native language in Finland. There is much anecdotal evidence to suggest, too, that Mexican children who emigrate to the United States after the sixth grade out-perform Mexican-American children who have been in the country since the first grade. Apparently, submersion in a second language before these children reach the age of 10 can exert a "destabilizing" effect on the development of their native language as a tool for mastering cognitive concepts, with the result that they become semi-lingual—not fully competent in either language. Since this condition applies to a large number of Hispanic children, who like the Finnish are members of a dominated minority group, such findings indicate that the students would fare better if they received instruction entirely in their native language for the first few grades before shifting into English.

Another serious problem has been the lack of adequately trained teachers. Teaching in two languages needs special preparation: a teacher who happens to be bilingual is not automatically qualified to undertake bilingual instruction; nor is a monolingual teacher who has taken a few courses in a second language up to the job. Yet, before 1974, no federal monies were appropriated for preservice teacher training, and only in 1978 were Title VII funds allocated for fellowship programs at the doctoral level.

In addition, determination of *Lau* violations by HEW and enforcement of remedies to comply with the law have proceeded slowly. Schools have been required to meet the needs of linguistically different children whether or not they receive federal assistance for the purpose. Thus, schools blame budgetary constraints for their failure to comply, and HEW, leery of applying the extreme measure of withholding funds, has allowed investigations to languish. Lack of government monitoring has also apparently permitted infractions in some schools that ostensibly have complied.

Practically speaking, then, the *Lau* remedies have not thus far had much direct effect; the leverage has consisted mainly in the implicit threat of sanctions. This may change in the future, however: monitoring and enforcement efforts have stepped up, and proposals to revise and formalize the *Lau* guidelines are under consideration. If approved, the new regulations would specifically mandate bilingual programs at both the elementary and secondary education levels, and children who have comparatively limited proficiency in either their home language or English would be covered—a measure that could vastly increase the numbers receiving bilingual instruction.

An influential study of Title VII projects begun in 1976 and sponsored by the Office of Education (OE) produced striking indications of many poor programs in the country—programs that were producing no academic gains for students or, in some cases, were actually allowing them to fall behind. This study was justifiably criticized for flaws in the research design, but it nonetheless dealt a blow to bilingual education's reputation.

Under the impact of the OE study, and in consultation with organizations working in the field of bilingual education, the guidelines for the 1978 Amendments to the Bilingual Education Act were strengthened. In addition to committing substantial funds for research and teacher preparation, the Act now covers linguistically different children who not only have difficulty speaking and understanding the English language but who need help reading and writing it. At the same time, it limits funding largely to programs aimed at helping children achieve competence in the English language, rather than, as in the 1974 Amendments, helping them "progress effectively through the school system." They affirm the desirability of parent involvement in decision making. They also allow for up to 40 percent of the participants to be children whose first language is English, and they authorize more money for curriculum development. Finally, the guidelines require that applicants demonstrate that federal grants would gradually be replaced by local or state funds to help achieve a regularly funded program.

The Prospects for Bilingual Education

Whether measures to bring about needed reforms in the implementation of bilingual programs succeed or fail, the *Lau* ruling will of course remain in effect. Schools will still have to meet the needs of linguistically different children and provide them with a meaningful education that meets the requirements of Title VI of the Civil Rights Act. On these grounds alone, it seems likely that some form of bilingual education will continue to be included among the methods chosen to deal with the language difficulties of these children—unless there is another major court decision that reverses or modifies the earlier ruling.

Whatever happens, the fact remains that at least 1.75 million Hispanic children have limited proficiency in English and need some form of special language assistance before they can fully participate in the educational system. Since neither quick submersion in regular classes nor ESL alone has worked well with children from low-income, non-English-speaking backgrounds, teaching such youngsters in their first language while they are learning English would appear to be a sensible alternative.

There is also the reality that many Hispanic organizations and parents want bilingual programs for their children, not only to help them master English-language skills but to help them maintain their first language. They have built an effective national constituency for it, with a leadership that has played a significant part in the formation of bilingual education policy. The growing Hispanic population and its increasing voting strength make this a group that all levels of government must reckon with. If Hispanic citizens press for bilingual programs, then educators and policy makers cannot avoid listening.

Furthermore, bilingual education has afforded Hispanic adults a significant route to social mobility and economic security. It has created bilingual teachers, administrators, bureaucrats at all government levels, curriculum developers, and researchers—the whole range of bilingual personnel needed to run this important new education movement. In the process, it has established positive role models for young people, holding out for them new types of satisfying career prospects.

Additionally, bilingual education has served as a stimulus for Hispanic parents to begin playing an active role in the schools, for the first time taking part in decisions affecting the quality of education their children receive. Whatever the results in the strictest terms of academic performance, bilingual education, they believe, has already helped to improve the way in which the educational system deals with their children. Schools have been less quick to shunt youngsters into low educational tracks or treat them with disrespect. Many parents are convinced that without bilingual education, the schools will go back to their former behavior, so they will continue to fight for it.

Then, since the concept of language rights has gained a recognized legal status, and since Hispanics are enjoying a more visible pride in their heritage, the use of Spanish in the schools has acquired great symbolic value. Hispanics can look forward to the day when their native language is no longer regarded as inferior, when it no longer offers the excuse for an ethnic slur and a means of destroying the self-confidence and self-esteem of a child.

Altogether, bilingual education has served as a vehicle to enable Hispanic people to press for their language rights at the same time giving them a major point of entry into all other issues having to do with opportunities and rights for Hispanics, and providing an avenue for their participation in the political process through election to school boards and other offices.

Historical and Future Context

Beyond these current trends there is, however, a broader context for thinking about bilingual education as an appropriate response to the educational needs of Hispanic children. One aspect of this concerns our special relationship with Puerto Rico and Mexico—a relationship established through two wars.

The United States annexed Puerto Rico in 1898 following its war with Spain. In 1917 the inhabitants became American citizens, albeit second-class citizens by virtue of Puerto Rico's status first as a U.S. territory and then as a commonwealth. Subsequently, the Unites States vacillated in its attitudes toward an English-language policy in Puerto Rican schools, causing a great deal of hardship for children and their families. Then, in 1947, it finally and officially declared the island Spanish-speaking in recognition of the reality and the desire of the people. Economic distress on the island after the Second World War brought millions of Puerto Ricans to New York City and elsewhere in search of jobs. Since 1970, however, there has been a consistent trend of net return migration. This two-way migratory flow has allowed mainland Puerto Ricans to sustain their ties to the island, but in doing so it has slowed the process of adaptation to American life and exposed Puerto Rican children to learning problems and discriminatory treatment in the schools. On the island, the so-called Neo-Rican children returning from the mainland are facing similar learning problems and discrimination.

Bilingual education would seem to be one obvious answer for dealing with these children. The argument for it can be made on practical grounds alone, but the claim for special treatment also gains emotional and political force because Puerto Rico is simply part of this nation. Following the Supreme Court's decision on *Lau*, a case brought by Aspira of New York against the New York City Board of Education was resolved by a consent decree mandating the implementation of bilingual education in city schools. Unfortunately, the law has proved difficult to enforce, and it covers only those students who are dominant in Spanish; it does not apply to children who are semilingual. Only in 1978 were federal funds finally authorized to help such children in Puerto Rican schools. Bilingual education for Puerto Rican children is obviously still more a goal than a reality.

The United States acquired half of Mexico's territory at the close of the Mexican-American War in 1848. At that time approximately 75,000 Mexicans living in what became U.S. territory were given the choice of becoming Americans or leaving the country. Most chose to stay. Although the treaty arrangements did not expressly guarantee the rights of the new citizens to retain their customs and language, the governments of the territories (later the states) of New Mexico, California, and Colorado acknowledged their constitutional obligations to Spanish-speaking citizens. Early legislative sessions were conducted in both English and Spanish. The 1891 constitution of the New Mexico territory mandated public bilingual education.

Subsequently, however, Mexican Americans came to be mistreated by their adopted country. In Texas, after the Civil War, no provision whatsoever was made for the education of Mexican-American children. When they were eventually allowed into the schools, they were segregated from Anglo children because of their "language handicap." Considered by school authorities to be children of an inferior race, they were often punished for speaking Spanish, heard their names involuntarily Anglicized, and saw their cultural background systematically ignored in textbooks. Indeed, with the exception of blacks and

Native Americans, no other ethnic group has been subjected to quite the same combination of racial and cultural insult as the Hispanics of the Southwest. Prior to 1940 it is estimated that only 1 percent of Mexican-American children of school age was actually enrolled in school.

This history is deeply etched in the minds of the present generation of Mexican-American leaders and encourages them to regard bilingual education as an instrument for redressing the wrongs of the past. Their attitude stems not only from the experience of the last century but from the knowledge that Spanish speakers were among the first immigrants to this country. The chronicles of the Spanish explorers of the 1500's predate those of the British. The names of important cities, towns, and states are a constant reminder of early Spanish settlements and governance in what is today the United States, reinforcing the feeling that Mexican Americans have a right to public recognition of their language.

Another aspect of our relationship with Mexico which has a bearing on bilingual policy concerns the influx of undocumented workers from there into the United States. The current wave began in the late 1950's and accelerated in the mid-1960's with the cancellation of a series of bilateral agreements which had allowed Mexican workers to come to this country for short periods of time and protected their rights to some extent while they were here. Since then, millions of Mexicans, attracted by the promise of jobs, have entered this country illegally, settling mainly in urban areas where they are vulnerable to abuse and exploitation. On the one hand, they are accused of taking jobs which rightfully belong to American citizens, including Hispanic Americans; on the other, they are said to fill jobs that no one else will take. To some extent their hidden presence places a burden on public services, such as the educational and health systems, because they are not counted in the formulas that determine eligibility for funding under federal and state aid programs. At the same time, they may be contributing more to the economy than they take from it: a U.S. Department of Labor study estimated that 77 percent pay social security taxes, the benefits of which they are unlikely to collect, 72 percent have federal income taxes deducted from their wages, all pay local and state sales taxes on consumer purchases, less than 1 percent are on welfare, and less than 8 percent appear to have their children in school.

Any solution to this situation will have to be worked out between Mexico and the United States and necessarily will be long in coming; it will not diminish migration to the north in the near future. In the meantime, something must be done to educate the children of illegal immigrants. Those who are born in this country are of course American citizens and entitled to a public education. That scarcely 8 percent of children of undocumented workers here are in school, however, should be no cause for satisfaction, for many of them will remain in this country permanently and grow up unprepared to compete in our increasingly technological society. The state policy in Texas of excluding children of illegal aliens from public schools has been challenged by Mexican parents, and the case is currently being reviewed in a federal district court. The state argues that any requirement to educate these children would siphon off resources from American citizens and that the schools, at least in the border area, cannot afford it. Just how much effect any liberalization in the state law would have on the actual enrollment of Mexican children remains to be seen, but the implications for educational policy seem clear and point toward forms of special language assistance that involve the use of Spanish, the only language most of these children speak.

Another perspective that bears on the schools' use of bilingual education has to do with the radically changed economic and social conditions of today as against those of the past and the circumstances in which Hispanics find themselves competing with other groups for jobs and a decent life.

Prior to the First World War the country needed large amounts of cheap labor, and it encouraged immigrants to come here by the millions. Jobs existed not only for them but for their children. Compulsory education existed in name only, and the school-leaving age was 12. If foreign-born students could not succeed in school, there was an immediate place for them in the factories or on farms. No one was surplus; everyone was needed.

It was only later, after the First World War, after there was a glut in the labor market of unskilled workers and immigration was restricted, that our rapidly advancing technological society began to need a better educated labor force. Then the schools took on a new importance, opposition to the new child labor laws and to compulsory education declined and disappeared, the school-leaving age was raised to 16, and immigrant families began to make the sacrifices necessary to see that their children got the high school credentials that would ensure their future success. The phenomenon of rising educational levels entered a wholly new phase after the Second World War, when an enormous demand developed for higher education, and a college degree came to be recognized as the minimum qualification for many jobs. Millions of young people whose parents had not attended college or even finished high school, including many who were the children or grandchildren of immigrants, flocked into higher education as it changed rapidly from an elitist institution to a vast democratic enterprise.

Poor people of Hispanic background, however, have come to this country late in the day, into a highly developed, mature society, offering less of the opportunity to build a nation enjoyed by new arrivals at the turn of the century. Their difficulties have been compounded by racial prejudice, by the language barrier, and by their isolation into segregated neighborhoods and schools, locking many of them into low-level, marginal jobs. Thus, even though the economic rewards are still great enough to encourage continued heavy migration, the promise of social mobility for the less educated has greatly diminished.

Bilingual education is certainly not a total panacea, but if it proves an effective measure for helping Hispanic children to develop the self-confidence and ability to perform well in school and stay there until they gain the needed credentials, then its implementation on the widest possible scale may be justified, for the alternatives are bleak indeed.

Working in favor of such special efforts to see that Hispanic students succeed are demographic trends. Hispanics, with their relatively high fertility and immigration rates, are producing a significant and growing part of today's relatively small cohort of children on whom the burden later of an aging American society is going to be exceedingly heavy. It may be asked whether in these circumstances the country can continue to afford treating any proportion of its youth as expendable. If not, we should not deceive ourselves into thinking that in furthering the education of Hispanic children we would be doing it out of the goodness of our hearts; we would be doing it for ourselves as well.

In at least one other respect conditions have changed from earlier days. A large proportion of the 13 million people who came here between 1900 and 1914 to meet the demand for cheap labor were from southern and eastern Europe. Growing fears that they would dilute the "basic strain of the population" and turn the United States into a "collection of foreign colonies" to some extent overlapped the anti-German sentiment already referred to and helped foster the Americanization program in the schools.

Perhaps such a policy, with the sacrifices exacted in human welfare and cultural enrichment to the nation, were necessary when a sense of nationhood had to be forged out of a multilingual, multicultural population. But the question can certainly be posed as to whether today's circumstances do not warrant a more humane approach to the education and acculturation of linguistic minorities. Are we not secure enough in our national identity to risk some relaxation of our earlier prohibitions and tolerate the kind of cultural and linguistic pluralism Hispanics are seeking without feeling that the cohesiveness of the nation is threatened? Should we not accept the assurances of Hispanic leaders that their goal is not separatism but simply the right to become active participants in the nation's economic, social, and political institutions without abandoning the language and culture that mean so much to them? If bilingual education offers adults and their children an opportunity for achieving this kind of participation, should opportunity be denied them?

Looking into the future, there is another way of assessing the value of instruction in two languages in schools at the elementary level. One consequence of the elimination of bilingual education during the First World War was to create our national bias against foreign-language acquisition and to make respectable our ignorance of other societies. In its late 1979 report, the President's Commission on Foreign Language and International Studies stated that, "America's incompetence in foreign languages is nothing short of scandalous, and it is becoming worse. . . ." To Commission members and many other observers of international affairs, the decline of foreign-language facility and teaching generally in the country is symptomatic of a short-sighted and dangerous ethnocentrism that has infected the nation. Pitifully few Americans can converse in a foreign tongue or read a foreign newspaper even where the language is one used by their parents or by themselves in childhood. Members of bilingual as well as monolingual groups in the United States are often surprised to learn that there are many nations where bilingual education is normal for all students and where the ability to speak more than one language well is a *sine qua non* for entry into the business, professional, and administrative elite of the society.

The most obvious corrective for the woeful situation in this country, of course, would be greatly increased foreign-language instruction for all children, starting at the elementary level and continuing through high school, and the most obvious choice of language in many regions would be Spanish. Today, the United States has the fourth largest Spanish-speaking population of any country in the western hemisphere. New York has the fifth largest Spanish-speaking population of any city. It is projected that by the 21st century two out of three inhabitants in the western hemisphere will be of Latin American extraction. More persons will speak Spanish than any other language of the Americas, including English. Spanish-language fluency in New York City and elsewhere has already become an advantage in employment opportunities. In all, a favorable environment is being created for the acquisition and maintenance of Spanish-speaking skills among members of the Spanish *and* Anglo communities, regardless of whether the Spanish language is taught in the schools.

The growing recognition of the importance of foreign-language acquisition is not inconsistent with the opinion of many Hispanic proponents of bilingual education, who believe that it should not be for their community alone, with the sole objective of assimilation into mainstream America, but should be for *all* children, English-speaking as well as Spanish-speaking, to help prepare them for the world of the future. Only when bilingual education becomes a desirable choice to English speakers, they add, will the movement be relieved of its stigma of being a compensatory program to help the disadvantaged and be protected from funding cutbacks and threats of extinction.

Final Thoughts

These pragmatic and broad historical and philosophical arguments, however, are not alone sufficient to justify the continuation of the bilingual education experiment as it is now conceived. Such a justification can only come from solid evidence that this new technique is succeeding—directly by improving the capacity of Hispanic children to learn *in English* and indirectly by stimulating parents and schools to give more serious attention to the educational needs of these youngsters. What is needed, now, is a determined effort by all concerned to improve bilingual education programs in the schools through more sympathetic administration and community support, more and better trained teachers, and a sustained, sophisticated, and well-financed research effort to find out where these programs are succeeding and where they are failing and why.

It goes without saying, therefore, that advocates of bilingual education should be wary of advancing rationales for it that go beyond its strictly educational purpose of helping children acquire the intellectual skills they will need to compete successfully in the American mainstream. Such arguments, surely, will simply exacerbate the considerable hostility that already exists toward bilingual education and heighten the resistance evident today among more affluent white Americans to any public expenditure aimed at improving the schooling of poor children of minority background. That trend, which has economic, racial, linguistic, and geographic dimensions, is already cause for deep concern, since its chief victims are children.

As for Hispanic children, their education is far too important a matter to be left to chance, vague hopes, rhetoric, or politics. All of us have an undeniable stake in their induction into the larger American society and their preparation to be effective, productive citizens. They are an inescapable part of the nation's future and therefore of all our futures.

A Foundation's Involvement in a Changing Society: Carnegie Corporation in South Africa

Foundations, existing as they do to promote the general welfare through charitable activities, and resting on an assumption of the possibility of betterment of the human condition, are by their very nature committed to a search for ways to use their resources to further nonviolent, constructive social change. How and where they go about this vary considerably and depend on such factors as the wishes of their creators, their charters and the judgment of their trustees and staffs.

Carnegie Corporation's long interest in South Africa, from 1927 to the present—a span of over half a century—reflects all of these considerations. Although the funds committed there have never been large because of restrictions on the proportion of its resources the foundation can spend outside the United States and competing claims in other areas, the interest has been continuous. There was, it is true, an interim of a few years when the hand of apartheid lay so heavily on the country it seemed that little could be accomplished. By 1975, however, the first glimmerings of a prospect for peaceful change, though faint and tentative, were beginning to appear, and it seemed conceivable that there might be new opportunities opening up for useful activity by the foundation. A decision, accordingly, was made by the trustees in that year to reinstate the program in South Africa, along the broadly educational lines mandated in the Corporation's charter.

In 1981, six years later, one can identify with a good deal more clarity and confidence certain positive forces for peaceful change that could only dimly be perceived in 1975. To mention these forces, of course, is not to claim that peaceful change toward a more just society is now a certainty. The chances of violence can never be ruled out where racial tensions and frustrations are involved, and both are at a dangerous level in South Africa today. It is simply to sugest that real and steady progress toward some new system that will satisfy the political, social and economic aspirations of all South Africans has become *possible* and will probably remain so for at least a short while to come. After that the outlook becomes very much more problematic.

Without question, the greatest force for change at the present time is the determination that has hardened among South Africa's twenty-one million African, Coloured and Indian citizens to gain their freedom from racial domination by the nation's four-and-a-half million whites, no matter what the cost. Pursuit of this goal has already involved some violence and there is evidence that more and more blacks, especially the young, have come to believe that change can be effected only through violent means. Nonetheless, peaceful change remains the goal of most blacks, and the moral force of such a course, when pursued by such numbers and with such passion, must surely be troubling the conscience of many whites.

Secondly, while the thesis that economic growth will *alone* solve South Africa's racial problems is hardly persuasive, the country's strong economy and prospects for continued economic growth do, if the will is there, offer a favorable environment for change. South Africa is a rich country with well-developed and strong agricultural, mining and industrial sectors. With an equitable and efficient use of its human and natural resources, it could provide a decent standard of living for all of its people, black as well as white. The claim, therefore, that the economic future of whites is dependent on the perpetuation of apartheid is simply not valid. Indeed, the full removal of present restraints on blacks, as producers and consumers, could stimulate a considerable amount of economic growth from which whites as well as blacks would benefit.

One can, in fact, already point to the rapidly growing importance of Africans, Coloureds and Indians in the economy, both as consumers, where they represent the principal growth potential in the market, and as skilled and semi-skilled workers. A concomitant of this development has been the rapid growth of black unions, to a point where they have become a substantial force in the country. It was the evidence that black trade unions were beginning to acquire political power that caused the government to decide not long ago to permit them to register, thereby offering them a new legitimacy and making it lawful for them to strike. Some black unions, however, have shown themselves reluctant to accept their new status, since registration gives the government extensive supervisory powers over them.

Thus far, blacks have used their growing economic power sparingly. Nevertheless, the power is there and will undoubtedly be used in the future to gain not only economic but also political concessions. As one looks at the demographic trends of the country, this becomes even more evident. The present ratio of blacks to whites, five to one, is expected to become eight to one by the end of the century. White South Africans will, therefore, have to choose between economic growth, with its built-in dynamic for social and political change, and artificial restrictions on growth to try to maintain the *status quo*. Given this choice, it seems likely that they will take their chances on the former. The rapid dismantling of job reservation, at least in the manufacturing and service sectors, and the recent announcement by the government that compulsory education will be introduced for all African children in certain areas in 1981 reveal a new recognition that increased participation of black workers in the labor force at a skilled level has become essential to further economic growth.

A third positive force for change would seem to be the considerable ferment that is taking place among white South Africans today in regard to the future racial disposition of the nation. Although the legislative framework of apartheid is still on the books and is still being generally implemented, there is now widespread recognition among the more educated and influential whites—Afrikaans as well as English-speaking—that separate development as an all-encompassing solution to the problem of racial relationships has failed. Admission of this failure is inherent in the far-reaching decision by the government to move away from the fiction that black South Africans, however many generations they have been there, are simply temporary sojourners in the cities. Indeed, beyond simply this official recognition of a *de facto* reality—the permanence of African urban residents—the new policy appears to be actively to encourage the growth of a stable black African middle class in the cities. Where this will lead is not yet clear, but it would seem that the purpose behind it is to offset the rapidly increasing disparity between the numbers of black Africans and whites by co-opting Coloureds, Indians and an urban African middle class into some form of closer association with whites. Meanwhile the black homelands, or national states, as they are now called, will serve as staging areas for large numbers of migrant and commuter workers for the white areas and as storage areas for those blacks who have little or nothing to contribute to the economy.

Thus, separate development, although still the official policy of the nation and still as onerous for most blacks as ever, has been breached in a seemingly significant way. Most importantly, the public admission of a reneging on the pure tenets of separate development has put into doubt the legitimacy of race as an absolute and inflexible organizational principle for the society, and this could have far-reaching long-term implications.

It is, of course, too early to tell what the consequences will be. The nascent urban black middle class could look only to its own interests—in effect be bought off—or it could gradually acquire considerable leverage in the society and use this as a potent force for significant change that will affect all blacks, those in the homelands as well as those in the urban areas. One can be hopeful that it will be the latter, although there can be no guarantee of it.

Additional evidence of the ferment stirring white South Africans is to be found in the widespread discussion of new constitutional arrangements through which

187

some measure of African, Indian and Coloured participation in the nation's political life can be accommodated. This discussion has led to replacement of the all-white upper chamber of Parliament, the Senate, with a new organ called the President's Council, composed of all races except Africans, who were offered membership in a separate advisory council but, not surprisingly, rejected it. The purpose of the President's Council is to serve as a forum for discussion of further constitutional changes and to be a body to make, from time to time, specific recommendations for such changes to the government. Although the Council has been boycotted by the opposition Progressive Federal Party and by many Coloured and Indian leaders because of its lack of African representation, to many white South Africans it seems a major step into an unknown future.

Still another area of active debate is the matter of a common South African nationality. Since none of the so-called independent national states, Transkei, Bophutatswana and Venda, has been recognized by any nation other than South Africa, serious passport difficulties have arisen when the "citizens" of these entities have wanted to travel abroad. There is much talk now of the establishment of a common South African nationality—which once again reveals the failure of separate development as a practical policy.

A fourth force for peaceful change is the continuing condemnation of South Africa's racial policies by Western nations. It can be argued that abhorrence of apartheid has been there for a long time with no appreciable effects, but that is a somewhat limited view. South African whites, both English- and Afrikaans-speaking, consider themselves to be part of the Western world, however much the Afrikaners, at least, also contend that they are as much part of Africa as Africans. Acceptance by a majority opinion in the Western community today, however, implies allegiance to principles of human conduct that are totally antithetical to officially mandated racial separation. Thus, the white South African cannot simultaneously practice racial discrimination and expect to be a member in good standing of the Western community. His dilemma, of course, is a feeling that, the more he abides by Western values in his treatment of the racial majority in his country, the more he will lose control of the nation to the people who he believes will have no regard for those very values once they gain power.

Despite this, most South African whites, uncomfortable in their group's isolated role of pariah of the world, have a deep psychological craving for acceptance in the West and yet understand intuitively that this will never be won until some measure of real racial justice comes to their country. It is, therefore, of the utmost importance to the achievement of peaceful change that the Western nations continue to make it clear to South Africa that such acceptance is absolutely dependent on evidence of real and continuous progress toward major reform.

These, then, are some of the more hopeful signs that peaceful progress toward a more equitable society is now at least a possibility in South Africa. Together they provide a sufficiently encouraging climate for a foundation such as Carnegie Corporation to be actively involved there on behalf of constructive social change.

The Corporation in South Africa

Since for many years Carnegie Corporation was the only American foundation to take a sustained interest in South Africa, it may be useful to review briefly the history of that involvement.

Prior to the Corporation's establishment in 1911, Andrew Carnegie, as part of his well-known effort to promote the development of free libraries throughout the English-speaking world, had made gifts out of his own pocket to several communities in South Africa for the construction of libraries. The first of these was at Vryheid in 1906, followed in 1907 by a similar gift to the town of Harrismith. In the following decade ten additional libraries, including one at Stellenbosch University, were given, either by Mr. Carnegie personally or by the Corporation.

In 1927 the president and the secretary of the Corporation, Frederick Keppel and James Bertram, made an extended visit to the then Union of South Africa to explore the feasibility of a systematic program of grants. The foundation's trustees had agreed to this exploration despite the fact that Mr. Carnegie's own intent with regard to South Africa in establishing a special fund for grants in "Canada and the British Colonies" was by no means clear. Nevertheless, evidently assuming that Mr. Carnegie, who had died in 1919, had meant by the term "colonies" areas of British settlement still linked to Britain as dominions, and recognizing the sovereignty of the Crown, the trustees concluded that South Africa qualified. Thus Dr. Keppel and Mr. Bertram, after visiting East and Central Africa, arrived in Johannesburg on August 5, 1927. Between then and their departure from Cape Town on September 2, they managed to get to all four provinces, each of the major cities, and a number of smaller places, and to visit a wide variety of educational and cultural institutions. They also held talks with numerous officials, including Prime Minister Hertzog and former Prime Minister Smuts, and with many private citizens. It was a visit that was to set the pattern for the Corporation's program in South Africa for many years to come.

In November 1927, following Dr. Keppel's report to the trustees, they approved his proposal that $500,000 be spent in East, Central and South Africa over the following years, a program that was subsequently extended to provide $1.5 million over more than twelve years. Grants were made in a variety of fields, including scientific research, public and academic library development, race relations, encouragement of adult education, the study of music and the arts, improvement of education for Africans, opportunities for technical education for Coloured and Indian students, and the support of visits to and from Africa by educational leaders. Most of the money was spent in South Africa, where grants were made on the recommendation of a specially constituted advisory committee of local citizens, known as the "South African Trustees." Travel grants to individuals were made on the advice of another local body, the "Visitors Grants Committee."

Perhaps the most important project of that pre-World War II period was the Carnegie Poor White Study. Addressed to the prevailing problem at that time of severe poverty among white South Africans, especially rural Afrikaners, and carried out over a four-year period from 1928 to 1932, this was one of the largest and most comprehensive multidisciplinary social science research efforts that had ever been undertaken, either in South Africa or elsewhere. The findings revealed the extent of the problem of poverty and helped the Afrikaner come to grips with it and to begin to devise solutions. For that reason the study has always been considered to have been of great importance in the subsequent revitalization of the Afrikaans-speaking community. The Poor White Study also played a role in the founding, with Carnegie support, of the National Bureau of Educational and Social Research within the Department of Education of South Africa. The Bureau in its early years made a number of valuable studies.

After the War, the South African grants program was continued, with special emphasis on the support of social and anthropological research at Rhodes University and the Universities of Natal and Cape Town. In the mid-1950s, however, institutional grants were phased out as the Corporation shifted its concern to emerging nations of tropical Africa such as Nigeria, Ghana, Sierra Leone and Kenya. Travel grants, however, were awarded to South African citizens until 1969 when a decision was made to bring the travel grant programs that the Corporation had operated for so long in Australia, New Zealand and South Africa all to a close.

In 1961 South Africa made its momentous decisions to become a republic and renounce its membership in the Commonwealth. These actions, however, did not disqualify it as a country in which the Corporation could make grants,* and in 1975 a special committee of the board, set up to review the future of what was then referred to as the Commonwealth program (now called the international program) recommended that the foundation's interest in South Africa be revived, but confined this time primarily to the needs of the African, Coloured and Indian communities.

Out of this mandate and under the leadership of the new director of the international program, David Hood, a wholly new program has developed related essentially to the changes that are beginning to take place in South African society. Thus, the new program, still broadly educational in its thrust,

---

*Because of the many changes taking place in the Commonwealth, the Corporation's charter was revised by the New York State Legislature on February 14, 1961, to make it possible for the foundation to continue to make grants forever thereafter in any country which on April 3, 1948, had been a British dominion or colony. South Africa, which had been a dominion as of that date, therefore continued to qualify.

is emphasizing three areas: intergroup relations, in accordance with the growing contact between blacks and whites in employment and elsewhere, career training for blacks to prepare them to assume increased responsibility in the nation's economic, social and political life and to participate more directly in the process of peaceful change, and, finally, action in the legal field, where it has become apparent that, despite a vast array of restrictive legislation and the absence of any constitutional protection for civil rights, there is a considerable amount that can be done through legal processes to improve the daily lives of blacks, and especially the black poor.

With regard to support for legal action, experience in the United States and elsewhere suggests that a key element in constructive, nonviolent social change is effective engagement of the conscience and talents of the legal profession. Evidence that the legal community in South Africa, or at least important elements of it, is now prepared to become socially involved has led the Corporation to participate in the establishment of two very important new enterprises, the Centre for Applied Legal Studies at Witwatersrand University in Johannesburg and the Legal Resource Centre, also in Johannesburg.

The Centre for Applied Legal Studies was created in 1978 to carry out public education in the field of civil rights and the law as it affects the welfare and rights of the black community, through teaching, research, publication, legal advice and litigation. Under the able and courageous leadership of Professor John Dugard and with the support of the University's administration, it has become a flourishing academic venture and is filling an important and clearly identifiable need on the South African scene. The broad sweep of its concerns includes such areas as labor law, restrictions on the movement of blacks (influx control), housing, administration of the Group Areas Act, censorship, citizenship and nationality, the protection of human rights, the security laws, prosecutions under the Riotous Assemblies Act, legal aid services, and consumer protection.

The importance of the Centre lies in the fact that in South Africa practicing members of the legal profession are inhibited from commenting publicly on legal matters by reason of their professional rules. Since the inhibition does not apply to academic lawyers, they are free—indeed, many would say, obligated—to perform this function. The scope, therefore, for such an institution as the Centre is large, and it has not hesitated to move vigorously into the previously inadequately explored fields of civil rights and the impact of the law on blacks, educating the public on these matters through providing information to the media and through a publication program.

Beyond these activities, the Centre contributed this past year to the formation of a new professional society in South Africa known as Lawyers for Human Rights. At an inaugural meeting held in Johannesburg and attended by some 200 judges, advocates, attorneys, academic lawyers and law students, a draft constitution for the new society was adopted. This read in part as follows: "The principal object of Lawyers for Human Rights shall be to uphold and strengthen in Southern Africa those human rights that are associated with the Rule of Law and the administration of law according to justice; in particular to assist in the maintenance of the highest standards of the administration of justice and in the furtherance and protection of the fundamental liberties of the individual and of groups."

The second new organization with which Carnegie Corporation has been deeply involved is supported also by the Ford and Field foundations, the Rockefeller Brothers Fund and by South African sources. This is the Legal Resources Centre (LRC), the first true public interest law firm in South Africa. Founded in 1978 and headed by Arthur Chaskalson, a leading Johannesburg advocate who gave up a substantial private practice to take on this responsibility, the LRC has quickly moved to a position of considerable importance in South African life. Its primary purposes are to provide free legal services to poor blacks, to develop test cases of wide significance to the black community, and to provide opportunities for law students of all races to gain practical experience in public interest law.

The LRC has taken on the responsibility of supervising the work of three law clinics run by students of the University of Witwatersrand. In addition, in 1979 it established its own clinic at Hoek Street close to the Johannesburg railroad station, where it is easily accessible to the several hundred thousand workers who pour into the city daily from Soweto. Staffed by employees of the LRC and by law students from the University of South Africa and the Rand Afrikaans University, the clinic now carries a load of over 200 cases per month and provides services to as many as 60 people a day.

Out of the mass of legal services being provided at Hoek Street and the other clinics, the staff of the LRC, consisting of two advocates, four attorneys and other workers, has identified key test cases that are representative of generalized forms of abuse or exploitation and in which a favorable decision would be widely beneficial. Dealing with such matters as the rise of bus fares, the hardships of influx control, abuse of prison labor rented out to white farms, the illegal discharge of domestic helpers without due notice, exploitation of night watchmen, the wrongful eviction of tenants from their homes, and widespread consumer fraud practiced against blacks, the cases on which the LRC has taken action have had far-reaching consequences.

The most notable of these cases is the Komani case, wherein a black worker living legally in Guguletu Township outside Cape Town brought suit, with the help of the LRC, in the Appellate Division of the Supreme Court, the highest court in South Africa, to overturn a ruling of a lower court that effectively barred his wife from living with him. Under Section 10 of the Black Urban Areas Act, an African can legally reside in an urban area only if he was born there and has lived there continuously ever since, or if he has worked in a city continuously for the same employer for ten years, or if he has worked continuously for one or more employers for fifteen years. Wives and children of such workers, however, prior to the Komani case, did not automatically qualify for urban residence. For them to so qualify their husband or father had to be the lessee of a house. Otherwise they were required by regulation to obtain a so-called lodger's permit. In practice these permits were extremely hard to get, with the result that many families were effectively separated—with all the adverse social consequences one might expect. In the Komani case the Appellate Division overturned a lower court ruling and declared the regulation requiring the lodger's permit *ultra vires,* a decision which opens the door to the reuniting of many thousands of black families in urban areas and enables many other thousands of Africans living illegally in urban areas to regularize their position. The decision, of course, does not affect migrant workers, who continue to be barred from having their families with them.

While the Komani case is perhaps the most dramatic of those taken on by the LRC, other cases have had equally significant effects in improving the lives of blacks. In one of these, the LRC succeeded in having a proposed increase in bus fares postponed for over 13 months during which the government increased its subsidies to the bus company. Eventually the transport authority granted permission to the bus company to charge fares which were approximately 30 percent lower than the fares it had intended charging 13 months previously. The result was a saving to the black commuters of Soweto and Alexandra Township of about $8 million and a raising anew of the entire question of government policy in regard to urban transportation for blacks.

Needless to say, pressure on the LRC to take on additional cases is heavy, so great are the legal needs of the black populace. There is also a real need for additional legal resource centers in other major cities such as Cape Town, Durban and Port Elizabeth.

It is heartening that a new sense of social commitment is arising in the South African legal profession, as evidenced by the blessing given to the LRC by the Transvaal Law Society and the Johannesburg Bar Council and by the devotion of their talents to the Centre by lawyers of the standing of Arthur Chaskalson and his colleagues. One hopes that the movement will grow and that the financial support for the LRC and similar enterprises from South African sources which is now beginning will continue to expand.

The record of Carnegie Corporation's involvement in South Africa over a 53-year span shows that 115 grants, totaling more than $2.5 million, were made to institutions and organizations in that country, and that travel grants were awarded to 324 South African citizens, to enable them to visit the United States, and to 41 Americans for visits to South Africa, at a further cost of about $1 million. Total expenditure, therefore, has amounted to approximately 3.5 million.

Beyond simply the value of the funds granted, however, there is evidence that the nature of the Corporation—a nonpolitical, independent private organization, with no vested interests and answerable to no special constituency nor government (except of course meeting the requirements of the law)—has been of very great importance in strengthening its impact. This has been of special significance in South Africa, a country where, as a general matter, activity by private voluntary organizations has never been particularly encouraged by public authority.

It is also important that over the years, through its travel awards to individuals, its grants to universities and other cultural institutions, and its support of the Carnegie Poor White Study, Corporation funds have benefited all racial groups. When the foundation first became involved in South Africa, only 12 years after the Act of Union, it was a small, relatively undeveloped, isolated nation, far removed from the main currents of European and North American intellectual activity. It was only natural, therefore, that the major object of the Corporation's attention at that time should be institutions that primarily served the needs of the white community, both English-and Afrikaans-speaking. White South Africa has, however, experienced tremendous development in the half century since then, and it should be taken amiss by no one and surprise no one that the foundation chooses now to concentrate on the needs of black South Africans. Indeed, its earlier attention to white needs perhaps now places it in a unique position to turn its attention exclusively to the needs of blacks.

Some Questions

The Corporation's involvement in South Africa has not been without its critics, especially in recent years. There are those in our country and in Africa, including South Africa, who believe with sincerity and fervor that *any* involvement in South Africa by an American organization, whatever its nature, is morally wrong. Those who hold this view claim that such involvement, since it must take place within the established framework of apartheid, implicitly lends legitimacy and respectability to that doctrine.

While their position must be respected, one can also be skeptical about the validity of this kind of sweeping moral judgment. There may be some forms of involvement which directly support apartheid, and they should, of course, be scrupulously avoided. Other forms may support apartheid indirectly, but they may, nevertheless, under certain conditions be justifiable because of compensating benefits that they bring, or may in the future bring, to black South Africans. Still other forms are directly antithetical to the perpetuation of apartheid. In short, opinions can and do differ about the net impact of any particular form of involvement, but no one can deny that, in their contacts with South Africa, American voluntary organizations, in the aggregate, offer an important means of communicating to a wide variety of South African citizens our strong attachment to a set of democratic values that, most importantly, includes a belief in racial equality. Over the long run, the communication of that message could be most beneficial.

This is not to suggest that selective ostracism of South Africa in ways that do not injure its black citizens is wrong or cannot be helpful. Such an option must always be kept open. The desegregation of some forms of sport in the Republic is unquestionably a result of the ban placed on South African participation in international competition. The point is that a blanket ostracizing of South Africa, while it may be advocated with the best of intentions, necessitates turning one's back on many people inside the country, both black and white, who desperately need outside moral support, encouragement and actual assistance. In taking such an extreme step one is, therefore, opting for a hypothetical future effect while forfeiting the chance to confer immediate benefit. The Corporation, therefore, has chosen to pursue an active program in South Africa, conferring such benefits there as it can.

Still, there is the question of why a foundation should decide to spend any of its funds at all in South Africa when it could just as well spend them in other countries that are apparently more deserving, since they do not practice systematic racial discrimination and exploitation as a matter of official policy. The answer, in part, lies in the very fact that South Africa does have these faults and for that reason has been judged to be a threat to world peace. How real this threat is at the present time is hard to say, but there can be little doubt that if racial tension continues to mount there and results in violence on a major scale, the threat to world peace the situation will then present, because of the possible intervention of external forces, will be real enough.

Furthermore, the fact that South Africa is a country where black people, who form a large majority of the population, are unable by law to participate, as does the white minority, in the major decisions that affect their lives makes it a place that is bound to be of special concern to all multiracial nations and particularly to the United States. Whether the interracial conflict that may one day erupt in South Africa as a result of this denial of rights could arouse strong enough feelings here to precipitate racial violence in our cities is an open question. But the worrisome possibility is there and is cause for us to have an immediate and deep interest in rapid movement in South Africa, with a minimum of racial violence, toward a more just society.

At bottom, therefore, the case for Carnegie Corporation being actively engaged in South Africa rests on the proposition that peaceful, constructive social change in that country is a matter of the highest urgency, and the foundation, through its grants program, is in a position to make at least a modest contribution to that cause. In the process, it can also give support and encouragement to deserving individuals caught in the entangling web of circumstances that so limits the human potential and diminishes the humanity of people of all racial groups in South Africa.

Trying to affect social change in another country, especially one as complex as South Africa, is, nonetheless, something that must be approached with considerable sensitivity, a great deal of humility and enough skepticism about the relevance of American experience to know that this country cannot be held up as an unquestioned model for South Africa, however useful certain pieces of our experience may be. Above all else, any American organization planning to work in South Africa has an obligation to become as thoroughly informed about the country as it possibly can, and this Carnegie Corporation, through periodic visits of its officers there, through seeking the counsel of well-qualified South Africans of all races and varying outlooks, and through other means, has always endeavored to do.

Some Cautions

It remains, of course, entirely possible that the impediments to peaceful change in South Africa will prove to be so formidable that little of a constructive nature can be accomplished. The impediments are there for all to see.

First, there is the almost total lack of communication today between whites and blacks in regard both to the ultimate shape of a new South African society and even the beginnings of a process by which to get there. There is, as we have seen, considerable ferment in the white community on the subject of change, and a number of proposed new constitutional arrangements are being widely debated. Blacks, however, have their own agenda for the future and consider what is being discussed by whites to be largely irrelevant. These two streams of thought, therefore, are likely to pass each other without ever making contact. This failure of communication would seem to pose great dangers, because at some point of crisis in the future, when negotiations between the two sides becomes obligatory, there will have been no preparation for it. Precious years of starting to sort out the issues and reach interim agreement on specific points will have been lost.

A second obvious barrier to peaceful change would seem to be the determination of a hard core of whites to maintain the *status quo* of white supremacy at any cost. How large this group is is difficult to say, but it is certainly sizable. It includes many working-class people, who naturally are fearful of black competition for jobs, much of the rural farm population, inhabitants of smaller towns and villages, and a good part of the police and the civil service. This group apparently feels betrayed by even the limited degree of change the present leadership has instituted, and it could at any time throw its support to the government's right-wing opposition.

For the 60 percent of whites who are of Afrikaner heritage, however, the issue is not simply the preservation of white supremacy in a growing sea of black disaffection. To them it is no less than the survival of the Afrikaner *volk* as a separate "nation" on the African continent. This purpose, being they believe, ordained by God, is mystical and spiritual in its nature and cannot be easily abandoned. They view their long history in Africa as a continuous struggle against the twin dangers of black aggression and British imperialism. The problem for the Afrikaner, therefore, is one of somehow reconciling two seemingly irreconcilable objectives—making the major social and political changes that will satisfy black aspirations, and which he knows in his heart must come, while at the same time being true to his mission to protect the social, cultural and political integrity of the Afrikaner nation.

Third, one must point to the sheer difficulty of dismantling apartheid once a decision to embark irrevocably on such a course has been made. Racial discrimination, of course, goes back three hundred years in South Africa as a principal feature of its way of life, but over the past three decades of National Party rule, this has been changed from a flexible, permeable, qualified practice, loosely enforced by a combination of statute and custom, to a rigid, inflexible, and absolutist official state doctrine reaching into every corner of the nation's life, enforced by literally thousands of statutes and regulations and administered by a large civil service and police force recruited and trained specifically to make apartheid work and believing firmly in the rightness of that mission.

Finally, beyond simply dismantling the intricate and all-embracing machinery of official apartheid, there is the matter of undoing the *effects*—both physical and human—of its 32 years of existence. On the physical side, the attempt to separate the several racial groups and—within the African population—tribal groups from each other spatially has resulted in the establishment of nine separate homelands, three of which are now "independent" and one moving toward independence, the construction outside the cities of vast African townships, such as Soweto, near Johannesburg, with its better than a million residents, and the forced removal of two million African, Indian and Coloured people from districts designated solely for white occupancy to new settlement areas often in remote, bleak places utterly lacking in amenities of any kind and providing few opportunities for gainful employment. All of this has necessitated the building up of an enormous infrastructure of housing, roads, transport, schools, churches, beer halls, and so on that has involved a great deal of effort and the expenditure of considerable sums of money. Whatever lies in South Africa's future, it will surely be living with the divisive physical infrastructure of apartheid for a very long time to come.

Undoing its human effects will also be troublesome. To the great majority of black South Africans, a fundamental, nonnegotiable part of any acceptable future dispensation is that there is a single South African nation, with a common citizenship for all its people. This obviously implies, at the least, some form of reincorporation of the three independent homelands into the nation—which will deprive their leaders and officials of a good deal of the power and privilege they now enjoy. After some years of benefiting from the perquisites of independence, are they likely to be willing to give all this up without a struggle?

There is, furthermore, the question of the millions of people who, having suffered the trauma of relocation under apartheid, have nonetheless tried to make the best they can of their new situation by building up new homes and new lives for themselves. Will these people, or some of them, elect to return to their former homes, and if they do, can the costs of the large-scale resettlement program involved be met? This could be a formidable problem.

Lastly, there is the psychological dimension of apartheid, both for blacks and whites, the full import of which can perhaps only be a matter for conjecture. Who can know what the effect on the human mind may be of three decades of having drummed into it day after day, year after year, the alleged moral rightness of racial separation? How deeply has that message penetrated and with what degree of permanence? Can people who have been subjected to such an assault on their psyches over such a long period of time, with all the authority of the state and, in the case of the Afrikaner, of the church, behind it, adopt a new set of values in which color becomes irrelevant? Will the people of South Africa, whether black or white, ever be able to think nonracially, or is the bitter legacy of apartheid to be a society permanently fractured along racial lines, where intergroup rivalry, suspicion and hostility are endemic and oppression of one racial group by another a constant danger? One hopes not, but the deeply entrenched racial attitudes fostered by years of apartheid will certainly be the most difficult barrier, and perhaps even an insurmountable one, to peaceful change. We have seen all too clearly here in the United States, with all our advantages, just how difficult it is to eradicate racist thinking.

At this point the impediments to peaceful change in South Africa are not sufficient to make the Corporation feel that its involvement there is a waste of effort and funds; indeed, the outlook is just the opposite. Nonetheless, there remains the grim possibility that increased violence and a consequent increase of repression might create a climate that would vitiate any possibility of constructive future action by a voluntary organization such as this foundation. One hopes otherwise, but the possibility cannot be dismissed.

Final Thoughts

As one becomes better informed about South Africa, one is more and more struck with how much its current problems are a product of its special history and how essential it is to know something about that history. Without this knowledge it is impossible even to begin to understand the character of the two great nationalist movements—African and Afrikaner—that are now locked in almost total confrontation. Even with such a background, it is presumptuous for outsiders to try to prescribe precisely what courses South Africa should follow in trying to solve its racial problems. They should not, of course, refrain from expressing a concern about the probable consequences of the racial injustice that now afflicts the country nor leave unspoken their desire to see the process of change that has now begun to gather strength and become much more meaningful, but this is probably as specific as they can be about the future. Only South Africans themselves—South Africans of all races—can ultimately

198

determine what new political arrangements will be necessary to allow the nation's varied racial groups to live in harmony and with justice for all.

Although it is possible to be cautiously hopeful about the future in South Africa, no one can say just how a new order will come into being in that unhappy land or how long it will take. One can only predict that, whatever the difficulty or length of the process, change surely will come. There may, in the event, not be much that outsiders can do to affect what happens, but this can be no excuse for indifference. Whatever the realistic chances that our help will be constructive, it is of the utmost importance that we make the effort to provide it, for South Africa, in its explosive social and cultural tensions, is a microcosm of the world's tensions. What eventuates there can affect not only the lives of South Africans themselves, about which we can properly be concerned, but also the future of a racially and culturally diverse world—a world in which all of us and our children will be living.

Carnegie Corporation in a Changing Society 1961–1981

The modern foundation is one of the few nongovernmental organizations in this country that addresses broad social issues. Its mission in the simplest terms is to better the world, not by assuming the conventional tasks of charity, as worthy and necessary as they are, but by using private wealth constructively and imaginatively in the search for basic solutions to human problems.

The charter mandates of large, general purpose foundations are as flexible as possible. The Rockefeller Foundation was endowed "to promote the well-being of mankind throughout the world," the Ford Foundation "to advance the general welfare." Carnegie Corporation was founded by Andrew Carnegie "for the advancement and diffusion of knowledge and understanding" among the people of the United States and the Commonwealth. This is the means by which he chose to better the world, and in his letter of gift to the trustees, dated November 10, 1911, he offered as examples of good works the aid of technical schools, institutions of higher learning, libraries, scientific research, hero funds, useful publication, "and other such agencies and means as shall from time to time be found appropriate."

Mr. Carnegie's examples reflect his own personal style of philanthropy. In the early 1900s he gave $43 million to set up 2,509 libraries in the English-speaking world. He was also deeply interested in higher education, creating the Carnegie Institute of Technology and The Carnegie Foundation for the Advancement of Teaching and also establishing the Carnegie Institution in Washington, D.C., to support scientific research, to cite only a few of the endeavors he underwrote to carry out his purposes.

Not surprisingly, the Corporation from its earliest days has been known as an educational foundation and, historically, most of its grants have gone to institutions of higher learning for activities aimed at finding a cure for one of the worst problems of mankind: ignorance.

Wise in the ways of giving, Mr. Carnegie counseled his trustees, in the simplified spelling he liked, that "conditions upon the erth inevitably change; hence, no wise man will bind Trustees forever to certain paths, causes or institutions. I disclaim any intention of doing so. On the contrary I giv my trustees full authority to change policy or causes hitherto aided, from time to time, when this, in their opinion, has become necessary or desirable. They shall best conform to my wishes by using their judgment."

Seventy years later, with the advantage of hindsight, it is interesting to see in what manner the foundation has tried to carry out Mr. Carnegie's will. The 1961 annual report contained a review of the first 50 years of the Corporation's programs. The following pages bring this review up to date, focusing particularly on grants to promote equal rights and opportunities. Our aim in looking back is not only to point to the Corporation's record of activity in this area during a period of extraordinary change in American life, but to reveal something of grant-making strategies and the way in which the foundation's interests have responded to shifting currents.

THE PAST TWENTY YEARS

During the years 1961–81, the Corporation developed a major commitment to the furtherance of social justice in our national life—to the right of every human being to enjoy equal opportunity and equal treatment before the law. Of the roughly $270 million the foundation has appropriated in grants during this period, an ever increasing share has gone for projects aimed at assuring the rights and opportunities of those less well served in the society—minority-group members, women, and children—especially children, because they are the least able to protect themselves and because they represent our future.

Concern for social justice was not lacking in the earlier years, as evidenced by the foundation's initiation and support of Gunnar Myrdal's pioneering study of race relations in the United States in the 1940s, entitled *An American Dilemma*. But other matters, by and large, commanded the foundation's attention between the Second World War and the early 1960s. In the decade prior to 1965, the grants program was concerned more with educational excellence—with the raising of educational standards and the identification and nurturing of the most gifted student. If the emphasis was on the opportunity, it was on individual opportunity, mainly the opportunity to attend college.

In the early 1960s, however, the staff and trustees became painfully aware of the urgent problems of race, poverty, and inequality that were besetting the nation. Public attention was riveted on a seeming paradox: the U.S. economy had never been stronger and per capita income had reached a record high, and yet more than 30 million people were living in dire straits—unemployed, on welfare, or working for less than the minimum wage. Studies pointed to a relationship between poverty, racial discrimination, and lack of educational opportunity. Children who were not doing well in school were more likely to have parents with low incomes and little education, and a disproportionate share of them were black or Hispanic or Native American.

Twenty years earlier, Gunnar Myrdal's study had pointed out the gigantic flaw in the fabric of American democracy—the stark contradiction between our belief in freedom, equality, and justice and the actuality of society's treatment of the Negro—but little heed was paid to the implicit warning in his analysis until black protest and the civil rights movement forced virtually every institution in American society, including Carnegie Corporation, to examine its own attitudes and actions toward this historically oppressed people. The year 1964 began the first of many comprehensive measures by the U.S. Congress, the Executive, and the Supreme Court to try to close the gap between principles and reality. Much of this new legislation was directed toward increasing education's role in promoting equal opportunity for the poor. The 1964 Civil Rights Act, among other measures, forbade federal funds to school districts not in compliance with desegregation guidelines. In 1965 President Johnson signed into law the Elementary and Secondary Education Act (ESEA), the first major federal intervention in public education to aid low-achieving, low-income children, appropriating in its first year about $1 billion to the schools for the development of compensatory education programs.

Between 1963 and 1967, the Corporation responded by appropriating roughly $9 million, or 19 percent, of its grant funds for programs directly related to disadvantaged minorities, largely to broaden the access of blacks to higher education and to strengthen predominately black colleges, a thrust that was in line with the foundation's traditional emphasis on higher education.

Then, in mid-1967, Alan Pifer, who had been acting president since 1965, became president, and the Corporation began a review of its entire grants program in relation to the persistence of poverty in our national life. Over three summers there had been rioting in the inner cities, associated in 1968 with the assassination of Martin Luther King, Jr., but also revealing deep discontent in black communities over the failure of the society to improve substantially the lot of the black poor. The violence, in turn, fueled a backlash among impatient lawmakers and the public against the allocation of more federal funds for social programs, aided, of course, by the drain on the federal treasury by the Vietnam War.

It seemed to the staff that, in view of the slowdown of federal leadership for social change, the Corporation as a private organization had a constructive role to play in keeping alive the idealism that had so galvanized the nation to action a few years before. The trustees and staff agreed that the promotion of equal educational opportunity and rights should henceforth cut across all of its grants programs. In the 1970s, this commitment to a more equitable society broadened to include equal opportunity and rights for women, which grew naturally out of an earlier program involving the continuing education of women.

Over the past 20 years, and particularly 15, the Corporation's programs* have had four principal objectives: first, prevention of educational disadvantage; second, increased access to legal representation; third, improved performance of the public schools and fourth, broadened opportunities for higher education. Strategies for achieving these objectives have included direct support of the formal education system as well as support of model and experimental programs, policy studies, social science research, leadership training, central services to educational institutions, minority-run organizations, monitoring and advocacy, and litigation. A number of these strategies are described below.

Preventing Educational Disadvantage

The nation's attention to poverty and its relationship to education under the Kennedy and Johnson administrations coincided with a new wave of research on the learning process, results of which offered new hope of ameliorating learning problems in young children before they became permanently handicapping.

Psychologists were amassing evidence in support of their hypothesis that intellectual and sensory stimulation of an infant or young child was critical to the development of language and problem-solving skills so necessary to success in school. Since there was plenty of evidence that poor children generally arrived in the first grade lagging behind middle-class children in these skills, the question was whether children with a high risk of academic failure could benefit from early education programs, givng them a "head start" so they could take full advantage of the curriculum once they entered school. The answer seemed to be yes, although in the early 1960s there was little solid information on whether intervention strategies would actually produce long-term educational gains for poor children. (Indeed, Project Head Start was mounted in the mid-1960s without much more to go on than theories and experimental data.)

Early childhood education. In early 1965, in part under the impact of expanding federal support for education, the Corporation staff saw an opportunity to help shape the direction of early childhood education, in which it had already made some grants, and the decision was made to make it a principal field of activity. By 1967, emphasis was mainly on helping disadvantaged children overcome the environmental obstacles to learning. Major goals of the program, as they evolved, were to encourage the production of sound scientific information about early learning, to promote use of this information in the creation of educational curricula, and to achieve a better understanding of the essential, most widely replicable elements of effective preschool programs. Altogether, the Corporation appropriated more than $18 million for these purposes and also for

---

*Approximately 7½ percent of the Corporation's grant funds each year are spent within the international program, which is not addressed in this report.

projects concerned with other aspects of child development, making it the leading foundation in the field of early childhood.

The decision to focus on cognitive development in preschool children had its roots in an earlier program, namely the nature of learning and cognitive processes generally and the application of research findings to education. For decades the fields of education and psychology had proceeded along separate tracks, with education drawing little or no vitality from the new knowledge that was being generated on human behavior and cognition. Corporation grants were made in part to help bridge the two fields. By the late 1950s, following the launching of Sputnik by the Russians, the climate for educational research had improved markedly, and the field began attracting the attention of high-calibre social scientists who brought their expertise to bear on the educational process and who, in their search for the origin of cognitive skills, moved to earlier and earlier stages of development and eventually to the newborn.

Corporation grants helped underwrite the theoretical and experimental research of such psychologists as Jerome Bruner, Jerome Kagan, William Kessen, Katherine Nelson, and others, each of whom contributed immeasurably to our appreciation of the learning capabilities of infants and preschool children and of the critical role of language development during the first few years of life.

From such work came additional research and experimentation, some of it supported by the Corporation, that concentrated on meeting the intellectual needs of disadvantaged preschool children. The Corporation began supporting a variety of experimental intervention strategies aimed at encouraging low-income children's own natural curiosity for learning and helping them acquire basic cognitive skills.

One experiment that has produced exciting results is the Mother-Child Home Program (MCHP) of the Verbal Interaction Project (VIP) based in Long Island and directed by psychologist Phyllis Levenstein. MCHP is a parent education program in which a trained "toy demonstrator" brings books and toys into the homes of low-income, mainly welfare families with two- and three-year-old children and unobtrusively models ways in which parents can use the material to stimulate verbal expression and the understanding of simple concepts by their children. Follow-up studies of the children in school show that they consistently outperform comparison groups on achievement tests. While the improvements do not appear to be dramatic, they are enough to make the difference between keeping up with their peers or falling behind.

Explanation of VIP's success seems to lie in the "parent-child network" engendered by the program—the positive reinforcement that parents and children give one another in play sessions, in which both are motivated to continue their verbal interaction and play long after outside assistance ends. MCHP has been adopted in at least 80 different locations around the country under the guidance of VIP's own demonstration center. Because it is relatively inexpensive and does not require long intensive training of personnel, MCHP appears to have potential for wider replication. An unexpected dividend of the program is that siblings not in the program have indirectly benefited from it and that many program mothers have become toy demonstrators themselves or have been motivated to continue their education.

An important issue which Carnegie-supported studies have explored is whether one kind of high-quality preschool curriculum produces better outcomes than another. Three different preschool programs were tested on low-income children and compared by the High/Scope Educational Research Foundation in Ypsilanti, Michigan, led by psychologist David Weikart. One was a highly structured program based on drill and repetition developed with partial Corporation support by Carl Bereiter and Siegfried Engelmann; another was a flexible program concentrating on social and emotional development; and a third was the cognitively oriented curriculum developed by Weikart and his colleagues that allows children to progress through a sequence of steps at their own pace. Contrary to expectations, all three curricula produced equally significant educational gains for children. By the end of the second grade, in fact, all but 20 percent of the project children were in the grade where they belonged.

Since 1962, Weikart and his colleagues have been conducting another study in cooperation with the Ypsilanti public school system, called the Perry Preschool Project. This study is testing the effects, over 25 years or more, of one and two years of High/Scope's cognitive curriculum on four successive cohorts of preschool children, many of them from welfare families. Possibly the longest-running and most scientific study of preschool effects, it has produced strong evidence that good preschool pays off, not only for children in their ability and motivation to "extract" a better education from the public school system and live a more rewarding life, but in savings to schools and to society in more productive citizens.

The Perry Preschool Project has served to mitigate the negative impact of the U.S. Office of Education study in 1969 of Project Head Start, which, in showing that children made only marginal gains in I.Q., created the public perception that early intervention was ineffective. Although the I.Q.s of the Perry Preschool children declined by the end of the third grade (after having risen during the program), achievement levels remained significantly higher than those of the control children, and they were less apt to have the behavioral problems associated with academic failure.

Both the curriculum demonstration program and the Perry Preschool Project suggest, according to Weikart, that any early education program that incorporates certain basic elements, such as parent involvement, qualified teachers, a proven curriculum, and just plain caring, will produce comparable long-term effects, whether or not the I.Q. gains of the children are sustained.

These and other projects aided by the Corporation have contributed valuable information on ways in which children can be helped to acquire the desired intellectual attributes for academic success, not only in experimental situations, but within the home and in regular center- and school-based programs. While there is little indication to date that federal funds will be available to support preschool education on a larger scale, studies by High/Scope staff suggest that public support for preschool through the states may grow in the years ahead.

Sesame Street. As early as 1966 Corporation staff members realized that providing quality early education for millions of children was not going to be a national priority for some time to come and they began to seek alternative means of educational delivery. What had not escaped notice was the mesmerizing effect of television on youngsters. Whatever their home situation, preschoolers were watching the "boob tube" a good 30 hours a week and learning to read numbers, letters, words, and sentences from the commercials, although not in a logical way. With this in mind, the Corporation commissioned a study of the possibility of producing and financing programs of outstanding quality which children would want to watch regularly and which would teach them basic cognitive skills.

The study was carried out by Joan Ganz Cooney, then a producer of public affairs programs for National Educational Television (NET). Based on her report, the Corporation, along with the Ford Foundation and the U.S. Office of Education, launched the production company, Children's Television Workshop (CTW), as a semi-autonomous unit within NET, and in the fall of 1969 *Sesame Street* was born. Within the first two months of broadcast more than six million children were watching the show. Today, *Sesame Street* is distributed in 50 different countries and territories. In the United States it is regularly watched by more than nine million preschoolers, and the production company that spawned it has become largely self-supporting from the educational books and toys and other projects spun off the program.

This fast-paced show featuring Muppets and human actors has demonstrated as no other children's television program that superior entertainment can be widely popular and also help children learn. Not only is it a model of excellence in programming that commercial networks must reckon with, but it has succeeded in its own terms: teaching preschoolers such skills as recognizing, naming and matching letters; recognizing and naming forms, shapes and numbers; and doing simple additions and subtractions. An evaluation by the Educational Testing Service has shown that "high-viewing" children from disadvantaged families make somewhat greater educational gains than those from advantaged families, and they surpass at post-test time advantaged children who watch little or none of the show.

The Corporation gave more than $3 million for the development of *Sesame Street* between the years 1966 and 1971.

Carnegie Council on Children. As more women with young children entered the labor force in the late 1960s and early 1970s, as the women's movement questioned the rigid role divisions between the sexes, as more families broke up and there were more single mothers, and as there evolved more variations in family life styles, many Americans became concerned about the impact of these changes on children.

The Corporation staff, as a consequence, began financing a number of studies that looked into these issues and in particular at American society's role and responsibility in children's education and care. In 1972, it established an independent study group, the Carnegie Council on Children, to draw together the facts about the status of children and to formulate recommendations for ways of meeting their developmental needs today and in the future.

Headed by psychologist Kenneth Keniston, with a membership of educators, social scientists, lawyers, and a pediatrician (most of them parents), the Council was first asked to focus on American children in their years of most rapid physical, psychological, and social growth—from conception to age nine. As the members went about their work, however, they saw that it would be impossible to deal with the subject of children without looking at families, and the reason was obvious: despite family fragmentation, 98 percent of all children were still being raised by one or both parents; hence, families would remain the critical factor determining children's fate.

In 1977, the Council issued its principal report, *All Our Children: The American Family Under Pressure*, a title that reflected the study group's dual focus. The report documented in graphic terms the damage done to families by the lag between traditional assumptions about family self-sufficiency and the reality that families, especially poor families, need outside help and yet too often the help, when it comes, does as much harm as good. The Council found that of all the "insults and injuries families face, none was worse than that of financial deprivation caused by the unfair distribution of economic rewards in society." It said, among other things, that it was not reasonable to expect that schooling alone could create equality of opportunity when equality did not exist in the world of jobs, of social relations, or of politics. Economic opportunity would have to follow educational opportunity if millions of American children were to grow up having any sense of a decent future. The Council made specific recommendations for the reform of private and public policies and services to make them more supportive of families and children. Beyond this it recommended a full-employment strategy, supplemented by a system of income supports, that would yield almost all American families with children a minimum of at least half the current median income for all families.

All told, the Council produced five reports before it disbanded, in the process causing a great deal of stir about its conclusions. While its recommendations may well be more far-reaching than the American people as a whole will ever be willing to accept, there is no question that the Council raised public awareness of the impact of larger social forces on children's lives, and it made a persuasive case for the collective responsibility of citizens toward all children if their optimal growth and development was to be assured.

Increasing Access to Legal Representation

Few events in American life so dramatically altered schools as did the 1954 Supreme Court decision in *Brown vs. Board of Education,* which struck down the doctrine of "separate but equal" and opened the way for desegregation of the schools. The action provoked years of struggle in the mind and soul of the South, served to raise black aspirations everywhere, and led to attacks on *de facto* school segregation in the North. During the period of 1964–79, additional court decisions and landmark legislation established important educational rights and entitlements to services for black, Hispanic, poor, handicapped, and female students. Clearly, the legal system and the courts, if a crude instrument, had become a major force for change in American education.

Although in the early 1960s the Corporation had occasionally made law-related grants to advance knowledge and understanding of a particular field or issue, it had not looked to the legal system to achieve educational or civil rights purposes. As the decade advanced, however, the Corporaton staff began turning its attention more systematically to legal representation and access to the law. Since then, grants for all law-related projects have totaled approximately $17 million.

Training black lawyers. In the South, where the law had historically denied justice to black people and was regarded by them with profound suspicion, there was a critical shortage of black lawyers—only 1 for each 37,000 black persons—and virtually no legal counsel for them on civil rights cases. This lack of representation meant not only that many of the newly won legal rights existed only on paper, but that southern blacks were not being prepared for the political leadership that was traditionally drawn from the legal profession.

One problem was that southern state law schools had only recently opened their doors to blacks, and they lacked either the resources or the determination to offer scholarship funds and tutorial programs to complement academic training—measures necessary to attract and hold black law students. Once blacks left the region for law school, they were unlikely to return to the South to practice, and thus the shortage of black lawyers persisted. The Corporation over a ten-year period gave more than $3.4 million to the Earl Warren Legal Training Program, the educational affiliate of the NAACP Legal Defense and Educational Fund (Inc. Fund) and to the Law Students Civil Rights Research Council (LSCRRC) toward a multi-foundation and corporation-supported effort to recruit and retain black law students in 17 southern state law schools and help them begin a civil rights practice in the South. Eventually, it was hoped, some of these lawyers would sharpen their leadership skills and work for the improvement of life for southern blacks generally.

Evaluation of the program revealed that, between 1969 and 1974, the number of blacks graduating from these law schools rose from 9 to 287, 183 of them assisted by the Earl Warren Training Program. Seven-year statistics showed that a high proportion of Earl Warren graduates were passing southern state bar examinations and staying in those states to practice. Indeed, by 1974, 177 Earl Warren graduates had become members of state bars in the South. Follow-up studies have not been carried out, but informal evidence suggests that a majority of these lawyers are still practicing in the South and a number have gone on to elective and appointive office.

The program addressed all aspects of the training and development of black lawyers and is a good example of what a well focused, coordinated effort can achieve. The Corporation subsequently built on this experience in its support, to a lesser degree, of a legal internship program within the Native American Rights Fund.

Use of the courts. In the late 1960s, the Nixon administration reversed the longtime policies of the U.S. Justice Department's Civil Rights Division and ordered it to cease supporting individual minority students and parents who were suing school boards and other state and local government agencies to ensure compliance with court orders to desegregate. This shift in Executive branch policy seemed to those representing minority interests to threaten more than a decade of progress toward educational equity through court action. Since it was clear that such activities could be effective in creating public enlightenment on an issue as well as in bringing about legal reform, the responsibility fell upon private organizations such as the NAACP and the Inc. Fund to enter the vacuum.

In the early 1970s, partly as a consequence of the stance by the federal government, the Corporation trustees approved a new program strategy—one that would support direct use of the legal system, including litigation, to promote equal opportunity in education. Prior grants to organizations working in the field of minority rights had gone for public and community education programs. Now the foundation would consider funding multi-disciplinary research and analysis, mobilization of expert witnesses, monitoring of governmental action, community fact-gathering, and other activities preparatory to litigation.

Recognition of the important role of the courts in social change underlay the trustees' decision. As a memorandum at the time expressed it, "It is clear that Americans have come to expect the courts to serve as a major institution by which conflicts are resolved, because it is a form of change based on tradition, respect for differing points of view, and constitutional principles." It was recognized, too, that in an adversary system of justice it was often the imbalance in legal representation and the lack of access to legal support that determined the outcome of cases involving the disadvantaged. The Corporation was concerned that, in education cases, its funds be used to help equalize the strength of the underrepresented, so that judges would have the best arguments and briefs on both sides of a case from which to fashion a fair and impartial decision. Criteria established by the Corporation limited support to cases brought on behalf of classes of people rather than private interests, in which major questions of public policy were involved, and where there seemed to be the potential for making major clarifications in the law. Support of the actual court costs was ruled out.

Since 1972, the Corporation has provided more than $4.3 million in grants to organizations which use the legal system to promote educational change, making the foundation the largest contributor to public interest law firms after the Ford Foundation. These organizations include the NAACP Legal Defense and Educational Fund, the NAACP, the Native American Rights Fund, the Puerto Rican Legal Defense and Education Fund (PRLDEF), and the Mexican American Legal Defense and Educational Fund (MALDEF). Corporation-supported activities include the legal research and back-up testimony of experts in northern school desegregation cases brought by the NAACP in Detroit, Boston, Cleveland, and Dayton; the monitoring by PRLDEF of the New York City Board of Education's compliance with a federal court mandate to offer bilingual education programs to over 85,000 Hispanic school children; and the creation within MALDEF of an education litigation component to work with a task force of educators, psychologists, sociologists, and linguists in developing an effective litigation strategy,

The lawsuits that these organizations have brought have helped not only to ensure educational equity for minority children, but to provide an outlet for minority disaffection and build minority leadership. It must be remembered, however, that use of the courts indicates the failure of the legislative and executive departments of government to deal fairly with the claims of excluded groups. Decisions have been left to the courts by default, and sometimes by design, because of the moral, as well as the legal, authority of the judiciary.

Improving the Performance of the Schools

As federal and state laws were passed to protect the right of all children to equal educational opportunity, many people confidently assumed that the educational system would use the dollars allocated for special assistance to students who historically had been underserved for their intended purposes, and the effects would show up in improved academic achievement. The facts told a disappointing story.

Studies of the implementation of these programs revealed that the new ideas and extra resources that were supposed to benefit children frequently never reached them in the form of better services. Important educational innovations did not result in the improvement of student skills because the programs were never seriously carried out. Making things work, it appeared, required a complex network of related actions, and this network was constantly breaking down, whether because of insufficient resources, bureaucratic inertia, political pressure, inadequate training and supportive assistance to educators, or a combination of all these factors.

Searching for underlying causes of failure, some social critics, among them Christopher Jencks whose controversial book, *Inequality,* was written with Corporation support, suggested that educational reforms were powerless to equalize educational achievement, much less reduce social inequities, when the society itself was inherently unequal. Others said that schools were at least concerned with knowledge and skills and that it was reasonable to think they could have an effect in those areas whether or not that affect translated into increased income or otherwise improved life chances for disadvantaged groups. As a matter of principle, they argued, the first concern of the schools should be to ensure that all children reached levels of skills adequate to effective participation in the society.

This second viewpoint is held within the Corporation, and a substantial number of its grants have been directed at the school community to bolster the willingness and capacity of its members to try to improve the educational outcomes of children at risk. Among the projects funded have been school-related monitoring and advocacy and the development of evaluation procedures that place greater responsibility on schools themselves to produce results.

Monitoring and advocacy. From early studies of the implementation of social legislation affecting children, it was apparent that the institutional arrangements within government to ensure accountability for the use of public funds were not always going to be adequate to the task, and it was left to independent organizations operating in the public interest to begin performing this function. The 1970s saw rapid growth in the number of such organizations monitoring governmental programs. According to a Corporation-supported study carried out by Designs for Change, those that served children with special needs increased from 117 to 665 between 1972 and 1977, a quarter of them focusing on the performance of the schools.

These organizations have not limited their activities to securing rights and entitlements under existing laws and regulations. They have also been concerned with stimulating the development of new laws and regulations. They often do casework involving parents and/or children, try to assist governmental agencies in devising alternatives to unacceptable practices, and identify needed services and try to secure them for clients. They conduct research and attempt to raise public awareness of issues through publications, and they train parents' groups and other advocates. As a last resort they will file lawsuits.

Since the early 1970s, the Corporation has committed $14.5 million toward such governmental monitoring and advocacy projects operating on behalf of minority, female, and handicapped children. More than one-half of the grants have concentrated on school-related issues.

One of the leading advocacy groups focusing on the welfare of children has been the Children's Defense Fund (CDF) in Washington, D.C. Established as an independent organization in 1973 (it was initially associated with the Washington Research Project), CDF, under the tireless leadership of Marian

Wright Edelman, has aimed at correcting selected serious problems faced by disadvantaged children in ways that lead to meaningful institutional reform and that raise more general questions about equality and justice in the society. The Fund's first report, *Children Out of School in America*, shattered the prevailing belief that all children who ought to go to school were in fact in school. Its second report, *School Suspensions: Are They Helping Children?*, revealed how education, a necessary if not sufficient ingredient for success as an adult, was denied to more than two million children each year. CDF also researches children's rights and needs in early education and day care, in health, in the juvenile justice system, and in medical experimentation; in addition it publishes handbooks to help parents gain a greater say over the decisions that affect their children's lives. The organization has had, over the past ten years, a considerable impact on public policy toward children.

A particular focus of groups supported by the Corporation has been Title I of the Elementary and Secondary Education Act of 1965, the largest source of federal funds ($2.4 billion in 1982, down from $3.1 billion in 1981) to local school districts for compensatory education and currently serving 5.4 million children in 68 percent of the nation's schools. Unfortunately, both program audits and independent studies have repeatedly demonstrated that Title I funds have, contrary to the law, been used to replace rather than supplement local expenditures, and there have been other problems, including the widespread failure to activate the involvement of the parent advisory groups mandated in the original legislation. The Federal Education Project of the Lawyers' Committee for Civil Rights Under Law, the Southeastern Public Education Program of the American Friends Service Committee, and the National Coalition of ESEA Title I Parents, have all received Corporation grants to investigate the oversight and management of Title I funds. They have done much to tighten the government's own monitoring mechanisms as well as lead the way to improved implementation.

Encouragingly, in recent years, Title I children have been demonstrating marked improvement in their academic achievement, according to a five-year evaluation by the U.S. Office of Education.

Testing and accountability. From its earliest years, the Corporation has had a major interest in strengthening educational standards in the United States, supporting, among other activities, the development of quantitative measures of ability and achievement in higher education. Since 1970 the foundation has granted more than $9.5 million toward test development and toward conferences, debates, and other mechanisms for the purpose of answering major questions regarding evaluation in elementary and secondary education.

The idea of national standards in education has always been anathema in this country, where education is a decentralized undertaking in which states and local areas have control over policy and curricula. Anything that can be construed as federal interference with these prerogatives tends to be resisted, as attested to by today's debates over the uses of federal funds for education (even though these make up only about 7 percent of all funding for education). One of the original mandates of the U.S. Office of Education, however, was that it make assessments of the state of education in the country and report to the American people. This had never been done until Francis Keppel,* U.S. Commissioner of Education in the Johnson administration, became interested in seeing whether and how the mandate could be carried out.

The idea for a census-like assessment of educational achievement had been discussed within the Corporation for some years, and in 1963 the foundation, with Keppel's encouragement, convened a group of educational and testing experts and representatives of other foundations to discuss its feasibility and desirability. Out of their preliminary work was formed, in 1968, the National Assessment of Educational Progress (NAEP), to which the Corporation contributed more than $2.5 million for the planning and test design before funding was assumed completely by the federal government. NAEP is now supported by the National Institute of Education and is administered by the Education Commission of the States, an educational policy compact supported by the states which itself was started with Corporation assistance.

Since 1960, NAEP has conducted periodic surveys of the educational attainment of nine-, thirteen-, and seventeen-year olds in ten subject areas, measured according to objectives established by local school personnel and others. The findings are communicated back to the schools and the public via the press, publications, and meetings in the hope that the information will be used to improve the educational process (but with no assurance that this will happen). To date it is the best mechanism, apart from standardized tests, for gaining a broad national and regional picture of what students are actually learning in schools.

In conducting the assessments, NAEP has had to develop new kinds of measures and sampling techniques that did not exist previously, and this work, along with dissemination, has in 12 years absorbed a great deal of federal and private money—$64 million or thereabouts—with uncertain impact on the schools. The Corporation has contributed to two outside "assessments of the Assessment" in the past few years, which have taken another look at its mission, testing techniques, and methods of communicating its findings to pertinent audiences, and recommendations have been made to make it more useful. Lurking suspicions that it might presage federal goal-setting for education, which it does *not*, have dogged it from the beginning. But with the growing insistence by the public that schools improve educational outcomes, educators may begin seriously to look to the Assessment for guidance in framing their

---

*Son of Frederick Keppel, who was president of Carnegie Corporation from 1923 to 1941. Francis Keppel also served as a trustee of the Corporation from 1970 to 1979.

policies. Much depends on the willingness of the federal government to reverse its declining support for NAEP in recent years.

In the early 1970s, as the so-called school accountability movement was gathering momentum, tests took on even greater importance as an index of educational outcomes. The Corporation began to seek through its grants not only to bring clarity to the debate about the functions and validity of standardized tests but to see how and whether measurement instruments could be developed for diagnostic purposes and for taking remedial steps in behalf of children who were doing less well than they should. The staff has also been concerned that the new minimum competency tests, which have been adopted by many states as a graduation standard, not be used to penalize students but to prompt schools to take corrective action with those in danger of being held back.

Up until now, in the absence of tests designed to yield information for public accountability purposes, standardized tests have been widely used to report to parents, school boards, legislators and citizens groups. Yet they are fundamentally unsuited for judging how well schools are doing their instructional job. They are useful at best in comparing the performance of one individual against another for sorting and selecting purposes.

The Corporation has been involved in the development of tests that exemplify more appropriate measures of educational outcomes and instruction. One of the most successful of these is Degrees of Reading Power (DRP), a test of reading comprehension developed for the New York State Department of Education by an independent research firm, Touchstone Applied Science Associates.

In the test, students are asked to read progressively more difficult nonfiction passages that have selected words deleted. Several options for completing the blanks are given, and in order to select the correct one, the students must understand the surrounding sentences. Their scores reflect the highest level of textual difficulty they can master.

One feature of DRP is that any expository writing a child might be asked to read can be rated on the same scoring system devised for the test, so that from a child's test results a teacher can judge whether or how well the student will grasp textbook material. Eventually, it is planned, teachers should be able to select reading materials at the level of the child's reading ability (or just above, in order to spur the child to learn more). Follow-up studies are now being conducted to determine ways in which teachers and textbook publishers can use information from the test results to organize and improve reading instruction and achievement.

DRP represents an important advance in measuring student achievement against criteria for what they should have achieved at their grade level and in assessing their progress. It has now been adopted by New York State, to be given to ninth graders in guiding their remedial work and to determine whether students meet minimum graduation standards in reading. Corporation assistance is enabling the College Board, in agreement with the New York State Education Department, to market DRP for use by other states and school districts for instructional, minimum competency, and accountability purposes as well as by other agencies, such as community colleges, for student placement.

One of the main difficulties involved in the promotion of better kinds of tests that serve the purpose of improving public education is that test development is expensive: it requires research on a subject area and on the ways a subject is learned at the same time, and this takes money. The Corporation has contributed more than $1.8 million for the development of DRP, which is only a portion of the true cost of the work. Commercial publishers appear not to be able to afford the investment. If further advances are to be made, then, the federal government may be the only agency that can marshal the required resources. This is not likely to happen without pressure from the public and corporation from the states and localities.

Broadening Access to Higher Education

The Corporation has had a continuing concern with lifelong learning as a logical sequel to Andrew Carnegie's interest in public libraries as "the university of the people." As early as 1919 the foundation initiated what was called the Americanization Study to explore educational opportunities for adults, primarily new immigrants. About 1960 the Corporation's interest took several new, related directions. One was in response to the desire for further education and careers on the part of women who had "stopped out" for marriage and child rearing. Another was in breaking down the rigidities of college and university structures so that degrees could be earned by individuals of any age for whom four years of campus residence was impractical or inappropriate. Still another was in liberating conventional attitudes about what constitutes learning and how it should be "credited."

The need to develop new opportunities for higher education took on special urgency with the coming of age of the baby-boom generation. (As one Corporation memorandum in the early 1960s put it rather melodramatically, "The projections of college enrollments for the years ahead are startling if not positively frightening. One estimate says there will be 12 million students in higher education by 1980—three times as many in 1960."* How the resources, the teachers, and the facilities for this "onslaught" were going to be found was seen as a major challenge for the future.

The other impetus came from the growing national consensus that higher education should be available to all who are qualified to benefit from it: not

---

*The projections turned out to be correct, but no one anticipated the dramatic drop in fertility of the 1960s and 1970s, resulting in a baby bust. They could not have foreseen, therefore, that undergraduate enrollments 20 years hence would include 2.5 million adults—more than a third of the total!

only minority-group members and adult women but individuals who, because of physical or economic handicaps, geographical isolation, or other reasons, were not able to attend a higher educational institution, even on a part-time basis.

Since the early 1960s the Corporation has expended well over $12 million in support of programs to introduce flexible arrangements that have provided higher educational opportunities for millions of individuals and served as well to break the traditional lockstep from high school through college.

Continuing education for women. In the postwar period, many women who had interrupted their education to have families wanted to return to the campus to complete their baccalaureates or pursue advanced or professional education. Yet they faced many obstacles. Higher education for the most part was designed for the full-time residential student of conventional college age. Many women with family obligations could be neither full-time nor residential, or if they were, felt uncomfortable around students years younger than they. Night school was inconvenient, and university extension programs offered only the first two years of undergraduate coursework.

At the advanced education level, graduate and professional schools were reluctant to provide the arrangements which would have made it possible for more women to enroll. Financial need was a major deterrent to graduate work for women. Many male students financed themselves by holding research assistantships, but these were seldom open to women of any age and certainly not on a part-time basis, a situation that was symptomatic of the prevailing prejudice against the idea of women pursuing advanced education at all.

By 1960 women made up about 35 percent of undergraduate enrollments and about 33 percent of the labor force, but their participation rate in the professions was only 10 percent and declining. The Corporation was seriously concerned about the talent loss entailed in the exclusion of thousands of able women from the higher professions, not only on social justice grounds but because of the growing shortage of teachers and other professionals.

In the early 1960s the Corporation made the first of many grants to colleges and universities to establish continuing education programs and to develop new models for advanced and professional study tailored to the needs of mature women. These programs demonstrated that there was no good reason why adult women could not pursue higher education on a flexible basis—that there was nothing, in short, standing in their way but the rigid rules and assumptions of the academic bureaucracy. The programs also demonstrated that there was a large and well-qualified clientele ready to take advantage of them.

The first grant went for an educational and career counseling program at the University of Minnesota. This was so successful that it was widely copied on other campuses. By 1965 approximately 70 other colleges and universities had initiated counseling services and special courses for mature women based to some extent on the continuing education model established at Minnesota.

The Corporation helped support somewhat similar programs at Syracuse University, the University of Pennsylvania, and Barnard College and also at Sarah Lawrence College which, with further grants, led to graduate programs in social work, elementary education, and librarianship taught by faculty members from New York University and Pratt Institute. Radcliffe College received grants for a program of fellowships at its Institute, most of which were post-doctoral, offered to talented mature women who needed encouragement and modest financial assistance. The Corporation in addition supported the first fellowship programs to women for part-time graduate study—one in the graduate school of arts and sciences at the University of Wisconsin, others at the University of Pittsburgh's library school and its graduate school of public and international affairs.

Nearly $2 million for the continuing education programs was appropriated by the Corporation from 1960 to 1972, when the foundation shifted its focus to the status of all women within higher education.

Nontraditional education. Another trend that the Corporation helped to shape concerns the diverse, unorthodox, and occasionally controversial movement that has come to be labeled nontraditional education. Support for the new forms, new structures, and new opportunities for higher education has over the past 20 years totaled more than $10 million.

Nontraditional study, which the Carnegie-supported Commission on Nontraditional Study called more an attitude than a system, departs from traditional education in its explicit recognition that learning should be measured by what students know rather than by how they have come to know it. Beyond that, it builds on two basic premises: that opportunity should be open to all who wish to learn and that education is a lifelong process not confined to age level or campus classroom.

The Corporation in 1960 had already been looking for some years to establish a degree program through independent study. Aware that the University of London had been offering a highly respected external degree since before the turn of the century, the foundation staff did not see why the decentralized system of education in this country need be a permanent barrier to recognition of a national system of credit by examination leading toward a degree. Such college-level examinations, moreover, could be credited by colleges for study not done on their campuses, something which could be invaluable to administrators seeking to evaluate previous education among the growing number of transfer students from junior colleges.

In 1960 the Corporation commissioned a study of the feasibility of developing such a national system of credit by examination, and in due course the College Entrance Examination Board (CEEB), using Corporation support, launched the College-Level Examination Program (CLEP).

CEEB, in developing CLEP, built on its experience with Advance Placement tests, which are used to exempt high-scoring students from taking courses in certain college subjects. Although acceptance of CLEP for college credit by the higher education community was slow and the participation of unaffiliated students was at first small, by now more than 90,000 people are taking the examinations each year in as many as 42 different subjects, and 1,000 colleges recognize the results of the tests for the purpose of course credit. They have been particularly useful in evaluating work done in the armed forces.

CLEP did not, however, create an external degree, since no college or university in this country was willing to award one solely on the basis of tests or off-campus learning experience. The major breakthrough came in 1970 when the University of the State of New York, the degree-granting authority of the state, announced that the Regents would award the first true external degree, one aimed at giving recognition to the skills and experiences of thousands of qualified citizens who might otherwise be barred from advancement in employment or from the realization of personal goals. The Regents External Degree (REX), which has grown into a national program, is open to individuals of high school age or older, who enter the program at any level their capabilities allow and progress at their own pace. All learning is validated through proficiency examinations which are a combination of the New York State Proficiency Examinations developed with Ford Foundation funds, the CLEP exams, and new examinations. Both Ford and Carnegie contributed heavily to the development of REX.

Currently, 20,444 REX students from every state are enrolled in eight different degree programs, divided between associate and baccalaureate levels, and there are approximately 15,000 degree holders. A high proportion of the enrollees are members of the armed forces and about half are women.

At about the same time that the Regents External Degree was announced, the State University of New York, with Ford Foundation and Corporation funds, established Empire State College as a separate unit for independent study within the New York state system of higher education. At Empire State, students of all ages work toward associate and baccalaureate degrees under the supervision of faculty mentors, with whom they develop an individualized plan of study and to whom they periodically report at regional learning centers. Empire State has awarded approximately 8,000 degrees to men and women in 11 different subject areas.

In the past ten years the Corporation has encouraged and supported the assessment of other ways in which people learn outside the formal educational system. A formidable array of educational courses, for example, is given by business, labor unions, professional organizations, government, cultural organizations, and other noncollege institutions to as many as 30 million Americans. The Corporation is supporting the Project on Noncollegiate-Sponsored Instruction of the Regents of the State of New York, which evaluates these programs and makes credit recommendations to the higher education community within the state. More recently it has been supporting the use of television and other

219

nonprint media as avenues for gaining nontraditional college degrees of superior quality.

Carnegie Commission on Higher Education. In 1960 a Corporation staff memorandum, referring to the baby-boom, spoke of the "extraordinary prospects facing institutions of higher education." The country's colleges and universities, it said, were entering a period of the most spectacular growth in their history, but there were no individuals, nor was there any group, engaged in long-term study of the fundamental forces, needs, issues, and conflicts which would shape the future of American higher education.

The Corporation saw this as an opportunity for foundation action, and over the next few years it financed a series of studies and projects aimed at providing a national perspective on higher education and at strengthening the hand of educational leaders and public policymakers as they faced the challenges ahead.

In 1965, this program took an unexpected turn. The Corporation's sister foundation, The Carnegie Foundation for the Advancement of Teaching (CFAT), which the Corporation's president also headed, had been created in 1905 to give expression to Mr. Carnegie's concept of free pensions for virtually all college and university faculty members of his day and to conduct educational studies. Many important studies had been carried out in the past but none recently, and the pension load had become insignificant. The question was raised about the CFAT's future.

The CFAT possessed a charter binding its activities to the welfare of higher education and a board of trustees drawn almost entirely from the academic community. These assets, it was felt by the trustees, were not lightly to be abandoned in the new era of universal higher education. The decision was made, therefore, to continue the Foundation's existence and revive its old mission of conducting education studies.

The Corporation, for its part, agreed to consider an annual request from the Foundation to support a major project in higher education, one which would actually be carried out by an appointed commission. The result was the formation of the Carnegie Commission on Higher Education, which Clark Kerr, former president of the University of California at Berkeley, agreed to chair.

Initially the trustees of both foundations had thought that the new Commission should carry out a comprehensive study of the future financing of higher education, but Mr. Kerr was of the opinion that this could not be done without looking more broadly at its structure and functions. The trustees concurred, and the project was designated the Carnegie Commission on the Future Structure, Functions, and Financing of Higher Education, which was then shortened to the Carnegie Commission of Higher Education.

The Commission was an *ad hoc* body fully independent of both foundations, with a life limited to six years. Financed by the Corporation in annual grants of $1 million, it was one of the Corporation's most important endeavors, although it had the indirect effect of reducing the support of higher education studies within its regular grants program.

The accomplishments of the Commission can scarcely be summarized in a few paragraphs. One can point to its publications—the 23 Commission reports, the 60 sponsored research reports, the 23 technical reports. In breadth of coverage, quality of research, sheer mass of data, and objectivity of presentation, these reports constitute possibly the most comprehensive and important body of descriptive and analytical literature about higher education ever produced.

One report, *Less Time, More Options*, issued in 1971, had a substantial impact on the academic community generally, in helping to break down unnecessary rigidities in the system and to popularize the notion that higher education should be available to all who seek it on a flexible basis, the very principle that had guided the Corporation's program in higher education for years.

Possibly the most important aspect of the Commission's entire effort was the conspicuous attention it devoted to equality of opportunity in higher education. While this was a general theme running through much of its work, the Commission dealt with it specifically in 11 of its 23 reports: *Quality and Equality*, 1968; *A Chance to Learn*, 1970; *The Open-Door Colleges*, 1970; *Quality and Equality* (revised recommendations), 1970; *Higher Education and the Nation's Health*, 1970; *Less Time, More Options*, 1971; *From Isolation to Mainstream*, 1971; *New Students and New Places*, 1971; *Institutional Aid*, 1972; *Opportunities for Women in Higher Education*, 1973; and the final report, *Priorities for Action*, 1973. These reports helped provide the impetus within higher education and government for making major advances toward the goal of equal educational opportunity.

They recommended, for example, the establishment in 1972 of the Basic Education Opportunity Grants (BEOG), now referred to as Pell Grants (for the U.S. Senator who sponsored the program), which awards students tuition assistance on the basis of need. They also led to the formation of the Fund for the Improvement of Postsecondary Education, a governmental foundation, to encourage innovation in higher education.

Altogether, the Commission's reports, testimony before legislative bodies, and advice to federal and state officials directly affected the spending of billions of dollars of federal funds for higher education, no small return on the Corporation's investment and suggesting that despite the massive movement of the government into areas which were once a private responsibility, there is an important role for foundations in public policy formation.

With the completion of the Commission's work, the CFAT decided to continue the study of higher education. The era of campus activism, anti-war protest, and radical changes in national values and personal lifestyles that affected campus life was past, bringing in a new set of challenges to higher education: declining enrollments, financial retrenchment, lowered optimism, growing conservatism, and the diminished capacity and will for experimentation. These now became the major issues dealt with by the CFAT in subsequent studies, a number of them supported by the Corporation.

Improving the Status of Women. In the years following the Presidential Executive Order of 1968, which forbade discrimination by federal contractors on grounds of sex, hundreds of formal charges of sex discrimination were filed against various institutions and entire state systems of higher education, requiring institutions to confront some bleak facts about the status of women on their campuses. Of all doctorates earned in the United States between 1960 and 1969, only 11.6 percent went to women, and in many fields there were virtually no women at all gaining Ph.D.s. Equally poor was the representation of women in the graduate and professional schools, which helped explain why, in 1970, they made up only 3.5 percent of lawyers, 2 percent of dentists, 7 percent of physicians, and less than 1 percent of engineers.

While women made up from one-fifth to one-quarter of the total teaching and professional staffs in colleges and universities, most of them were located at small colleges, junior colleges, and institutions with lower prestige. Less than one-tenth of all women faculty members were full professors, whereas a quarter of the men held that rank. Finally, they earned considerably less than men. The Carnegie Commission on Higher Education in its 1973 report *Opportunities for Women in Higher Education.* estimated that, as a group, women faculty members administrators earned $150 to $200 million less per year than men in comparable positions.

Many explanations were put forward for the underrepresentation of women in higher education, not least, the lingering effects of the "headlong rush into maternity" by young women after the Second World War, which had kept many of them at home during the critical years when most career choices were made. But discriminatory practices and attitudes on the part of a male-dominated system loomed as the most intractable barrier to women's advancement in the present and future. The academic community, however, declined to acknowledge this or to take remedial action. As a consequence, women began to look to the federal government for redress. Individually and collectively, they sued the systems over hiring, pay, promotion, nepotism rules, part-time appointments, and a host of other issues under the anti-discriminatory laws and regulations.

In the early 1970s the Corporation, building on its program in continuing education for women, began to make grants addressed to women's position in higher education generally. Since then it has appropriated more than $7 million for programs aimed variously at increasing opportunities for women in nontraditional fields; studying women students and the college environment; training women in academic administration; researching administrative policies and practices; providing career counseling for women Ph.D.s; and facilitating promotion of women faculty members to tenured positions. In addition, the foundation has supported a number of projects that offer continuing appraisals of women's progress, or the lack of it, in the field. One of these is the Project on the Status and Education of Women.

In 1970, as women began to seek remedy through the courts and through new laws and to broaden the examination of higher education's relationship to women, institutions found themselves in a difficult position to respond. Burdened with staggering financial problems and shrinking enrollments, their attention was fastened in extreme instances on simply staying solvent. Moreover, they had no firm base of information about discrimination and sometimes an erroneous notion of the laws and regulations that dealt with it or the ways of correcting inequities. The federal government, which had driven home the illegality of discrimination by delaying federal contracts at some 40 universities, did not seem prepared to make things any clearer.

To help institutions gain a better understanding of the issues, the Corporation, along with two other foundations, funded the newly organized Project on the Status and Education of Women, sponsored by the Association of American Colleges, in Washington, D.C., and headed by Bernice Sandler. Its specific aims were to make the education world aware of the federal regulations and statutes concerning women in education and to keep administrators, academic and nonacademic women, and government abreast of developments on all college and university campuses.

Eleven years later the Project is still operating at high speed, issuing summaries of federal rulings, writing and reprinting issue papers, digging out statistical data on women's status in every category of higher education, and beyond that serving as a basic clearinghouse for people and institutions interested in education. In doing so the Project, more than any other single agency, has managed to authenticate the existence of sex discrimination on campus and aided greatly in the ability of institutions to comply with federal policy, helping government in the process to set goals for affirmative action that are reasonable and fair.

The climate for women in higher education has improved markedly in the last decade. Women students now make up more than half of undergraduate enrollments, and institutions battling enrollment declines are glad to have them on campus. A recent study showed that a quarter of all women entering college today plan a career in one of the professional fields of law, medicine, engineering, or business. Progress toward sex equity in academic employment, on the other hand, has been slow, mainly because the economic retrenchment in higher education has resulted in little hiring, and competition is fierce for the few jobs available. Women are still badly underrepresented in the academic and administrative ranks or are locked in sex-stereotyped roles and fields. Today, women make up about 25 percent of full-time faculty positions but only 11 percent of tenured faculty. The more prestigious the institution, the lower the percentage.

There are many ways of interpreting the figures, but most analysts conclude that sex discrimination is still an important factor in the discrepancies. There will be a role for the Project on the Status and Education of Women for some time to come.

CONCLUSION

The preceding pages have described aspects of Carnegie Corporation's grant-making program over the past 20 years to help those less advantaged in society to gain a greater say in the policy decisions that affect their lives and to broaden opportunities for them, particularly in the field of education. The aim explicitly has been to help close the gap between our democratic ideals and the reality that millions of American citizens historically have not enjoyed equal opportunity and rights as guaranteed them by the laws of the land. Looking toward the next 20 years, it seems evident that a continuation of this effort will be more important than ever, not only on grounds of principle but for the pragmatic reason that we are entering an era in which no individual can be counted as expendable. Our population as a whole is growing older. The median age today is 30. The number of young persons below the age of 15 has dropped by 7.8 million since 1970, while that of adults age 25 to 34 has swelled by 12.8 million and that of the elderly by 5.2 million. The next generation will be assuming an unusually heavy burden to produce the nation's cadres of professional, administrative, technical and skilled workers, to ensure the well-being of the generation behind it, and to provide assistance to the 12 to 15 percent of the population of elderly people that the nation will have by the next century. Without doubt, an increasing share of this responsibility will fall upon members of minority groups who, by natural increase and immigration, will constitute a rising proportion of the young.

For these reasons the Corporation can be expected to continue investing its limited resources in young people, with a special emphasis on minority-group members, women, and girls, who remain a comparatively neglected pool of talent for the nation and whose services will be desperately needed to maintain the nation's standard of living and its very capacity to defend itself. Much has been achieved in the society during the past 20 years to bring these groups into the mainstream; much remains to be done.

Final Thoughts

This annual report essay is written with considerable sadness—sadness not because it is my last as president of Carnegie Corporation but because of the nature of our times. A short-sighted and uncharitable spirit seems to be abroad in the land, as a result of which investment in human resources generally and meeting the needs of the less fortunate members of the society specifically have been downgraded as national priorities. The nation's future dependence on a broadly educated citizenry seems to have been forgotten, while the poor have come to be treated with more obloquy than sympathy. Before discussing this disturbing state of affairs, however, I must explain why this is my final essay.

Two years ago I informed the trustees of the foundation that I did not plan to continue in the presidency until I reached the official retirement age of 65. A year later I set a firm departure date with them of December 9, 1982, the day of the annual meeting for this year. Having been an officer of the foundation for going on 30 years and its acting president or president for over 17, and having passed my 61st birthday, I felt a distinct need of "repotting." It was not so much that I had outgrown the size of the pot, for that would never be possible at a place like Carnegie Corporation, with the infinite possibilities it offers for constructive work; it was simply an urge to be in a position to have fewer daily obligations and constraints on the use of my time for my remaining active years.

As for the Corporation, I felt that it would benefit from some new leadership. Change in the management of any institution is better made too soon than too late. As a foundation officer, I had had ample opportunity to observe the wisdom of that dictum. It was only a matter of facing reality and applying it to myself. Accordingly, arrangements were made with the trustees under which a new president would be selected and I would become president emeritus and senior consultant, free to pursue my interests in public policy issues while available to take on any specific tasks the new president might wish.

Following the agreed course, the trustees set up a special selection committee which, under the conscientious leadership of the board's vice chairman, Helene Kaplan, conducted an extensive six months' search for a new president. The committee, having looked at a large number of candidates, concluded without hesitation that the best choice lay within the board's own membership and recommended the selection of David Hamburg. He was unanimously and enthusiastically elected to the foundation's presidency by the full board on June 10 of this year, to take office in December.

I wish to record here, as both a trustee and head of the foundation's staff, my own delight and satisfaction at the choice of Dr. Hamburg as my successor. I have no doubt that he will provide the kind of sensitive, imaginative, and socially conscious leadership I would wish the Corporation to have, and I envisage an exciting new phase in the foundation's history under his able direction.

This, therefore, is my final annual report essay. And since it is the last occasion on which I will write as the president of the Corporation, it seems appropriate that I give some account of the personal outlook that I have brought to my 17 years of its leadership. In my view, a foundation, if it is to be worth anything at all, cannot be morally neutral. It must be guided by a set of values—must stand for something. Necessarily, in developing the foundation's set of values and publicly articulating them, the role of the chief executive officer will be of great importance. Certainly, that has always been the case at Carnegie Corporation.

Looking back over the years since 1953, when I joined the Corporation, I am impressed with what a tumultuous period it has been in the world's history. On the international scene, we have witnessed the demise of colonialism and the rise of Third World consciousness, the reemergence of China as a dominant power, the first impressive forays into space, the proliferation of nuclear weaponry, and mounting competition for such essential resources as oil and food, to name only a few changes.

Here in the United States we have seen established social and political systems challenged by the civil rights, women's, and youth movements, the massive entry of women into the labor force, and the emergence of new sexual and cultural mores. We have endured unprecedented national traumas in the assassination of major public figures, urban violence, the Vietnam War, and Watergate. We have seen, moreover, rapid growth of the Hispanic minority, the rise of the computer age, and, finally, a seemingly conservative counterrevolution against the general welfare state and the liberal political and social trends of the period.

Truly the past three decades have been remarkable ones. So great have been the changes both in the world and at home that I look back now on the early 1950s as belonging to an altogether different age, as remote from the present as the Victorian era was from those years.

A number of these great movements and events impinged on the Corporation only indirectly or not at all, while others affected it directly. Whatever their nature, they interacted with one another to form an ever-changing context—a swiftly flowing river of immediacy—within which those of us who served the foundation seemed to be inescapably immersed. Seldom did it seem possible to climb out onto the bank to rest and get one's bearings. Always there were the pressures of the moment—new funds which had to be spent, new claims on the funds, new issues demanding attention, and simply the day-in, day-out requirements imposed by administrative responsibility. Very occasionally, of course, I did make a determined effort to step outside the rush of the immediate and try to comprehend the deeper meaning of some of the changes that were taking place and to communicate my thoughts on these matters in articles, speeches, and annual report essays. I talked variously about the role of the voluntary sector in democratic society and its relationships with government, about the impact of rapid growth in higher education, about the problems of the developing nations, about racial intolerance in this country and in South Africa, about the needs of children, about women in the work force, about the Hispanic community, and about the social role of government.

Despite the great variety that has characterized my daily existence at the Corporation, however, virtually everything I have done as its president, whether it involved public statements or the internal responsibilities of program formulation and grant making, has been guided by a single motivating force—a lifelong belief in social justice and the equality of all people under the law. This was a passion I inherited from parents who were deeply imbued with democratic values and brought me up to share them. The conviction was strengthened during the war years when, along with many other Americans, I took part in the defense of freedom against Nazi and Fascist tyranny, and it became firmly set in the years immediately after the war when I was working abroad and had the opportunity to travel widely in Europe and Africa. By the time I came to the Corporation in 1953, the commitment had become an immutable part of my very being. The key questions for me here with respect to any proposed action have always been: Will it promote equality of opportunity? And will it to some degree make the world a fairer and more just place?

As time went by this outlook was supplemented by a second perspective that gradually became as strong and as clear as the first. The new outlook grew from an interest I began to take during the 1960s in human resource development or, as it is sometimes called, "human capital formation," which over time has led me to the view that the very future of our society depends absolutely on the broad development of all our people, and especially of our children, irrespective of race, sex, economic status, or any other consideration. Investment in such things as nutrition, health, decent housing, education—for the poor as well as the more affluent—is, therefore, not only a matter of social justice but of practical necessity.* Failure to appreciate this fundamental truth, I have come to feel, is more dangerous for this nation than any alleged missile gap or other short-coming in armaments. This second perspective was considerably sharpened when I began to appreciate the full significance of major alterations taking place in the structure of the American population. As the consequence of increases in the fertility rate (the average number of children born to all females aged 15 to 44) over the three decades from the early 1930s to the early 1960s, the number of births rose from a Depression low of 2.3 million in 1933 to a high of 4.3 million in 1957, bringing into being the baby-boom generation. The baby boom is a demographic phenomenon of major proportions whose chronological progression through successive decades has been likened to the passage of a tennis ball through the belly of a snake. Its impact on education, societal values, the job market, political attitudes, and in other realms is already enormous and will continue to be well into the next century.

Similarly, the precipitous decline in the fertility rate from 3.7 in 1957 to 1.8 today, well below the replacement rate of the population, has produced yet another demographic phenomenon, the baby-bust generation. Seven million fewer young people will reach working age in the 1990s than did so in the 1970s. This aberration may pose serious problems to the not-too-distant future in the form of a shortage of entry-level workers for the economy and, possibly, depending on the needs at that time, of young men and women for the armed forces. Over the greater run, as the number of older, no-longer productive people in the nation mounts, and especially after about the year 2010, when the members of the baby-boom generation will begin to retire in large numbers, the proportion of active workers paying for the benefits of retired persons—in 1950 about sixteen to one and presently about three to one—will be only two to one (if present fertility trends continue). That, surely, unless there is a spectacular increase in productivity over the next four decades, will be a time of unprecedented economic difficulty and intergenerational social tension.

The special significance of this demographic quirk or twist in fertility rates is that it places a very high premium on making the most of the much smaller number of Americans now being born—getting them off to the best possible start in life as children and then continuing to invest in them at later stages of development. Human capital formation, always important, has become many times more so because casualties result from poor nutrition, poor health care,

---

*In this respect, I should say that I am simply subscribing to Andrew Carnegie's belief in a broadly available educational system as the essential foundation for a democratic society, although the issue in my time has been one of increasing access to education by overcoming barriers of discrimination and poverty, whereas in his it was promoting an understanding of education's value. In any event, he had instructed the Corporation's trustees, and their successors after them, to spend the foundation's funds for the "advancement and diffusion of knowledge and understanding among the people of the United States," and I have felt that in my concern for the development of all Americans, I have been true to his wishes.

inferior education, low motivation, and so on simply can no longer be afforded. The need to avoid talent loss is particularly important in the black and Hispanic communities because the higher fertility rates of these groups are making their offspring a steadily increasing proportion of each successive cohort.

Among basic demographic trends, one must also take note of the rapidly rising numbers of elderly people in the nation, the product of greatly improved life expectancy for Americans of all ages over the past half century or more. In 1900 only three out of ten Americans could anticipate reaching the age of 70, whereas now seven out of ten can expect to do so, and four out of ten can expect to live to 80! The proportion of the population 65 or older, in 1900 only 4 percent, has risen to 11 percent today. By the year 2030, when the baby-boom cohorts have retired, it will be 20 percent. At that time, the number of people past the age of 65 will be about 55 million.

What is important about this trend is that 16 percent of the voting age population is now 65 or older, a figure that will continue to rise in the decades ahead as the population ages further. Even more important, recent elections have shown that the elderly actually vote in much higher proportion than younger citizens. There is, thus, a growing presumption that issues affecting older Americans will get favored political attention. Expenditure on these citizens, has, indeed, expanded rapidly. As a proportion of the federal budget, it was 13 percent in 1960, rose to over 25 percent by 1981, and, if nothing is done to check the rate of increase, will rise to as much as 35 percent in 2000 and 65 percent in 2020!

It should not be difficult, in view of these trends, to see what two of the nation's principal challenges will be in the coming years: How to make the most of the limited number of productive workers there will be then in proportion to nonproductive Americans by better preparing today's children for the heavy responsibilities that lie ahead for them and how, in a period when resources will inevitably be limited, to reconcile, in an equitable and humane manner and with maximum long-range benefit to the nation, the insatiable demand for expenditure of public and private funds on the elderly with the competing needs and claims of younger age groups.

In a sense, these problems are simply different formulations of the same basic issue—how Americans generally can be persuaded to be concerned about the nation's future needs when they are fully absorbed with their own present wants. The problem is particularly acute in regard to the elderly who have a powerful sense of having earned, and, therefore, of being entitled to, the benefits they are getting and, presumably, are not particularly concerned about the longer-run future, since they are not going to be here to experience it. Furthermore, they have the justification for their position that their poverty rate, despite the public programs designed to help them, is still, at 15.3 percent, higher than the general rate, with another 10 percent living close to the poverty line.

It may, however, not be the elderly alone who have a diminished sense of concern about the future. This may also be a characteristic of the large baby-boom generation whose formative years have been marked by expectations of ever-rising real incomes, by the initiation of large new social insurance programs and the growth of private pensions, by the appearance of new conventions that advance immediate self-gratification as a worthy social goal, and, finally, by sustained high inflation that discourages saving. For all of these reasons one would not expect this generation to have a particularly keen appreciation of the necessity to balance the claims of the present against the needs of the future.

In view of the seriousness of these demographic issues, it is not surprising that I am deeply saddened and disturbed by current efforts to dismantle many of the social programs established over the preceding decades—programs that were not confined simply to helping those members of the society who are least able to help themselves but were aimed broadly at developing the nation's human potential. My concern now is that there will be societal and individual costs involved in this reversal of direction many times greater than the costs of the programs themselves and ultimately a loss of talent to the nation that could seriously weaken its future competitive ability in the world. It took years to summon up the national will to put these programs in place, and now they are being torn down with a degree of haste and thoughtlessness that is truly astonishing.

In 1982, it is clear beyond any doubt that moves are under way to bring about a fundamental change in the social policies of the nation and the social role of the federal government. No longer are the government's taxing and spending powers to be used to achieve social equity or as a mechanism for the redistribution of income. No longer are they to be used to try to ameliorate the effects of poverty and discrimination or to solve social problems. No longer are they to be used for the broad development of all the nation's human resources. Government, it is claimed, can accomplish those purposes better by promoting economic growth and reducing inflation.

This, of course, is an attractive proposition to those who are not poor because it offers the prospect of reduced taxes. It seems suddenly that a magic way has been discovered to meet the nation's social needs without anyone having to meet the cost. That is pure self-delusion. Economic growth has never by itself guaranteed that the necessary investment will be made in broad human resource development. Nor has such growth ever raised substantial numbers of those at the bottom of society out of poverty. The metaphor of all the boats rising with the tide may be good imagery, but it is poor social analysis, and it will be even poorer in the type of economy we can expect in the future where there will be little or no opportunity for the unskilled or for those suffering the varied debilitating effects of prolonged social deprivation.

The argument is also made that the states can better meet society's needs than the federal government. However, only if the states receive sums of money from Washington equivalent to what it would have spent, with strict instructions that those funds are to be used for the same purposes, will this be possible, and on neither count is that the intent. The predictable result will be that the states with the most resources and the most sense of social obligation will do the best they can. Many states on the other hand will do little or nothing to take up the slack, thereby compounding the already existing problem of the inequitable treatment of some Americans simply because of their place of residence.

The contention is also made that the shortfall in federal dollars can be made up by the business sector, foundations, voluntary organizations, and churches. This claim is, frankly, ridiculous to someone who is well informed about the entire field of philanthropy. These groups are of enormous importance and essential to a healthy society, but they do not have the capacity even to begin to substitute for the federal role. Indeed, as federal programs are cut, many of the nation's most valuable voluntary organizations, which have depended heavily on federal support, are seeing their capacity to provide services to the needy disappear. They are, thus, in the position of being asked to do more by the same administration that is simultaneously weakening their viability as organizations. This situation naturally makes for considerable bitterness and dismay within the social welfare community.

In short, there simply is no feasible way for the federal government to transfer its social role elsewhere in the society without causing a national abdication of responsibilities that we have no choice but to meet if we are to have a prosperous and secure future. Amidst all the rhetoric about the alleged mischief inherent in the federal social role this is a central reality of which we cannot afford to lose sight.

Approaching the end of 1982, more than 11 million workers are unemployed, and huge deficits are anticipated in the federal budget for the next few years. Generous tax cuts have failed to stimulate economic growth and have so increased the federal deficit that the country has been obliged to institute a large tax increase. In this situation of a depressed economy and looming federal deficits, further cuts have had to be made in social programs by the Congress. The principal sacrifices, therefore, have been made by the poor rather than equally on the part of all income groups. Fortunately, questions are at last being raised about reductions in defense spending, which was vastly increased during the past year on the illogical and unconvincing grounds that the decline in the *proportion* of the federal budget going to defense over the previous decades was *prima facie* evidence that our defense capacity itself had also declined.

One can see now that the nation is at a fork in the road. If it goes down one road, the guiding philosophy will be clear: This is the view that a federal social role is wrong in principle and cannot, in any event, be afforded if we are to retain a strong defense capability. It must, therefore, be reduced, if not totally eliminated. There will be a legitimate social role for the states if they choose to exercise it, but, essentially, a growing economy will largely obviate the need for public provision of social services by making it possible for virtually all families to purchase them privately out of their earnings. The federal taxing and spending power should be used for no other social purpose than basic social insurance and the provision of assistance to the "deserving poor"—those who qualify by viture of old age, illness, or physical handicap.

If the nation goes down the other road, the guiding philosophy will be equally clear but totally different. The basic assumption will be that the federal social role is entirely legitimate—indeed mandated in the general welfare clause of the Constitution—and that it should be reinstated as soon as possible and even, perhaps, expanded into new areas of need. The assumption, further, will be that, no matter how buoyant the economy becomes there will always be a sizable group in society whose members must receive public assistance if they are to live decently and if their children are to have anything like an equal chance in life. Finally, it will be assumed that, since a vigorous social role by the national government is fundamental to the maintenance of a stable society and to the development of its human resources and hence its security, the country will give the social role the priority necessary for it to be fully funded.

While conceding that there are very powerful, well-financed interests working to see that the nation continues to go down the first of these two roads, it is my firm conviction that sooner or later, and probably sooner, the nation will revert to the second road. I say this because I believe that down the first road there lies nothing but increasing hardship for ever-growing numbers, a mounting possibility of severe social unrest, and the consequent development among the upper classes and the business community of sufficient fear for the survival of our capitalist economic system to bring about an abrupt change of course. In short, just as we built the general welfare state in the 1930s and expanded it in the 1960s as a safety valve for the easing of social tension, so we will do it again in the 1980s. Any other path is simply too risky.

It would, of course, be fine if the free enterprise system were functioning in a way that ensured equality of opportunity for all, employment at decent wages for everyone who wanted to or needed to work, and a distribution of economic rewards sufficiently equitable to meet basic standards of fairness. But, unfortunately, as well as our modified capitalist system serves most of us, it serves some of our fellow citizens very poorly. Because their lives have been blighted by such misfortunes as racial or sexual discrimination, poor nutrition, lack of medical care, inferior schooling, and substandard housing in dangerous, depressed neighborhoods, these citizens are simply unequipped to compete in the type of post-industrial society we have today and will have increasingly in the future.

One of the purposes behind the expansion of the general welfare state in the 1960s and early 1970s was to remove the barriers that inhibited the upward mobility of disadvantaged Americans and to help at least some of them reach a point where their further progress would be self-sustaining. With all its faults, this was an undertaking characterized by hope, dignity, and compassion, and in many cases it did work. We are abandoning this strategy now for harsh policies that deny assistance to many who need it desperately, that take support away from people who have the will to succeed but need some help, and that shift the blame for misfortune from society to the victims.

It is possible, of course, that the majority of Americans—those of us who live comfortable, secure lives—will be able to abide the contradiction of poverty and human misery amidst plenty, our consciences dulled by facile rationalizations of one kind or another. We did, after all, live for much of our history as a nation with legalized segregation of the races and with discrimination against women. We were content to allow some 20 percent of our people to live in poverty until as late as the 1960s. We permitted all kinds of injustice to endure while giving lip service to a Constitution that prohibits it. And these, alas, are evils toward which we are now returning in the name of "getting the government out of our lives."

Nevertheless, I remain hopeful. I believe that some Americans will begin to understand the longer-term negative consequences for the nation's economy and for its security of a prolonged failure to invest adequately in human resource development. Others, I think, may find that they were more deeply affected by the great democratic advances of the 1960s than they realized and will become increasingly uneasy about a society that not only condones inequality but promotes it through its basic public policies. A third group may begin to comprehend that the existence of the general welfare state, far from being a disaster for the nation, has been a great boon to it, in that the reform and social amelioration it has provided over the past half century have offered an alternative to revolution and have served thereby to preserve our American economic and political institutions through a turbulent period of world history.

For my part, although I will no longer be at the helm of the foundation, I will be continuing to exert my fullest efforts in other, and I hope, no less productive, ways to help build the kind of society in which I believe so staunchly— one that is humane, caring, and provident in developing the talents of all its people.

In closing, I should say that I have been privileged to serve this great institution as its leader, and I shall always be grateful for that opportunity. Leadership, of course, is rarely the work of one person but is a shared enterprise. My deepest thanks and appreciation go to my colleagues on the staff and the board of trustees and especially to David Robinson, the Corporation's executive vice president, who for the past 12 years has consistently offered both wise and supportive counsel.

Index

ABOUT THE AUTHOR

Alan Pifer is President Emeritus of Carnegie Corporation of New York, where he served as President for
over seventeen years. He serves as a Director of
McGraw-Hill, Inc. and American Association for
Higher Education, and as a trustee of The Carnegie
Foundation for the Advancement of Teaching. He also
serves as Chairman of the National Conference on Social Welfare Study on the Federal Social Role, Carnegie Corporation's Project on the Aging Society, and
The Corsortium for the Advancement of Private
Higher Education. Throughout his distinguished career, Mr. Pifer has been active as a Director and
Trustee of numerous organizations concerned with
philanthropy, education, and social and public policy.
Alan Pifer has been awarded honorary doctorate degrees from six major universities and was given the
Cleveland E. Dodge Medal for Distinguished Service
from Teachers College, Columbia University, in 1982.